ADVANCE PRAISE FOR

The Mediation of Financial Crises

"With the benefit of hindsight, Sophie Knowles is able to look back on the great financial crisis of 2008 to see how little has changed and why we still need investigative journalists to educate the public and hold companies to account."

—Anya Schiffrin, Director of Technology, Media, and Communications, Columbia University, New York

"This crisply written and compelling book does the business press the honour of taking it and its role seriously, giving credit where it is due, acknowledging the challenges it faces, but forthrightly and illuminatingly holding it to account where deserved. And it often is.

The book's historical and comparative approach, comparing coverage of the 2008 crisis to previous modern crises, provides vital context for the Press's buy-in to a deregulatory agenda and other pro-industry assumptions. And by comparing the Press's role in different countries—in the U.S., U.K. and Australia—it exposes how 'group-think,' as she rightly calls it, crossed borders and took over Anglo-Saxon newsrooms. And to her great credit, Sophie Knowles gets out into the field to ask the Press for its side of the story, through qualitative interviews that add another essential dimension to the analysis.

As we continue to struggle through a post-crisis world, Knowles challenges the Press to do better—to marshal its formidable resources and talents to puncture the myths that got us here and to help build a more stable future.

The Mediation of Financial Crises is a vital contribution to our understanding of the financial Press and of the Press in general."

—Dean Starkman, Senior Editor, International Consortium of Investigative Journalists, Author, *The Watchdog That Didn't Bark: The Financial Crisis and the Disappearance of Investigative Journalism*

"Well-grounded and solidly illustrated with several case studies, Sophie Knowles provides a powerful indictment about the history and current state of financial journalism. An incisive account that revisits what have we learnt since the financial meltdown of 2008 that almost brought down the world economy and that has cost years of austerity against the poorest in society. In a time in which financial corporate players are back to many of their 'esoteric' greed and unregulated practices, this book presents not only a welcomed reflection but an urgent call for action by those of us who believe in a better and more just society."

—Jairo Lugo-Ocando, Professor, Northwestern University, Qatar

The Mediation of Financial Crises

Simon Cottle
General Editor

Vol. 25

The Global Crises and the Media series
is part of the Peter Lang Media and Communication list.
Every volume is peer reviewed and meets
the highest quality standards for content and production.

PETER LANG
New York • Bern • Berlin
Brussels • Vienna • Oxford • Warsaw

Sophie Knowles

The Mediation of Financial Crises

Watchdogs, Lapdogs or Canaries in the Coal Mine?

PETER LANG
New York • Bern • Berlin
Brussels • Vienna • Oxford • Warsaw

Library of Congress Cataloging-in-Publication Data

Names: Knowles, Sophie, author.
Title: The mediation of financial crises: watchdogs, lapdogs or canaries
in the coal mine? / Sophie Knowles.
Description: New York: Peter Lang, 2020.
Series: Global crises and the media; v. 25 | ISSN 1947-2587
Includes bibliographical references and index.
Identifiers: LCCN 2019056157 (print) | LCCN 2019056158 (ebook)
ISBN 978-1-4331-5230-6 (hardback: alk. paper)
ISBN 978-1-4331-5231-3 (paperback: alk. paper) | ISBN 978-1-4331-5232-0 (ebook pdf)
ISBN 978-1-4331-5233-7 (epub) | ISBN 978-1-4331-5234-4 (mobi)
Subjects: LCSH: Financial crises—Press coverage—Great Britain. |
Journalism, Commercial—Great Britain—History—21st century
Classification: LCC PN5124.F5 K56 2020 (print) | LCC PN5124.F5 (ebook) |
DDC 070.4/493309410905—dc23
LC record available at https://lccn.loc.gov/2019056157
LC ebook record available at https://lccn.loc.gov/2019056158
DOI 10.3726/b16560

Bibliographic information published by **Die Deutsche Nationalbibliothek.**
Die Deutsche Nationalbibliothek lists this publication in the "Deutsche
Nationalbibliografie"; detailed bibliographic data are available
on the Internet at http://dnb.d-nb.de/.

This book is dedicated to Gail Phillips and Steve Schifferes.
Two shining examples of the good that exists in media and academia. Thanks also to Johan Lidberg for steering me out of a corporate magazine toward this important research.

Contents

List of Figures

Foreword

STEVE SCHIFFERES

Professor of Financial Journalism (retired), City University of London

The scale, scope and extent of the global financial crisis of 2007–8 was unprecedented. It was also a moment of truth for the financial press, whose role is effectively evaluated in the comparative and historical perspective in this book.

Not since the Great Depression of the 1930s had a financial crisis had such a wide-ranging and long-lasting effect on the economy, on living standards and on the banking system. The strain on public finances, due to the costs of a government rescue, led directly to the austerity policies were introduced in many countries.

The speed at which the crisis spread around the world, shaking the economies not just of the developed world of the US and Europe, but also developing countries from Zambia to China who depended for economic growth on exports, was a demonstration of the power of globalisation. With interest rates at all-time lows, public finances still stretched, and a growing burden of private debt, it is unclear how the world would be able to cope with the next financial crisis.

Underlying the global financial crisis was 30 years of globalisation. A liberalized world trading system, underpinned by the creation of the World Trade Organisation (which strengthened and extended existing trade rules), led to huge increase in international trade, with the creation of global supply chains linking developing and developed countries in the production of goods from smartphones to T-shirts. Even more important was financial globalisation, which led to an unprecedented flow of capital across national borders, encouraged by the IMF and World Bank, which urged countries to abandon exchange controls and integrate in to the world financial system.

The result was the huge increase in the power, scale and reach of the large banking groups, whose interests and influence soon spanned the globe. Although these global banks were largely American – such as Citigroup, JP Morgan, and Bank of America – UK and European banks such as Barclays, RBS, and Deutschebank joined in the quest for international acquisitions and revenue streams. The close integration of the global financial system, as well as its size and scale, was a major reason that the financial crisis spread with lightning speed across the world.

These developments were broadly applauded and indeed aided by the policies of most Western governments. The banking sector was deregulated and encouraged to expand, for example, by the opening up of the City of London to global investment in the 1980s, and the ending of the division between retail and investment banking in the USA. The introduction of 'light touch' regulation in the UK under Labour, and the belief in the self-correcting nature of financial markets by the head of the US Federal Reserve, Alan Greenspan, led to a relaxed attitude towards the continued expansion of the financial sector at the expense of the real economy, and indeed the domination of short-term financial gains rather than long-term investment in the corporate sector.

The failure to regulate the exotic financial instruments, such as CDOs (collateralized debt obligations) and CDSs (credit default swaps), created by the banks to boost profits led directly to the highly leveraged and increasingly unstable architecture of the financial system. And outside the official banking sector, unregulated "shadow banks" were able to take even greater risks and become an ever bigger part of the global financial system.

For most of this period, the benefits of globalisation were largely uncontested, both by politicians and the financial press. The benefits of globalisation – increasing prosperity and economic stability, growing government revenues to fund tax cuts or further spending, and the integration of all countries into a global economic system – seemed obvious and overwhelmingly positive. The downsides of globalisation – the growing disparity of wealth and income, as a global elite gained the most economic benefits, while workers in developed countries suffered job losses and reduced wages; the overweighting of finance against manufacturing in the real economy; the instability of the financial system, and the inability of national governments to manage their economies in a global economic system – were overlooked. The idea that there were going to be losers as well as winners from globalisation, both between and within countries and regions, was not on the radar.

This embrace of globalisation has been generally subsumed in the broader term "neo-liberalism" or "market fundamentalism," which seeks to embed this policy change in a general shift away from state intervention in the economy (such as Keynesianism), which arose after the Great Depression in the 1930s, to the laissez-faire policies embraced by the Thatcher and Reagan governments in the 1980s and continued by their successors.

The financial press, which itself had greatly expanded during this period, was predominantly a cheerleader for this process, embracing and covering the emergence of global finance on terms that sometimes bordered on adulation. It rarely questioned the consensus between policy-makers, politicians and businessmen. The specialist financial press, in particular, whose audience was precisely these business and finance professionals who were benefitting from globalisation, saw its role as an enabler rather than a critic of the rapidly changing financial landscape.

This book provides vital evidence and a deeper understanding of this process and in particular, the reasons why the Press was unable to play the watchdog role that might have warned the public about the inherent dangers in the path the global economy was taking.

It takes a new and fresh approach to the problem in several ways.

First, it benefits from the strengths of its historical and comparative approach, considering not just the coverage of the global financial crisis in 2007–8 but referring back to the coverage of two previous crises stretching back to the 1980s

This helps understand the evolution of the growing support for neo-liberalism over time and the decline of any questioning of this pathway.

By looking comparatively at the role of the Press in three different countries, the USA, the UK and Australia, who were differently affected by the crisis, it reinforces the notion that there was indeed a global consensus – a kind of group-think – on the benefits of globalisation, at least in the Anglo-Saxon world, that was reflected in press coverage.

Another strength of the book is its use of not just quantitative data, but interviews with journalists to a get a more detailed picture of what was going on and, in particular, the pressures faced by journalists in covering the global financial crisis.

This reveals not just the ideological but also the practical pressures on journalists that limited their ability to rise to the challenge of covering the crisis – the shortage of time and resources, the reliance on PR professionals for access to key actors, and difficulties caused by over-specialization. This meant that it was more difficult to make the connections between the banking sector, capital markets, house prices, and the real economy.

A further challenge for journalists in all countries, which the comparative coverage throws light on, is the difficulty in understanding the global nature of the crisis and the linkages between their own economies and the origins of the crisis in the US banking system. Much of the early coverage across the world focused on the problems in the US and failed to recognize how quickly the crisis would spread worldwide.

Another key element in the story is the ideology of the journalists themselves. How do financial journalists define their role? How much importance do they give to the investigative role of journalism in holding power to account? How can they reconcile this with the need to appeal to a specialist audience with strong vested interests in the current system? And how can they gain access to the resources and the critics who can provide alternative explanations?

The challenges facing journalists in covering future financial crises might be even more acute. The question of time and resources has become even more critical as the internet has both reduced the financial ability of the traditional media to employ a large staff of journalists, and put more pressure on existing journalists to write shorter, quick news stories that are published immediately online. The pressures of group-think are ever-present, particularly as the financial sector has emerged from the crisis virtually unscathed, with fewer but larger global firms still dominant. Journalists need even more to be able to take a longer-term historical perspective to learn how the lessons of the past apply to the present. Even more challenging is bringing a global perspective to developments that are still covered in a national perspective – where, for example, it might be Chinese debt that triggers the next financial crisis.

The backlash from globalisation has led to the rise of populist politicians across the world, from the UK, the USA and Europe to Brazil, who seek to find scapegoats for their economic problems in immigrants, criminals, and scroungers, and who encourage an economic nationalism that blames other countries for what are global problems. Probably the most important task facing economic and financial journalists in the future is in deconstructing these mythsand working towards an understanding of a global economic system that is more equitable, more stable and more sustainable than that which we have seen so far.

CHAPTER ONE

Financial Journalism Then and Now: Why Should We Care?

> Given the scale and complexity of business and finance in the modern world, the existence of a press equipped to analyse and hold it to public accountability is a necessary component of democracy in a market society. (Parsons 1989, 228)

In 2007–8 esoteric financial products associated with the US subprime mortgage market, which had spread globally via our complex financial market system, caused a meltdown on a scale comparable with the Great Depression of the 1930s. The events began to unfold on August 9, 2007, when the investment bank BNP Paribas suspended trading of three investment funds and announced that they could no longer value assets associated with the US subprime housing market (Soros 2009, xii), but the story did not grace our mainstream news pages and TV screens until the following month. Then, in the UK, in September, BBC business editor Robert Peston broke the story that one of the biggest UK-based retail banks, Northern Rock, was going to be rescued by the Bank of England after experiencing financing problems – causing a run on a UK bank for the first time in more than a century. But despite this, both US and UK journalists were taken by surprise when, one year later the bankruptcy of the US investment bank Lehman Brothers led to the collapse of the world financial system and a global recession (Tooze, 2018).

Parsons – one of the first academics to write in-depth about the development and implications of financial journalism in the UK, US and Australia – wrote about the importance of journalism in shaping a new economic paradigm, which switched from Keynesianism (government expenditure, especially during times of economic crisis) and then back to Monetarism (government control over money). To what degree did they fulfil the important role of critiquing the system? Fast forward three decades later to the Global Financial Crisis and the world has experienced a downturn and economic crisis, the likes of which have not been seen since the 1930s. The scale of complexity of business and finance has grown exponentially, as evidenced by the way the crisis caught fire and spread from one sector and industry to the next and from one geographical region to the other.

From greedy mortgage brokers in the US to retail banks in Iceland, and charities in the UK, the web of the financial products that underwrote the GFC had spread the world over. But, when the story broke in August of 2007, it seemed that the journalists telling the story were mostly playing catch-up, having been caught up in the financial system themselves, by welcoming the new financial instruments that caused the problem; by being too passive and not critical enough in their investigative approach; and in their journalistic newsgathering practises, being too dependent on the financial actors they used as sources for information.

As the events continued to play out the true scope and global nature of the crisis continued to unravel in 2008 and 2009 – most notably when Lehman Brothers collapsed in the US in 2009, a year after the run on the Northern Rock – journalists that reported on the economy, business and finance (hereafter referred to as financial journalists) came under increasing criticism for the part they played, and in some cases failed to play, in the Global Financial Crisis (hereafter referred to as the GFC). An unsuspecting public wondered why financial journalists had not acted as soothsayers and provided an element of forewarning. Journalists were blamed for not being sufficiently independent from or sceptical of their sources and the financial institutions that they were reporting on. The title of the 2009 book, *Playing Footsie with the FTSE? The Great Crash of 2008 and the Crisis in Journalism* (Mair and Keeble 2009), encapsulates the sense of a too-cosy relationship between the financial press and the financial world. While a few luminaries had sounded alarm bells, such as the economist Nouriel Roubini and *Financial Times* journalist Gillian Tett, they were ignored, swept away as irrelevant voices in the market euphoria, or else labelled doomsayers—Nouriel Roubini was regularly referred to as 'Dr. Doom' by the media.

Journalists were needed, before the crisis hit, to play the role of watchdogs – a role they mostly failed in.

The roles financial journalists play have been interpreted according to three broad categories: as watchdogs who provided some forewarning for the public (Roush 2006); as lapdogs who peddled unquestionably the line offered to them by financial PR practitioners and politicians (Starkman 2009); and as canaries in the coalmine, who reported reactively to events in a way that was not productive, but instead reactive and arguable exacerbated the situation. This latter point is best encapsulated by the fact that in early 2009 a UK Parliamentary select committee pulled in a group of the most eminent financial journalists – including Robert Peston who had broken the Northern Rock story – to ask whether journalists had contributed to the global panic and whether they should self-censor themselves during periods of crisis to avoid stoking the fire. (See Schifferes and Roberts 2014 for an edited transcript of the proceedings.)

Just a brief foray in to the literature makes it clear that these criticisms are not new. It is argued elsewhere that during a global crisis the news media plays a pivotal role, not just as a "conduit", but also in the development of the "definition" and "elaboration" of the crisis (Cottle 2008, 2). The public has frequently been dissatisfied with mainstream financial, business and economic coverage – especially around the time of crises. This book asks whether quality in financial reporting has declined in recent years as criticism would suggest, and what broader developments need to be understood to make any sense of these trends? To what degree does the financial press operate with the public interest in mind and how far does it go in fulfilling a watchdog role for the general public?

These questions around the quality of financial news and the role of financial journalists as watchdogs are as pertinent now as they were in 2007–8, as the financial crisis continues in its various transmuted economic and political forms. After the financial crisis, after governments spent billions bailing out the stricken banks, economies across the UK, the US and much of Europe fell into recession. In response to the cost of the bail-outs a number of governments, rather than trying to boost the economy, favoured austerity policies to cut public spending, reducing the welfare state and maintaining low tax rates for the wealthy and for businesses. What we are witnessing now are associated socio-political phenomena: the collapse in public trust in politics and institutions; and a subsequent rise in popular politics, seen most evidently in the UK's separation from Europe and the rise of support for populist and nationalist parties in Europe and the US.

So, if the financial media had such an important role to play in the story of the financial crisis, what lessons were learned and what has changed in the tumultuous decade that has passed since?

The main theme of the book is its critique of the watchdog role played by the financial media in three economically developed and democratic countries with well-established financial centres – the US, UK and Australia – during the past three decades. Each could be described as being culturally and politically similar, with each having a tie with Europe. This book looks at how and why we got in to this situation by taking a more longitudinal glance at other crises, to place the reporting of the GFC in to context. There has been no longitudinal study of financial journalism since an analysis in the 1980s of content from 1930–1970 (Barkin 1982). Since that time, not only have there been a number of financial and economic crises but also the media industry itself has undergone unparalleled change both structurally and technologically. Overall it shows the extent to which financial news standards have declined since the 1980s.

The case studies were chosen as three important economic and financial booms and busts to have affected the developed world economy over the past three decades. The 1990 recession was an economic crisis that affected a number of developed economies in the first years of the decade (Chapter 3); the dot com boom of 2000 emanated from a boom in investment in Internet-based stocks and shares, which eventually collapsed after several years of hype and very little return on investments (Chapter 4); and the GFC of 2007–2008 was just outlined to some degree and still lives in our more recent memory (Chapter 5). A comparison of the reporting in these countries offered some interesting and illuminating examples of how powerful a narrative can become when news media perpetuate the same values and adopt a similar journalistic approach. The chosen news outlets are three of the country's influential and mainstream newspapers, which now have reach online – the *Guardian*, *New York Times* and *Sydney Morning Herald*.

In addition to an analysis of the content of three financial crises in three countries, there is a discussion about the pressures that journalists now face when trying to report on finance, the economy, and business and interrogation of these issues through interviews with some preeminent journalists that operate in the UK, Australia and the US (Chapter 2). So while this book discusses various meta institutional, ideological and industrial pressures that journalists face, it also takes the views of journalists in to account, with the view that news stories are shaped by individuals and discursively produced (Boukes and Vliegenhart 2017; Cooper and Ebeling 2007).

The interviews are with financial, economic and business journalists and editors who have worked for decades and have witnessed the reporting of more than one financial crisis – and witnessed the way technology has changed the way journalism is practised. A number of them were conducted between 2012–14 and updated more recently to track any changes. They include (among others): former BBC editor (now with ITV) Robert Peston; former *Times* finance editor (now with Sky News) Ian King; economics editor at the *Sydney Morning Herald*, Ross Gittins; economics editor for the ABC network in Australia, Steven Long; economics columnist for the *New York Times*, Eduardo Porter; Economics editor in

Europe at the *New York Times* Peter Goodman; and Rana Foroohar, global business columnist at the *Financial Times* and economic analyst for CNN.

At the end of the book there is an assessment of the watchdog role financial journalism can and should play in the future – especially online and in alternative forms (Chapter 6).

The Fourth Estate Tradition and the Financial Press

For now, we will consider the goals that underpin the meaning and existence of journalism as a watchdog to protect civil society and the more idealistic concept of the Fourth Estate. From its establishment in the 18th century, the Fourth Estate came in to being to be able to educate and enlighten its readership; to promote democratic debate to reach a common good (Hampton 2010, 4). This idea is complicated by McNair (2003, 32), who argues that the liberal and Enlightenment principles, when applied to the media, are only possible when there is competition and diversity of ideas and views – the corollary of which means a press that does not encourage diverse views is in fact obscuring the truth.

In Australia, as early as colonial times, the Press was "unlicensed, distributed post-free and uncensored" and watchdog-style journalism prevailed despite strict libel laws (Schultz 1998, 26). Some of the earliest examples of Fourth Estate journalism in Australia are criticisms of the Governor Arthur of Tasmania in the *Hobart Town Gazette* (1816–1836), and the establishment of the *Australian* (1824–1848) without official approval and "in the interests of self-government against autocracy" (Green, cited in ibid., 31). As the nineteenth century progressed, news became more conservative and liberal, and the Press in Australia—although unlicensed since its establishment—became encumbered by political and economic constraints (Schultz 1998, 3).

The power of the Press had also been growing in the UK. Laws that had subjected the Press to both censorship and taxation, and limited its distribution had been scrapped in the mid-to-late nineteenth century. Simultaneously a 'new' form of financial journalism emerged, which contemporary journalist Charles Duguid described as providing a "crisp note" "straightforward advice" and "fearless criticism" (Porter 2005, 2). It is argued that Harry Marks of *Financial News* in the US was the leading creator and proponent of this new style that brought articles to life and moved away from insipid Victorian money articles. Marks generated this new more popular and lively style of financial writing from his training at newspapers in the US. The financial press was also growing expanded exponentially – the number of financial titles grew from 19 in 1874 to 109 in 1904 (Porter 2005) – with titles we still know to this day; the *Economist* was established in 1843 and the *Financial Times* in 1888. It was growing in popularity, reflecting the financial markets and system which was being accessed more freely by amateur investors and all classes in society.

Its development was not, however, straightforward. Financial news was chiaroscuro in its contrast of public service ideals and corrupt practices of bribery and puffery. Financial journalism was viewed as both depraved and requiring a new set of codes of ethics. The *Economist* gave its description of the financial press in 1913 as providing "First blackmail, then puff, then the suppression of facts which could be inconvenient to advertisers, and the insertion of those which are favourable. Lastly … there is abstention from criticism" (Porter 2005, 12).

In the US, freedom of speech and the Press were enshrined and protected by the First Amendment of the US Constitution introduced in 1791. The rise of mass market newspaper in the 1890s–1920s led both to more investigative stories and more popular yellow journalism as papers competed for readers. There was sharp growth of investigative journalism in the US in the early 1900s – the muckrakers who attacked monopolistic companies, exploitation of the workers and corrupt governments. They were certainly the model for investigative journalism in the US – as Starkman makes clear (2015). They were also part of the New Journalism movement, which was partly a reaction to press manipulation during World War I, as expressed by Walter Lippmann in his book Public Opinion (1922).

A renewed enthusiasm for Fourth Estate reporting principles and watchdog investigations emerged from the mid-1900s out of a feeling, encapsulated in the Hutchins Commission's recommendations of 1947, that the Press might better serve the public if it took a less partisan approach to news reporting. According to the theory of social responsibility, the Press should critique the free-market and any of its failings to address what society needs (Lacy and Fico 1991b, 364).

In the US a renewed commitment to investigative journalism emerged with the Hutchins Commission in the 1940s,[1] the publication of the Pentagon Papers in the 1960s, and the Watergate scandal in the 1970s. And in the UK, there were three Royal Commissions from the Second World War to the 1970s, which had started to challenge media monopolies and promoted the ideal of the Fourth Estate as an independent press activity that should be encouraged by government. Australia's "golden age" of watchdog journalism arrived in the 1980s (Schultz 1998, 43), and is described by Schultz (ibid., 13) as a transformative decade in Australian journalism." Through Schultz' work, examining the attitudes of journalists in Australia during this period, she found strong commitment to watchdog journalism in the 1980s, as practitioners lobbied for greater autonomy and independence in their working practices.

1980s onward

Financial journalism, caught between Fourth Estate ideals of the enhancement and protection of democracy on the one hand, and increasing competition and commercialisation on the other, faced new challenges from the 1980s onward, with larger and more open financial markets, and a subsequent increase in demand for financial news from a widening audience. This juncture, which can be linked to Thatcher and Reagan policies to deregulate and privatize the financial sector, can also be pinpointed as the juncture at which financial journalists were more challenged to operate as watchdogs for a general public – and paradoxically as the time when they were most needed to critique the political economic and financial system that was developing under the auspices of a free-market neo-liberal paradigm.

Although it is a crude delineation, in many ways the 1980s could be described as a formative decade for financial journalism (and journalism more generally). This is mostly due to the number of changes to the financial and media industries that took place during this decade, the growing popularity of this genre of news, and global reach of specialist publications like the *Financial Times* and *Wall Street Journal*. Rather than writing with the general public in mind, however, and critiquing the still developing neo-liberal paradigm, journalists were instead swept up in the developments and the dominant political narrative.

The main effects of neo-liberalism for the public are described well by Couldry (2010, 2) who calls neo-liberalism a discourse which places the financial markets as a central concern for politics and, subsequently, cancels out the "voice" of the public:

> [neo-liberalism as a discourse] has come to dominate the contemporary world (formally, practically, culturally and imaginatively). That discourse operates with a view of economic life that does not value voice and imposes that view of economic life on to politics, via a reductive view of politics as the implementing of market functioning.

In the UK Peston describes the beginning of this process as the end of "financial paternalism", because the general public is now faced with a deregulated economy and a financial system that requires them to secure their own financial futures:

> There was a time when jobs were for life and a decent income in retirement was guaranteed by a benign employer, with the welfare state rescuing the unlucky or feckless few. Those were the days. Whether its pensions, or buying a house or acquiring new skills so that we can remain in gainful employment, the onus has been put much more on individuals to make decisions that will determine whether they'll be prosperous or paupers (Peston 2009, 18).

Moreover, free market theory, and neo-liberal ideology generally, were adopted by the media in the US, UK, and Australia – and eventually by large and developing economies such as India and China (Seaga-Shaw 2015). Particularly in the UK, while the free-market position was espoused by some academics in institutions like the London School of Economics and London Business School, Parsons contends that "the most vital territory occupied by the forces of economic liberalism was not academia but the financial press (1989 172) (See also Kitchener for a discussion on the role of the Press in spreading the ideology associated with the neo-liberal paradigm in Australia 1999, 238). In the US, academics such as Milton Friedman were more successful in taking their case directly to the public and politicians through the Press.

After the GFC, the neo-liberal paradigm was challenged to some degree, by politicians, the media and the public (Lewis 2010. They called for more regulation of financial markets and the separation of retail and investment banking activities. While some legislative changes were introduced, the banks fought back fiercely to limit deregulation and as the issue faded from public consciousness, the system of financial deregulation that had emerged in the previous three decades emerged unscathed and bolstered by the very crisis it had contributed to (Blythe 2013).

In addition to political economic and ideological pressures, other pressures and challenges to the practice of financial journalism have grown incrementally as the financial and media industries have had to transform since the 1980s. Henriques (2000b, 19)—a financial reporter at the *New York Times*—believes many publications in the 1980s and 1990s suffered from the proliferation of financial news and publications that were increasing their size, or what she describes as "the expansion-team syndrome". She says the personal finance magazines and local newspapers were most affected, as most financial journalists learned their trade with them and then moved on. The audience being targeted was also changing from "readers" in the 1980s, to "consumers" in the 1990s, and "investors" by the year 2000 (ibid., 29). This is echoed by Solomon (2002, 3), who notes that even "the 'general circulation' press had become transfixed by the investor." In contrast to investors, the general audience and "their very human needs come across as clunky impediments to economic progress".

Newsgathering techniques were also under pressure from technological advancement. Where finding a story once meant searching archives and "fat envelopes of fragile clippings", in the 1990s this newsgathering technique changed, as "everybody's old stories are a click away" (Henriques 2000b, 19). Therefore, time pressures had become worse than ever, while—due to globalisation and technological advances—the stories were gaining complexity. These increasing pressures on the practice of financial journalism, experienced by Henriques during the 1980s and 1990s, continued with some momentum throughout the 2000s.

At the turn of the twenty first century the dot com boom and Enron exposed the dangers of a decline in the quality of financial news for the general reader. Doyle (2006) argued that the financial press did not equip the general public with the kind of knowledge their specialist counterparts at the *FT* did before Enron and the dot com boom story imploded. A similar view was expressed by economics editor Jeffrey Madrick (2002, 3), who argues financial reporters during the 1990s "reported well on neither the Enron story nor the economic stories impacting the American people in the 1990s." There was, he says, "little sense that they served a public watchdog during this time."

Just before the financial crisis imploded, in 2007, Tambini (2008, 2010) identified some of the key challenges for the practice and integrity of financial journalism. His study was based on interviews with journalists and their lawyers in the UK and the US (Tambini 2010, 165–168). They confirm some of the issues that were noted by Henriques some ten years earlier:

- New communications technology that has increased the need for speedier reporting;
- The increased complexity of stories based on complicated financial products;
- A lack of financial training to cope with time and complexity pressures;
- A growth in business and financial PR that skew stories, and prevent source access;
- A lack of resources in a competitive industry with dwindling profits; and
- A lack of support from defamation law.

With pressures on the practice of financial journalism, there is – rightfully – significant concern about the public interest and quality standards being produced. Journalism standards have been increasingly under pressure since the 1980s, and time pressures on journalists have increased with the advent of the 24/7 multi-platform news operations. Chapters 3, 4 and 5 demonstrate empirically the degree to which standards have fallen since the 1980s.

There is also the question of the degree to which journalists view themselves in a watchdog role. While the ideal role for a journalist may be that of a watchdog, investigating corporate and political malfeasance, the role of the journalist is not a one-size-fits-all approach (Josephi 2013), and the roles journalists perceive for themselves can vary by political and economic context (Hanitzsch, Hanusch, and Lauerer 2016). Interviews with financial journalists demonstrate a mixed self-perception of their role (Tambini 2010; Usher 2013). In the US, Usher (2013) showed that a large number of financial journalists view their roles as passive mirrors that reflect what is happening in the markets. Meanwhile, interviews conducted more recently (Damstra forthcoming) – including in this book – show strong desire among financial journalists in the Netherlands, UK, US and Australia to investigate malfeasance and to write for a broad audience.

The Relevance of the Fourth Estate in a Digital World

A discussion on values and quality are arguably part of the same concern that the establishment of a set of global news ethics, values and standards is becoming increasingly crucial as news consumers, outlets, and journalistic practices are brought closer together by globalisation and technology. There is debate surrounding the applicability of the normative relationship between journalism and democracy, and watchdog function of the media, to a digitally connected world.

There is growing consensus amongst academics and, arguably, amongst the public, that the media needs to reorientate itself within a more ethical and balanced version of itself with regards to quality and inclusiveness of voices and values. This idea of a set of global ethics, values, and standards, is only made more expedient by scandals like the phone-hacking scandal in the UK at the *News of the World*, which saw its closure, and the Leveson inquiry in the UK and the Finkelstein inquiry in Australia – government-led inquiries in to press culture and ethics. More recently, we are witnessing a global debate around fake news, which is being exacerbated in the US by President Donald Trump's antipathy towards the news media and the extreme polarization of the news audience.

A brief analysis of Google trends shows the way fake news has manifested in the public's consciousness in the past few years, creating the perfect storm for doubt and a call to arms to challenge the status quo. Figure 1 below shows the number of times the public 'googled' the phrase, which rose from January 2016 and peaked in January 2018.

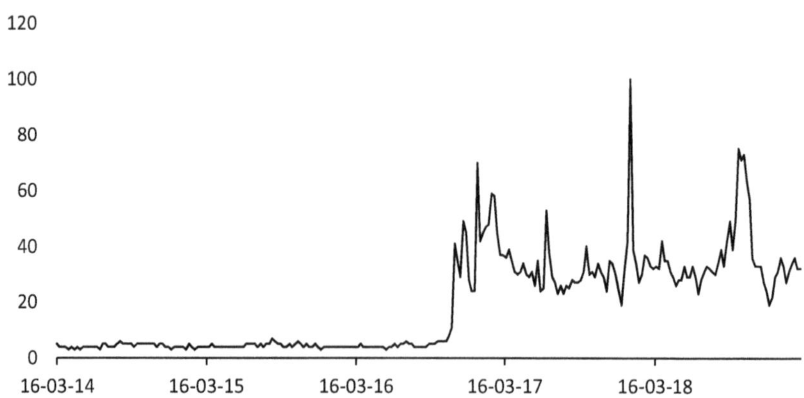

Figure 1. Number of times "fake news" has been searched on Google worldwide

Levels of trust in the news media have scarcely been worse. A helpful barometer of the health of the relationship between the public and its Press is usefully provided on an annual basis by the Edelman Trust Survey, which has access to 33,000 respondents worldwide. The media is now the least trusted institution in 21 out of 28 countries surveyed, with more trust placed in governments, businesses and the judiciary. The titles of Edelman's trust surveys are a useful indicator of how things have shifted over time, and they illustrate the close relationship between trust, the economy and political leadership. In 2002 (post-Enron) they refer to the "fall of the celebrity CEO"; in 2009 (post-GFC) "business must partner with government to regain trust"; in 2013 as the economic crisis in Europe continues we see a "crisis of leadership"; and now in 2018, as populism is growing worldwide, and we are plagued by discussions around "fake news", things are described in fatalistic terms as "the battle for truth". It is unsurprising then that in 2018 Edelman has recorded the steepest decline in trust in media ever recorded in the US. The polarisation of this trust is seen in the cleavage that exists between the level of trust Democratic voters have in media (61%) and levels displayed by Republicans who support Donald Trump (35%). And worldwide 7 in 10 worry fake news will be used as a weapon. (Edelman 2018)

But there is a more nuanced shift if we compare trust in journalists with media platforms, as the public seems to trust journalists more in 2018 than they did in 2017, and trust has particularly declined for online platforms and search engines. This trend can be explained by UK-based political consulting firm Cambridge Analytica's unethical use of 87 million personal Facebook user profiles for political advertisement purpose; data that was used by Donald Trump's 2016 election campaign and by the leave campaign for Britain to leave the EU. So the debates and scandals that have surrounded fake news have evidently had an influence on the public, with 21 out of 28 countries losing trust in platforms. Edelman suggests three trust-building mandates: guarding information quality, educating the public on important issues, and informing good life decisions. Globally the media falls on each criterion: across the 28 countries surveyed 36% of the public thinks the media guards information quality; 50% think they educate, and 45% inform good life decisions.

Therefore, there is plenty of evidence of the need for support of journalism that revises old Fourth Estate traditions and generates new ones that are ethically sound, globally adaptable, and sustainable for the long-term trust and respect of media industries. There are a few clear ideas that have emerged which could instruct journalism on how to fit within normative democratic values. An argument has developed in favour of story boxes (boxes are described as providing a better metaphor than frames) that encapsulate nuances and alternative versions of events in such a way that it is accessible to news consumers (Anderson 2013, 15).

Meanwhile a survey of academics, journalists, and members of the public in the UK – one of the relatively few studies to seek the public's view on what they consider the "public interest" – made it clear that "public interest" itself needs to be defined (O'Leary and Tryhorn 2012, 33). The public want to know more about the main point—the 'what'—of a story and its significance rather than who is involved in a story, which can lead to unethical news practices that encroach on peoples' private lives. They also believe newspapers must be more accountable and transparent about how they have gathered a story and where it has come from. Finally, they believe the public must be involved in press regulation (ibid.). The fact that public trust of the Press is waning points to the urgent need for journalism to reassess its values in contemporary society.

It will also be essential to provide an inclusive version of journalism, which incorporates the "voice" of the public, to borrow the words used by Couldry (2010). This idea speaks to the social responsibility theory that emerged around the time of the Hutchins Commission (discussed earlier) in the 1940s; that journalistic fairness and balance are at the heart of journalism's goal to serve society. Fairness and balance are achieved by representing "all voices" in the public debate (Lacy and Fico 1991b, 364). The focus on the broad spectrum of society also avoids the threat of capture of the media by political elites eager to exert their influence on governments and business (Brown, Bybee, Wearden and Straughan 1987, 46).

This version of journalism is espoused by Cushion (2012, 44), who argues for journalism that appeals to a large section of society. Cushion argues that regardless of the nation, outlet, medium, or ethical codes that influence individual journalists and create news values, all media should be bound by the same democratic principles. Democratic news is defined as providing "information, analysis and context on issues that identify audiences as citizens rather than consumers" (ibid., 59). Like Brown and others (1987), Cushion (2012, 44) also rejects the pluralist perspective that considers audience reach or numbers of news outlets as measures of quality, as this ignores the calibre of the content that is provided by the news outlet.

Moreover, journalism in a modern environment, which reaches and often combines several different cultural, political, and social contexts, may need to devise a paradigm that is flexible but draws from the normative values of the Fourth Estate tradition. Wright (2014) provides the practical compromise that it should be somewhere between what Couldry (2012, 189) describes as philosophical and 'Aristotelian' in its approach to the idea that practitioners should, as individuals, work towards the same goals and the prospect that "we can live well together"; and something more utilitarian – a set of standards that can be agreed upon between transnational news organisations, which takes in to consideration the everyday practices and routines that journalists work with.

The idea that a normative framework can be built and agreed upon, and the assumption that a link still exists between journalism and democracy, was critiqued in a special issue of *Journalism*, where it was argued that journalism can in fact be 'de-coupled' from democracy (Josephi 2013). This is not to say that the authors of the various journal articles believe that democracy no longer needs journalism and vice versa, but that journalists can uphold the values that are necessary for democratic debate even if they operate outside a functioning democracy.

Josephi (2013) uses the Arabic news service Al Jazeera as an example to illustrate how fair and balanced watchdog reporting can take place outside of a democratic political system. In the same issue, Nerone (2013, 456) argues a new journalism paradigm is needed that addresses the requirements of new mediums and more demanding audiences. It must be a flexible journalism paradigm that works within Fourth Estate ideals, without assuming the "hegemonic western model" of journalism. He cautions against throwing the baby out with the bathwater:

> Journalisms are never invented out of the whole cloth; they are always patchworks of older traditions. Much of the tradition of hegemonic journalism, including its professions of populism and its deference to the intelligence of the people, can be useful. It is hard to imagine a journalism of any value that does not include some version of these elements [...] In systems in which journalists look for the ideological resources to support a vigorous critique of concentrations of power and abuses of authority, the norms of western journalism can be inspirational, but not if treated with too much reverence (Nerone 2013, 456).

This discussion shows how the ideal of watchdog journalism, far from being stuffy and out-of-date, is still relevant while needing reinvention in the modern age of global digitised media. This has been confirmed in a poll by the Pew Research Center (2017), in the US, which found 65 per cent of the public believes in and supports the watchdog role that the press are playing for them, up nearly 10 per cent from 2011. This is down from a high of 75 per cent in 2016 and, as illustrated by Edelman, PEW also finds huge variation depending on political affiliation: again Democrats trust the media more than Republicans (82 per cent v 38 per cent), whose trust has declined dramatically and reflects the President's views about a fake media. In addition to this polarisation and delineation between party supporters and trust in news, Republican support for a watchdog press has declined from a whopping 77 to just 38 per cent.

Overall, a continuing and voracious contemporary debate demonstrates that watchdog journalism embodies a vital and timeless news value, which politicians and the public continue to see as central to society's functioning, and journalists should uphold regardless of what company they work for, what medium they work in, or where they are located.

What the General Public Want and Need from Financial Journalism

It is fair to say that financial news is moving on from being political news' less attractive cousin to a rather important and popular sibling sister. Once relegated to the back pages, and focused on narrow financial topics, news about the economy, business and finance can be found on front-pages and prime-time TV news bulletins. And periods of financial crisis bring this genre of news even closer to its audience. During critical junctures such as these, people question what will happen with their money, their jobs and their pensions. This can extend more broadly to the way political power is shaping the economic system.

This was certainly true of the 2008 financial crisis, which prompted a surge of interest from a wide audience. (See Schifferes and Coulter's 2012 study on the dramatic increase in interest in online financial news from the BBC during the crisis.) The Reuters Institute's 2012 Digital Survey of 11,000 people across Europe, Japan and the US shows that between 36 and 46 per cent of those polled consume news on the economy, while between 15 and 27 per cent consume news on finance (Newman et al. 2013). Some of the highest demand for news about the economy comes from the UK and the US at 53 per cent and 52 per cent respectively (Schifferes 2012).

But, even though consumption is on the rise, the content is not always satisfactory to an audience that is not elite and is consuming mainstream news. The public themselves desire more information on topics that relate to them as non-shareholders. A UK wide poll of 2,000 people revealed they want more information on topics like personal finance, government spending, and jobs. Moreover, they would like them written in a way that addresses them as non-elite, non-shareholders with minimal jargon (Schifferes 2012).

A sound grasp of economic and financial topics is needed to better understand the growing political and economic debate and the turn to populist answers to complex questions. This fact is expressed most acutely by a rise in populist politics and the increasing popularity of simplistic solutions that has paralleled a decline in trust in institutions and experts, which has grown from a prolonged global economic crisis – and which has been reflected in Britain's referendum on exiting the EU and the rise of Donald Trump. But simplistic narratives in the press did little to engage and inform an audience that is growing in size and shifting in profile – as those who consume financial news are still disproportionately male, old and well-off (Knowles and Schifferes 2020). Mainstream coverage often ignores the broader systemic issues that caused the financial crisis, focused on greedy bankers, an indebted government and provided few narratives and ideas to offer alternatives to austerity policies (Basu, Schifferes and Knowles 2018). The wider public, unsurprisingly, distrusts the financial press more than ever (Schifferes 2014) and has looked for their own political alternatives and scapegoats.

If the audience for financial news is increasing, and engagement is at a peak during times of crisis, the potential this has for informing the audience and enhancing democracy is limited by the public's persistently low financial literacy. International studies have repeatedly found the public's insufficient knowledge when reading topics on finance and the economy in the news (Lusardi and Mitchell 2011; Nicolini et al. 2013; OECD 2017). The public in the US had a poor understanding of basic economic topics when trying to understand the GFC (PEW 2009). Moreover, those with low incomes, those who are not employed, and those who are young, are less likely to understand the meaning of economic or financial terms like GDP or the Dow Jones industrial average (ibid., 3). Only one out of four understands economic policy well (ibid., 6).

The public's interest in this genre of news peaked during the GFC, as many turned to outlets like the BBC to stay abreast of economic developments (Schifferes and Coulter 2012). Since the crisis, the public has continued to get its financial and economic information from mainstream media (Knowles and Schifferes 2020).

Indeed, the way the media frames and shapes issues and events is of increasing importance. Since the GFC consumption of financial and economic news has risen and remains at a permanently high level. In 2005 only a third of the UK population were using the media to keep up with financial matters weekly. In 2011 this figure had risen substantially to 70% who said they were keeping up weekly or daily (Atkinson 2006; Knowles and Schifferes 2020). These surveys show that at the peak of the GFC and the height of the Brexit debates, the public were consuming financial news frequently (Newman et al. 2013; Schifferes 2014; Knowles and Schifferes 2020).

And when asked what they use to keep up with news about finance and the economy in 2018, as with the earlier surveys, TV news is still the most important medium; with 35% using this as a source to keep up with news about business or the economy, followed closely by online news at 31%. Newspapers were only 10%, radio 5%, social media 7%, and friends, family and work colleagues at 5%.

And globally it is usually those on low incomes, the young and women who are most likely to rely on mainstream media for financial news when compared to those on higher incomes who pay for specialist advice and specialised information.

Low-income earners, in particular, use mainstream news media for their financial information in the US (Rhine and Toussaint 2002). The same is true of South Africa (Roberts, Struwig, Gordon, Viljoen and Wentzel 2012).

Surveys of the public, therefore, show that two challenges in particular stand in the way of increasing engagement and preparing citizens for when another crisis hits: lack of knowledge about finance and the economy and a lack of trust in the financial news press (Schifferes 2014).

Economy, a charitable foundation in the UK, also found social class to be a barrier, with those from lower social classes talking about economic issues less, and feeling socially inhibited from economic discussions. The charity Economy also found that the public want to be involved in discussions about the economy, but cannot decipher the language in the news which they describe as being too abstract, alien and expert-dominated. More worrying, it was the participants who could not understand this economic language who were the least likely to get involved in the democratic process. Trust in economic news can also predict political decisions, with those who voted for the extreme right-wing UK party UKIP in the UK general elections least likely to trust economic news and those who voted to leave the EU unable to engage in a conversation about the economy (Economy 2018, 21).

All of this would be irrelevant if it weren't for the public's news consumption patterns, which show increasing consumption of mainstream news about the economy, especially during times of crisis (Schifferes 2014). The same variables which impact financial literacy can be found in the variables that dictate patterns of financial news consumption. And more recent focus groups by Berry (2018) indicate the wide cleavage that exists between what the public knows and understands about the economy and the dangerous degree to which the media frames these issues for them. Berry conducted 16 focus groups in the UK at the height of the GFC, and the responses highlighted the lack of knowledge and the degree to which media was driving their perceptions and understanding (p. 113). As one individual, from a low-income group in Glasgow, put it: "I have a bit of difficulty with the media and how they portray a lot of what's happening because they expect you to understand it and they don't actually get down to a level where you can actually understand what they're talking about" (p. 105). More worryingly still, Berry traces the way conservatively-framed media explanations and simplistic narratives about a growing deficit contributed to "long-term media socialisation", which inevitably lead to public support for austerity policies.

Journalists and academics think the media should be helping to resolve this gap in knowledge. At the peak of the crisis Robert Peston (2009, 18) argued that in financial journalism "there is more-then-ever a requirement ... to empower people to participate fully in democracy". Doyle (2006, 434), like Peston, bestows on financial journalism an imperative to provide "sound public grasp" to ensure both civic empowerment and democracy (ibid., 435). Doyle (ibid., 433) blames differences between specialist and mainstream publications—and specifically the "in-depth analysis" which is "confined to specialist media"—for the failure in "facilitating a sound public grasp over the significance of financial and economic news."

In other words, financial journalists in the mainstream media, like their specialist counterparts, need to provide more in-depth reports on financial issues for the general public in a way they can understand.

Conclusion

In the wake of the GFC, the role of the media in reporting financial and economic topics was a hotbed of discussion and debate. It prompted several new studies and renewed interest in this reporting beat. For the first time in the past two generations, the interconnectedness of the world economy was made more apparent than ever. The impact that financial markets can have on the real economy and the public's lives has been made tangible, as the latter carries the burden of the prolonged recession in the form of stagnant wage growth, tightened bank lending, and a cutback in the welfare state and the public sector.

This Chapter has argued that we should continue to care about the role of the financial media in our lives, and particularly the mainstream news that shapes so many worldviews. Meanwhile, while the general public is consuming more financial news, it is limited by a lack of financial literacy, which limits the ability to fully participate in public debate – something that is affecting young women across the globe in particular.

In the next chapter, we discuss the various challenges – ideological, organisational, ethical and industrial – that journalists have faced in doing their jobs and acting as effective watchdogs. It interrogates those criticisms that journalists have faced during the GFC and previous financial crises, among them: for being too uncritical, too cosy with elite sources, and limited by the narrow horizons of the conventional wisdom. The literature and the criticisms that have been levelled at financial journalism are discussed with experienced journalists working in the US, UK, and Australia.

This is followed by a discussion of the method used to analyse three case studies then the case studies themselves: the 1990 recession, the dot com boom and the GFC. In the last chapter there is a discussion of very recent content that can be found in blogs and social media, and a continuation of our discussion with journalists themselves about how financial journalism has changed in the past ten years since the GFC – and what role they played in the entrenchment of the neo-liberal free-market paradigm, the rise of populism and the prolonged commitment to austerity policies.

Note

1. The Hutchins Commission on Freedom of the Press was launched in 1942 with the brief of inquiring into the proper function of the press in a democracy, in response to the widespread attacks in the press on the New Deal reforms prompted by the Great Depression, and called for industry to be more accountable and socially responsible. Its final report, presented in 1947, established the parameters for what became known as the social responsibility model of journalism.

References

Anderson, Peter. 2013. "Defining and Measuring Quality News Journalism." In *The Future of Quality News Journalism: A Cross-Continental Analysis*, edited by Peter Anderson, Michael Williams, and George Ogola, 7–34. London: Routledge.

Atkinson, Adele, Stephen McKay, Elaine Kempson, and Sharon Collard, 2006. *Levels of Financial Capability in the UK: Results of a Baseline Survey*, consumer research 47, prepared for the Financial Services Authority by the Personal Finance Research Centre, University of Bristol, Financial Services Authority, March.

Barkin, Steve. 1982. 'Changes in Business Sections, 1931–1979.' *Journalism Quarterly* 59 (3): 435–439.

Basu, Laura, Steve Schifferes, and Sophie Knowles. 2018. *Media and Austerity: Comparative Perspectives*. London: Routledge.

Berry, Mike. 2018. *The Media, the Public and the Great Financial Crisis*. London: Springer.

Blythe, Mark. 2013. *Austerity: The History of a Dangerous Idea*. Oxford: Oxford University Press.

Boukes, Mark, and Rens Vliegenthart. 2017. 'A General Pattern in the Construction of Economic Newsworthiness? Analyzing News Factors in Popular, Quality, Regional, and Financial Newspapers.' *Journalism* : 1464884917725989.

Brown, Jane, Carl Bybee, Stanley Wearden, and Dulcie Straughan. 1987. 'Invisible Power: Newspaper News Sources and the Limits of Diversity.' *Journalism Quarterly* 4 (1): 45–54.

Cooper, Geoff, and Mary Ebeling. 2007. 'Epistemology, Structure and Urgency: The Sociology of Financial and Scientific Journalists.' *Sociological Research Online* 12 (3): 1–12.

Cottle, Simon. 2008. 'Global Crisis? What Crisis' In *Global Crisis Reporting: Journalism in a Global Age*, edited by Simon Cottle. London: McGraw-Hill. pp. 1–25.

Couldry, Nick. 2010. *Why Voice Matters: Culture and Politics After Neoliberalism*. London: Sage.

Couldry, Nick. 2012. *Media, Society, World: Social Theory and Digital Media Practice*. London: Polity.

Cushion, Stephen. 2012. *The Democratic Value of News*. Basingstoke: Palgrave Macmillan.

Damstra, Alyt, and Knut De Swert. 2020. "The Making of Economic news: Dutch Economic Journalists Contextualizing Their Work." *Journalism*: 1464884919897161.

Doyle, Gillian. 2006. 'Financial News Journalism: A Post-Enron Analysis of Approaches towards Economic and Financial News Production.' *Journalism* 7 (4): 433–452.

Edelman. 2018. Edelman Trist Barometer. January 21. https://www.edelman.com/research/2018-edelman-trust-barometer (Accessed Jan 1 2020).

Elliott, A., P. Dolan, I. Vlaev, C. Adriaenssens, and R. Metcalfe, 2010. *Transforming Financial Behaviour: Developing Interventions That Build Financial Capability*, CFEB consumer research report 01, Consumer Financial Education Body (CFEB), July.

Hampton, Mark. 2010. 'The Fourth Estate Ideal in Journalism History' In *The Routledge Companion to News and Journalism*, edited by Stuart Allan. London: Routledge. pp. 3–12.

Hanitzsch, Thomas, Folker Hanusch, and Corinna Lauerer. 2016. 'Setting the Agenda, Influencing Public Opinion, and Advocating for Social Change: Determinants of Journalistic Interventionism in 21 countries.' *Journalism Studies* 17 (1): 1–20.

Henriques, Diana B. 2000b. 'Business Reporting: Behind the Curve.' *Columbia Journalism Review* 39: 18–21.

Hung, Angela, Joanne Yoong, and Elizabeth Brown. 2012. 'Empowering Women through Financial Awareness and Education.' OECD Working Papers on Finance, Insurance and Private Pensions, 14, OECD Publishing, Paris.

Jappelli, Tullio. 2010. 'Economic Literacy: An International Comparison', *Economic Journal*, 120 (548): F429–F451.

Josephi, Beate. 2013. 'How Much Democracy Does Journalism Need?' *Journalism* 14 (4): 474–489.

Kitchener, Jennifer. 1999. 'Business Journalism in the 1980s.' In *Journalism: Print, Politics and Popular Culture*, edited by Ann Curthoys, and Julianne Schultz, St Lucia: University of Queensland Press. pp. 229–241.

Knowles, Sophie. 2020. 'Women, the Economy and the News: Undeserved and Underrepresented?' *Journalism Studies*, 9(1): 61–83.

Lacy, Stephen, and Frederick Fico. 1991b. 'Fairness and Balance in the Prestige Press.' *Journalism Quarterly* 68 (3): 363–370.

Lewis, Justin. 2010. 'Normal Viewing Will be Resumed Shortly: News, Recession and the Politics of Growth.' *Popular Communication* 8 (3): 161–165.

Lippmann, Walter. 1922. *Public Opinion*. Greenback Publications. Reprinted 2010.

Lusardi, Anna M., and Mitchell, Olivia S., 2011. 'Financial Literacy Around the World: An Overview', *Journal of Pension Economics and Finance*, 10 (4): 497–508.

Mair, John, and Richard L. Keeble, eds. 2009. *Playing Footsie with the FTSE? The Great Crash of 2008 and the Crisis in Journalism*. Suffolk: Institute of Communication Ethics and Abramis Academic.

McNair, Brian. 2003. *News and Journalism in the UK.* 4th ed. London: Routledge.

Nerone, John. 2013. 'The Historical Roots of the Normative Model of Journalism.' *Journalism* 14 (4): 446–458.

Newman, Nic, and David A. L. Levy, eds. 2013. *Reuters Institute Digital News Report.* Oxford: Reuters Institute for the Study of Journalism.

Nicolini, Gianni, Brenda J. Cude, and Swarn Chatterjee. 2013. 'Financial Literacy: A Comparative Study across Four Countries.' *International Journal of Consumer Studies* 37(6): 689–705.

OECD (2017), G20/OECD INFE report on adult financial literacy in G20 countries. http://www.oecd.org/daf/fin/financial-education/G20-OECD-INFE-report-adult-financial-literacy-in-G20-countries.pdf (Accessed 01 May 2020).

O'Leary, Duncan and Chris Tryhorn. 2012. *Voicing the Public Interest: Listening to the Public on Press Regulation.* Better Journalism. Dunfermline: Carnegie UK Trust and Demos.

Parsons, Wayne. 1989. *The Power of the Financial Press: Journalism and Economic Opinion in Britain and America.* New Brunswick: Rutgers University.

Peston, Robert. 2009. 'In the New Digital World, There Is a Stronger Need Than Ever for Subsidized, Public-Service News.' In *Playing Footsie with the FTSE? The Great Crash of 2008 and the Crisis in Journalism*, edited by John Mair and Richard L. Keeble, Suffolk: Institute of Communication Ethics and Abramis Academic. pp. 10–22.

Pew Research Center. 2009. 'Public Knows Basic Facts about Financial Crisis.' https://www.people-press.org/2009/04/02/public-knows-basic-facts-about-financial-crisis/ (Accessed 01 May 2020).

Pew Research Center, May, 2017, 'Americans' Attitudes about the News Media Deeply Divided Along Partisan Lines.' https://www.journalism.org/2017/05/10/americans-attitudes-about-the-news-media-deeply-divided-along-partisan-lines/ (Accessed Jan 1 2020).

Porter, Dilwyn. 2005. "A Trusted Guide of the Investing Public: Harry Marks and the Financial News 1884-1916". In *Speculators and Patriots: Essays in Business Biography*, edited by Richard P. T Davenport-Hines, London: Taylor & Francis. pp. 1–6.

Rethinking Economics. 2018. Doing Economics Differently: How Can Rethinking Economics and Economy Support Professionals to Find New Ways of Doing Economics? https://www.ecnmy.org/wp-content/uploads/2018/10/RE-Economy-Doing-Economics-Differently-Report-September-2018-DIGITAL.pdf (Accesed Dec 1 2019).

Rhine, Sherrie L. W., and Maude Toussaint-Comeau. 2002. 'Consumer Preferences in the Delivery of Financial Information: A Summary.' *Consumer Interest Annual* 48.

Roberts, Benjamin, Jarè Struwig, Steven Gordon, Johan Viljoen, and Marie Wentzel. 2012. 'Financial Literacy in South Africa: Results of a Baseline National Survey.' Pretoria: Financial Services Board.

Roush, Chris. 2006. *Profits and Losses: Business Journalism and Its Role in Society.* Illinois: Marion Street Press.

Schifferes, Steve. 2012. Austerity News: The Financial Crisis and the Digital Revolution, pp 61–64 in Reuters report. http://media.digitalnewsreport.org/wp-content/uploads/2012/05/Reuters-Institute-Digital-News-Report-2012.pdf (Accessed Feb 1 2020).

Schifferes, Steve. 2014. 'Why We Don't Trust the Financial Press.' In *Soothsayers of Doom: The Media and Financial Crises*, edited by Steve Schifferes and Richard Roberts. London: Routledge.

Schifferes, Steve and Richard Roberts, eds. 2014. *The Media and Financial Crises: Historical and Comparative Perspectives*. London: Routledge.

Schifferes, Steve, and Stephen Coulter. 2012. 'Downloading Disaster: BBC News Online Coverage of the Global Financial Crisis.' *Journalism* 14 (2): 228–252.

Schultz, Julianne. 1998. *Reviving the Fourth Estate: Democracy, Accountability & the Media*. Cambridge: Cambridge University Press.

Shaw, Ibrahim S. 2015. *Business Journalism: A Critical Political Economy Approach*. London: Routledge.

Solomon, Norman. 2002. 'Money Makes Headlines in Today's News Coverage.' *Nieman Reports*, June 15.

Starkman, Dean. 2009. 'Power Problem: The Business Press Did Everything but Take on the Institutions that Brought Down the Financial System.' *Columbia Journalism Review* 48 (1): 22–30.

Starkman, Dean. 2015. *The Watchdog that Didn't Bark*. New York: Columbia University Press.

Soros, George. 2009. *The Crash of 2008 and What It Means: The New Paradigm for Financial Markets*. New York: Public Affairs.

Tambini, Damian. 2008. *What is Financial Journalism For? Ethics and Responsibility in a Time of Crisis and Change*. London: London School of Economics and Political Science.

Tambini, Damian. 2010. 'What Are Financial Journalists For?' *Journalism Studies* 11 (2): 158–174.

Tooze, Adam. 2018. *Crashed: How a Decade of Financial Crises Changed the World*. New York: Viking.

Usher, Nikki. 2013. 'Ignored, Uninterested, and the Blame Game: How the New York Times, Marketplace, and the Street Distanced Themselves from preventing the 2007–2009 Financial Crisis.' *Journalism* 14 (2): 190–207.

Wright, Kate. 2014. 'Should Journalists be 'Virtuous'? Mainstream News, Complex Media Organisations and the Work of Nick Couldry.' *Journalism* 15 (3): 364–381.

CHAPTER TWO

Challenges and Pressures in Financial Journalism

> All this would be of no more than academic interest were it not for the fact that the media is the single most powerful influence in democratic society. No other institution, including government or the judiciary, carries the same power to shape lives and thought. (Beecher 2005, 68)

We interrogate the criticisms that financial journalists have faced from a practical, measured, and industry-facing perspective, drawing on in-depth interviews with leading business Journalists in the UK, Australia and the US. They provide some much-needed practical explanations which address some of the criticisms of the media coverage of financial crises. Among those criticisms are that they have become lapdogs rather than watchdogs (Starkman 2015), that they are too cosy with the players on the financial markets (Mair and Keeble 2009); too narrow in their explanations and sources used for information (Berry 2015, 2018); and lacking the foresight that is needed to forewarn a general public about economic developments and impending downturns (Starkman 2009a, 2015).

Political Economic and Ideological Pressures

The development of the financial press and capitalism are inextricably intertwined, with one struggling to exist without the other. The development and success of market capitalism relies on the existence of economic communications for price discovery (Parsons 1989, 1), and the emergence of merchant capitalism in the seventeenth century was paralleled by the early development of financial news. By the late nineteenth century the development of industrial capitalism led to creation of the modern specialised financial press with the founding of the *Financial Times* (1884), the *Financial News* (1888) and the *Wall Street Journal*. By the late 20th century the financialisation of the economy and its global reach led to the widespread adoption of neo-liberalism with its emphasis on the benefits of free-markets, globalisation and deregulation.

The role of the financial press as a cheerleader for business and globalisation poses a serious ethical dilemma for financial journalists: a theme that academics have discussed for the past few decades. (See Butterick (2015), Tiffen (1989), Schultz and Matolcsy (1993), Craig (2001), Greenfield and Williams (2002), and Kitchener (2005, 44).) The main issue that arises is that the financial media are too embedded within the capitalist system to be able to think independently and critically about the values and practices that shape the business environment. As a result they become a constitutive part of the capitalist process rather than taking on a watchdog role with reporting that is fair and balanced, impartial, and intent on representing reality to the public-at-large.

Financialisation and the Role of the Financial Media

The acceptance of a neo-liberal ideology that favours minimal government intervention in economic and financial affairs, and the overall acceptance of a free financial market, was reinforced by – and contributed to the pervasiveness of – the process of "financialisation." Financialisation means the focus and growth of the finance sector in relation to other areas of the economy – i.e. the manufacturing industry shrank to 10 per cent of GDP in the US compared with the finance sector, which in 2010 grew to 20 percent, by 2010 (See World Bank data: https://data.worldbank.org/indicator/NV.IND.MANF.ZS). The financialisation of the economy with the creation of global financial markets led to increasing support of neo-liberal policy from the 1980s in the US, the UK, and Australia. As governments espoused neo-liberalism and economic liberalisation, the media was normalising the trend through supportive coverage. The views of leading proponents of the neo-liberal attitude, such as Frederick Hayek, Milton Friedman, and Alan Greenspan, were widely and favourably reported by the media (Chakravarrty and Schiller 2010a, 677; Parsons 1989).

Many financial journalists accepted the consensus view that these developments were both inevitable and desirable, instead of questioning whether market forces benefitted all. In the US the reportage around market forces, deregulation, and privatisation was steeped in "language of 'inevitability'" (Frank 2000, 313). Financial journalists accepted business as king and business sources as the preferred voices representing the status quo (ibid.). This has resulted in a certain elitist attitude within the media that tended to ignore alternative voices and favours expert opinion over real-world experiences of ordinary people. Frank sees this as part of a larger, more worrying trend, which is that journalists cannot address questions of institutional power (ibid., 315).

This tendency to report positively about financial and business investment decisions is found in an analysis of mainstream financial news content from the US and the UK. Davis finds a wave of reporting that supports the justification for financialisation and the growth of some "dangerous creations" (Davis 2011, 241). The "dangerous creations" are those synthetic financial products like collateralised debt obligations (CDO), which packaged and disseminated the US subprime mortgages around the globe and contributed to the GFC. Consequently, financial institutions have become more powerful and pervasive in public life.

A similar development has been found in Australia, as financialisation has dominated both government policy and financial reporting. In the 1990s the deregulation, globalisation and marketization of Australia's economy was viewed as a reason Australia managed to escape the Asian Financial Crisis. In reporting from the *Age* and the *Australian Financial Review* during the Asian Financial Crisis in 1997 Australia was represented as protected and "blessed with free market policies" (Bryan 2001, 20). An analysis of broadcast material during the same period of the 1980s and 90s shows a mix of praise and criticism for a turn toward deregulation and free market activity in the reporting (Greenfield and Williams 2002). Journalists, such as Robert Gottliebsen, columnist for the Australian Financial Review, and economics writer at *The Australian*, reported on the benefits of finance for the "ordinary person" while Max Walsh, former editor of the *Australian Financial Review* and anchor on ABC, is viewed as a "voice of reason" as he praised elements of deregulation but called for "humane" and constrained limits (ibid., 421–422). By 1997, there is a shift to outright acceptance of finance above all else. For example, Charles Woolley's reporting on the Asian Financial Crisis on the TV Channel 9 *Sunday* program is concerned above all else with the extent and speed of the markets correction and the effects on interest rates, rather than the more general public (ibid., 423–424).

Focusing on the reporting of the GFC in Australia and Canada, Mickler reveals a series of writings from conservative columnists and exponents of market deregulation that tried to transfer blame from "finance and investment groups" to "liberal values" within the public, such as excessive borrowing (2012, 5).

The role that the financial press played in the financialisation narrative and ultimately in the GFC is a topic taken up by media scholars who also consider the everyday realities of the practice of financial journalism. For instance, Chakravarrty and Schiller (2010a, 677) argue that the ideology was normalised to such a degree that it became a language of its own, or what they refer to as the business journalists' "neo-liberal newspeak." In this way, the financial media were not only complicit in their espousal of the neo-liberal attitude that allowed privatisation and financial markets to grow exponentially, but they also played an important role in the dissemination and acceptance of neo-liberal logic.

Many commentators now see neo-liberalism as the central assumption and accepted as the norm within the media and within financial journalism. Preston and Silke (2012, 1) share Chakravarrty and Schiller's (2010a) view that ideology is embedded in everyday routine journalistic practices, such as the favouring of certain narratives over others, and through the use of biased sources "in favour of officialdom or corporate business." The authors support their position through a content analysis of the *Irish Times* three weeks before the 2007 general election (ibid., 12).

These ideological pressures have been reinforced by organisational pressures, which we will turn to in the next section. Hamilton (2009) describes cultural biases within media institutions that encourage optimistic pro-business reportage and discourage speculation that something may be wrong with business or the economy. Likewise, former editor of the *New Statesman*, Peter Wilby (2009), argues that business and economics writers are more vulnerable than other journalists because commercially driven newspaper proprietors who benefit from an economic system that is driven by less regulation and more speculation on financial markets. He believes as a consequence that advice offered by a business journalist who makes a prediction about the economy or share prices should be taken with "the same cellars of salt as you would take the football writers' predictions of who will win Saturday's top-of-the-table match" (ibid., 86).

The literature describes the synonymous relationship that exists between the financial markets, capitalism and the media. And there are academic studies in the UK, US and Australia that point to a press that has mostly buoyed these financial developments, with very little critique or discussion of alternatives. Financial journalism has always been closely aligned with the development of capitalism. It has been embraced as an ideology and its reporting standards have been defined by it. In particular, the literature points to its recent support of the narrative of financialisation, and of minimal government regulation to buoy financial markets. It also suggests that ultimately this sort of uncritical reporting serves no-one's interest – neither those of the elite investors nor those of the general non-shareholding public.

Views of the Journalists

The journalists interviewed for this book tend to agree that journalists were not as critical as they might have been when deregulation started in the 1980s or after the GFC. They explain that there is not pressure to write in a way that is pro-business or pro-deregulation – at least not in terms of being told what to write and what not to write by editors or managers. But there is the sense that it is difficult to challenge a paradigm, or indeed write about an alternative that does not exist. Much of this comes from the inevitability of reflecting the views of those individuals being covered. In the views of many of the journalists, there were some strong political personalities in this period, many of whom were enthusiastic about changes to an economic system that hadn't been working in the 1970s, and they were simply doing their job of reporting and reflecting what was happening.

One of the journalists most vocal and supportive of capitalism was the Australian journalist Alan Kohler, the founder of *Business Spectator* and long-term presenter on the Australian Broadcast Corporation (ABC). He argues that "Financial journalists are operating in a capitalist world, that's what it's all about. If you don't believe it's an acceptable world, then you're not going to be a financial journalist." While he thinks that the primary set of people critiquing deregulation after the GFC were journalists, during the 1980s and 90s he believes that no-one was as critical as they should have been.

Also working in Australia, a previous editor of the *Australian Financial Review* and journalist at the *Sydney Morning Herald*, Colleen Ryan, argues there is no other alternative economic system to write about; with the only likely alternative being "socialism." While journalists were "swept along" in the 1990s, she thinks the alternative view is not an attractive one: "If you suggest that we go back to socialist planning, I don't think there'd be too many financial editors that would think that would be a great story."

A similar view is held by Eduardo Porter, economics columnist for the *New York Times* in the US, who does not see that there is an option for writing about a system that does not yet exist: "Any intellectual endeavour in writing news articles are embedded in a context: an economic and political system where you accept some things and critique others. I think we have no experience of a system of economic organisation that does a better job than markets and capitalism."

These responses, therefore, raise the additional question, how do you cover a system objectively if you are a constitutive part of it?

In contrast, there are a few journalists that express their desire to critique the capitalist system. Larry Elliott, long-serving economics editor at the *Guardian*, is one of them. He says the *Guardian* has been "quite open to critiques of capitalism." Other newspapers are not, in his mind, as critical and tend to "go along with neo-liberal mainstream," which is a story he says he has fundamentally rejected. The neo-liberal story that he rejects is the idea that "the world economy was on its knees in the 1970s and needed a strong dose of neoliberal medicine, which it received under Thatcher and Reagan, deregulation, privatization. [That] smashing the trade unions was a good thing and resulted in the good times returning."

But overall, the consensus view from the journalists is that the job of a journalist is to report and reflect a political culture that has few left-wing critics of the status quo. This is particularly the case when the economy is being directed and shaped by influential personalities in politics. For instance, while Elliott argues that the *Guardian* and he are driving forces behind the critique of capitalism, he adds that:

> Under Tony Blair it [capitalism] became a much more pro-business force, Clinton accepted far more of the new order that had been established by Thatcher and Reagan in the 1980s, which makes it inevitable that that is how politics and the economy is reported – [that] the market is the way forward and the more free market the better. That is going to colour the way it is reported. That's even leaving to one side the fact that newspapers are themselves run by people who are right wing and use their newspaper to reflect their own views.

A similar narrative is told by Robert Peston, the BBC's former business and economics editor, and now political editor for ITV. He describes a culture which, before Mrs Thatcher's reforms, was far more sceptical of business claims for the benefits of free markets. He also places a lot of the explanation for a lack of critique of capitalism, or lack of a left-wing perspective as he describes it, on a lack of a political alternative and the support of business coming from New Labour:

> There have been progressively fewer left-wing voices in newspaper articles, partly because Thatcher undermined the power of the unions, actually probably even more importantly it was the attitude of Tony Blair and New Labour, who had very little respect for trade unions. So if you had an ostensibly left-wing government, that prefer wealth creators to unions, what's the media going to do in those circumstances? In that case nobody is underwriting the trade union viewpoint or the more left-wing

> viewpoint. So I would say if you want to look at the powerful influence on the absence of an alternative left-wing perspective in the media I would say probably the Blair government was more responsible than Thatcher.
>
> There was a period when there was such a massive punch up between unions and business during the Thatcher years that of course there was a lot of union coverage as part of the existential battle.

Very similar views are held by the other journalists and the same names are referred to: Thatcher, Reagan, Clinton, Blair. Again in the UK, Ian King, formerly city editor at the *Times*, and now a presenter on Sky, argues that "A lot of was driven by Bill Clinton's government. It was Clinton that abolished Glass-Steagall under pressure from Wall Street."

In Australia, Paul Clearly refers to "strong and charismatic individuals" and the leading political proponent for deregulation there, former Prime Minister Paul Keating: "Newspaper journalists and editors embraced these new [neoliberal] ideas in an enthusiastic way because this was a new way of thinking."

The fact that journalists are expected to report on events and others' views can often be the cause of source "capture" – when a journalist is so taken by a source that he or she throws scepticism out of the window. This is referred to both implicitly and explicitly by the journalists. In the US, Peter Goodman, at the time of the interview at the *Huffington Post* (and now back at the *New York Times* and based in the UK), discusses the ways "you tend to reflect the thinking of the people you are covering and not for nefarious reasons, but because that's who you are supposed to." He refers back to the 1990 technology boom and the journalists that were competing with one another for a scoop. These journalists, operating with tight deadlines, would return time and time again to the sources that were accessible and provided good quotes quickly, a process he describes as a feedback loop.

Certainly, if only sources with similar views are being used for quotes frequently, then alternative and contrarian voices are not being used to provide different interpretations. While this may be viewed as a by-product of the challenges and circumstances of journalism practice, which report and reflect what is happening and their sources' views, there is also an element of choice in terms of what sources are chosen for quotes and explanations.

Referring directly to deregulation in the 1980s and 90s, Ross Gittins, long-serving economics editor at the *Sydney Morning Herald* in Australia, believes journalists "... should have been more critical than they were, and they probably should have stayed more critical. There's a tendency among journalists to line up with the new fashion." And he refers explicitly to source capture as a particular consequence of this (a theme we will pick up again further down) and "the great occupational hazard in all journalism." The tendency to be captured has improved for him, he says, with age and experience: "It's only as I've got older that I've been less inclined to just swallow the values of my sources and I've become more critical."

Organisational and Cultural Factors

Lack of Corporate Transparency

The job of a financial journalist is challenged quite significantly by the limited company information that is accessible. Financial journalists often have to rely on the good grace of their sources, which can lead to a dangerous co-dependency. In the 1980s in Australia Tiffen (1989, 44) described a sycophancy which can lead to "envy": "It is a make-believe world, hob-nobbing with the rich as observers, which sometimes leads to envy, especially if you realise that (some are) not bright and you could do better." Indeed, this is a challenge that financial journalism has faced for some time.

In the US, there was a shift in the 1960s toward the increased and pervasive influence of business (Welles 1973, 40–41). The increasing power of business was not, however, accessible or transparent. Welles goes so far as to compare business with the CIA in terms of levels of secrecy. This, he argues, is a worry for all of society, as "they determine to a substantial degree the entire economic structure of society, the quality of our environment, the values that guide our lives" (ibid.). This stymies investigations into business and in the US, with the exception of the *New York Times,* he argues that the rest of financial news is a "bleak wasteland" (ibid.).

The situation is described similarly in Australia. In his comprehensive study of journalism in Australia, Tiffen (1989) describes financial journalism as a beat that is particularly dependent upon its sources both for access and for information. Veteran Australian business journalist, Robert Gottliebsen, has described the hurdles he faced when reporting on one of Australia's biggest resource companies, BHP in the 1980s: "I was the first journalist to interview Ian McLennan, chairman of BHP. There was enormous preparation. The editor checked the questions from Sydney … The first interview with BHP was like a summit. BHP was a shut shop" (cited in ibid., 41).

Today defamation laws and a lack of publicly available information augment the problems faced by financial journalists. They are tasked with taking on big companies when media companies are struggling financially. Journalists in the UK and Australia are not always protected by defamation laws, which tend to protect business interests rather than the press. The revised Defamation Act 2013, provides more protection, in journalist's favour, with more onus on the claimant to prove that defamation has indeed occurred. The Freedom of Information (FOI) laws are also often less than helpful as they offer no recourse to access private company information, only that which is public (ibid., 170). And there have been increasing legal constraints placed upon access to business information by companies with big profits and therefore big legal teams.

Journalists interviewed for a study in Australia portray financial journalists as particularly susceptible as companies have big purse strings (Kitchener 1999, 50). But these same interviews with journalists working in Australia revealed that Internet searches have made it easier for financial journalists to access company information on the public record and thence facilitate their watchdog role (ibid., 45).

The literature shows how restricted access to company information impacts on the practice of financial journalism in the US, the UK, and Australia. Not only does this limit the range and scope of stories, and prevent watchdog-style investigations in the public interest, but it also creates tensions between journalists and the sources they depend on for information. Government regulation is not always supportive of journalistic activities in the private corporate realm. Private companies do not need to provide annual statements, unlike publicly held data that is held at Companies House in the UK, for instance, and which anybody can access.

So how have these attitudes impacted on the practice of journalism in areas such as the selection of sources and voices, and the diversity of views?

Sources and "Voices" that Shape Financial News

If we take the social responsibility theory articulated by the Hutchins Commission in the US, in 1947, financial journalism would be fair and balanced and take "all voices" into account, including those from inside and outside of the business world (Lacy and Fico 1991b). Giving "voice" to points of view other than those that are simply "conventional" provides another, arguably more accurate, picture of events. This is a change that financial journalist Carswell (1938a, 191) called for in the US in the 1930s, as he showed that before the stock market crash of 1929, the financial press was catering to speculators, brokers, and bankers instead of aiming to reach "the majority." "Fair and balanced" was also a requirement of the FCC in regulating radio and TV news broadcasts from the 1930s, and Ofcom has similar rules for impartiality in the UK.

Carswell argued plaintively in the 1930s: "Business affects everybody; everybody talks about it. It would be possible to present business news in such a manner that everybody would read it, understand it and enjoy it."

Nearly a century later and accessibility for everybody is something journalists and academia are still calling for. The Columbia Journalism School began an annual collection of "best business writing" in 2012 and, based on the principle of social responsibility, they argue that "The debate can't be left to experts and cognoscenti (clearly) and must be opened to as wide a swath of society as possible, even people who don't normally think of business news as their bag" (Starkman, Hamilton, Chittum and Salmon 2012, xiii). This is part of a continuing debate about business journalism and its intended audience.

While a journalist in the 1930s and one of the world's top journalism schools called for a picture of business that more people can relate to, other studies have discussed the fact that speaking to sources outside of the expert and elite status quo will be beneficial, not just for engagement purposes, but also as a way to investigate and find malfeasance.

Giles and Sussman (2011, 180), in their analysis of the GFC, argue that speaking with sources that offer varying and different perspectives will offer "cautionary perspectives." In other words, a focus on the same sources for information and a narrowing version of reality can actually be damaging for the economy and society, as past events such as the dot com boom have illustrated.

Indeed, the dot com boom – a culmination of the speculation on new Internet companies, many of which had not turned a profit – and the second case study we look at in Chapter 4 – is an excellent example of a period when finance journalists, consulting a narrow range of sources, presented a narrow version of reality to the public. Richard Lambert, editor at the *Financial Times*, recalls it as a time when journalists would take "dictation from analysts" (Page 2002, 54). And while analysts were issuing buy recommendations for technology shares during the dot com boom, they were describing the same stocks as being "crap" to their colleagues (Shefrin 2002, xvii). The picture would have been distorted further by corporate executives who were caught up in a game of recommendations with analysts (ibid., 269). This is a case-in-point that the sources financial journalists seek and rely on to support the status quo and provide much-needed information are often tightly aligned with the values and motivations of the institutions that they represent. Therefore, commitment to business sources, as well as analysts and investors, does not only present a distorted representation of reality, but it also means that financial journalists risk bias and capture by their sources and their points of view.

An illuminating example is provided by journalist Bethany McLean's reporting (in *Fortune* on March 2001) on the company Enron – a company which, as it turned out, was not based on profits but on a Ponzi-style scheme that used people's investments as profit. It borrowed money to expand against its rising stock price and hid the resulting debts in secret "special purpose vehicles" so that the company continued to appear profitable. The question McLean asked yielded no clear answers, as it was simply, "how exactly does Enron make its money?" (ibid., 179). Instead of listening to the questions Mclean posed, the financial press chose to ignore the issues she raised. It was not until Enron collapsed that the press looked retrospectively to where they went wrong.

A decade on and the GFC presented much of the same. The irony is that the GFC provided the press with an opportune moment to question the status quo. Starkman (2009a) argues the press in the US were inflicted by "Stockholm Syndrome" – or implicit cognitive capture by their sources of information. Lewis argues that after the GFC the press could have launched a "radical, popular challenge, not just to the neoliberal orthodoxy but also to consumer capitalism as a model for human progress" (Lewis 2010, 162). And while neo-liberalism was criticised after the GFC, this lasted only for a short time (Basu, 2018; Blyth 2013); the status quo remained largely unchallenged along with the sources used to explain the events (ibid., 163). Lewis says the lack of critique and narrow range of sources used for information results in the "narrow worldview, [that] what is good for business (or, more specifically, the people who run businesses) is good for everyone" (ibid., 164).

The journalists interviewed for this book provide some highly practical explanations for the preponderance of business and executive voices – and address the criticism that they have been captured by elites at the expense of the more general public's interests.

The message they present isclear: business sources in the private sector are quicker to respond than sources in the public sector they provide more useful quotes than those working in academia because their knowledge about market movements and business cycles is more clearly attached to business and economic realities. Academics and other voices from charities and NGOs are seen as part of the bloated public sector, which is less well resourced, with less expertise and less available personnel. The public is not viewed as a valuable sources of information, usually made relevant only in times of crisis.

This view that business voices provide more relevant knowledge and perspectives is shared by Ian King in the UK who thinks "A lot of academics don't tend to have real-world experience [while] Members of the public can often be ignorant and ill-informed."

In the UK, Larry Elliott is of the same view that the business sector provides more timely and relevant quotes. He refers to the public, not as irrelevant, but as difficult to reach. This, he says, is more of a challenge in recent years as journalists have less time than they used to have: "As time's gone as, as deadline pressures have become more intense, the media has become 24/7, so people are under enormous pressure to get stories out very quickly and so they tend to go for the sources that are easily obtainable." Also, the business sector is far more adept to agenda-setting than members of the public or the public sector. Elliott explains that he receives around 200 emails a day. Of them only five are usually from members of the public. The rest of them are from investment banks, business groups, trade union movements, and occasionally academics.

Robert Peston, again, provides a practical reflection, and this time his explanation is told through the prism of running a journalistic investigation. He explains that sources needed for information are naturally part of the elite sphere. Those who have the information you want usually wish to remain anonymous, and are involved in some way in the thing being investigated: they are usually bankers, the regulators orpoliticians.

Chris Roush, founding director of the Carolina Business News Initiative in the US expresses disappointment in the constant use of business sources, explaining: "It is a kind of journalism that is concerned with seeing the world through a specialist perspective and the perspective of the people who are making the decisions rather than from those who are on the receiving end of the consequences of the decisions." This extends to being captured by sources. He says, "Any business journalist, no matter how objective, if they think they can be friends with the people they are covering, then it affects their coverage, ideas, and the types of stories they write about."

Academics are less relevant, abstract, and hardly available for a 24/7 news cycle

while business sources appear to be king, academics are viewed with much less relevance. Larry Elliott in the UK thinks academics can be useful, but for secondary commentary, insight and analysis. But reading their work can be quite cumbersome and time-consuming. He explains, "Academics in the UK – I can't say for anywhere else in the world – are quite poor at writing pieces that get to the heart of the issue straight away." Robert Peston views academics in a similar way to Elliott, as secondary sources that provide explanation and analysis after an event.

According to Alan Kohler in Australia, business sources are "the most useful and desirable because they are engaged generally in what the story is about … Likewise, academics are more theoretical than practical." A very similar explanation is offered by Colleen Ryan, who says, "I tend not to use academics because they're not involved in business. For the sort of business journalism I was doing I don't really see that academics have a lot to offer."

But overall, the general sense is that academics are less relevant, too abstract, unavailable and not used to the news cycle. Colleen Ryan in Australia argues that the academics who do have more to offer are those with a more famous profile, and knowledge that fits with markets and business cycles: "If you're talking economists for the GFC, Nouriel Roubini was the most often quoted economist of the time and he's an academic [he was also known as Dr Doom before the GFC], similarly of Paul Krugman."

Goodman, *New York Times'* European economics editor, agrees that journalists do not view academics as important:

> With rare exception there are people like Nouriel Roubini or Ken Rogoff on CNBC. There isn't a flock of people following them through big events. Also, there aren't that many who are willing to engage with even the well-intentioned financial reporter. They also tend to be difficult to reach. They are less likely to wander around with blackberries and respond in real time to a reporter on a deadline. They can be impatient talking to people who don't have the same expertise or grasp that they have. It's very rare to find a credentialed, insightful academic, who is willing to take the time with a neophyte financial journalist or even someone who is up-to-speed.

Ross Gittins in Australia provides an interesting parallel to Goodman and paints academics as recalcitrant:

> If they're not specialized in the area you want to talk to them about, they're probably reluctant to talk to you about it. By the nature of their academic discipline, they tend not to give very colourful quotes. Another reason is that academics often aren't up with the latest news. You want to talk about something that's just happened recently, but they don't want to talk about anything they haven't read for themselves, they don't want you to tell what the story is. There are exceptions to these rules, but this is the general situation. The fourth is you can never get the bastards when you want them, because they're always away giving a paper in America.

Source Capture

Colleen Ryan in Australia regards source capture as a genuine dimension of financial journalism, and one which we may be getting back to: "In the mid-80s, as the entrepreneurs were rising – like the Alan Bonds and the Holmes a Courts – there was a very big tendency for journalists to get too close and applaud their achievements. As they started to collapse there was a much more forensic and critical approach, but I think we're getting back to some of the business hero coverage which is a real worry."

And Ian King in the UK provides a view of capture that is not mentioned by any of those interviewed for this book. He argues that the dynamics between journalists and business people has changed over the years so that journalists are less affluent and have less in common compared to those in business: "If what you mean by captured also means socializing, then I have no doubt that it used to be the case, when business journalists were paid more, had a lot more common with them than they used to and were a similar age to them. They're more likely now to be in their twenties or early thirties and probably not as especially well paid."

Robert Peston sees capture on several levels. First, that during the GFC regulators were effectively captured by the banking industry, which was increasing its risks and not reducing it, and "journalists too believed too much of the mythology around innovation in finance." He adds another dimension, which is that "Too many newspapers in particular were too dependent on housing boom-related advertising and therefore, were probably not sufficiently critical of the bubble that was emerging in both banking and property."

An approach to reporting, which seeks sources beyond the usual set of business voices, is advocated by economic columnist at the *New York Times*, Eduardo Porter (and the author of one of the earliest warnings available in the Chapter 5 case study of the GFC). He explains that he will "rarely quote business sources" and most of the time he quotes "academic sources, non-profit organisations, policy makers" and he rarely speaks to the general public. He says he writes about policy and therefore what academics have to say, is much more relevant. The idea of capture, he thinks, is incidental, and argues that is not surprising that the views of others bleach into journalists' work.

Members of the Public Are Ghettoized as a Source until a Crisis Occurs

As opposed to business sources, the general view among the journalists interviewed is that the public is generally irrelevant as a source of information. Members of the public are, however, used more frequently when market conditions decline and the economy slides in to recession. For instance, Colleen Ryan explains, "As the value of their stocks declines dramatically, then you would go to members of the public. I know in the *Financial Review* in the smart money and so forth it was full of examples of people who had lost everything because of collapses of various property funds and share funds."

At the *Guardian*, however, Larry Elliott explains that the public is desirable as a source of information – he mentions former *Guardian* editor Alan Rusbridger's efforts to incite a culture change that includes a more iterative news process with the public at its center: "He's [Rusbridger when he was editor] trying to affect a culture change here and get away from the idea that newspapers are like citadels firing bits of information from the parapet at the masses outside, to what members of the public are thinking and saying." And journalists are time-poor, with less opportunity to get out on the streets as they used to. He explains, "the website is more important than the physical product now so whereas a quarter of a century ago you had an entire day to produce a piece, and you could go out in the street and talk to people, now you're stuck behind the desk most of the time, churning out stories."

Former reporter at the *Wall Street Journal*, Dean Starkman, explains his theory of the difference between access and accountability reporting, and who journalists speak with plays an integral role:

> I categorize the two schools as access reporting versus accountability reporting. Access reporting is precisely what your study is finding; it's about seeking information from powerful people that might have relevance for markets. Accountability reporting is seeking information about powerful people.
>
> My argument is that of these two schools access is the default mode of business journalism – its initial function was to gain access to inside information for markets. So it's always had the upper hand. The accountability school had its moment in the sun, but it's clear to me that this narrow definition of business news – who gets spoken to, who the sources are, who is allowed to appear in the sphere of business news – is being very narrowly defined. In the end it really is about who you are talking to, and if you are only talking to CEOs, you are going to get a dangerously distorted picture of reality.

He cites as an important example of the way the story of the subprime mortgage market was told (which the very foundation of the GFC rested on), and the moral is that journalists were not talking to a wide enough range of sources – and more conversations with the public would have opened the story frames and pinpointed some of the undersides of the market. (We pick up this theme again in Chapter 5 when we discuss the GFC as a case study and find some of the earliest and most prescient warnings came from discussions with the public.)

Goodman provides a very similar interpretation to Starkman in the US. He too thinks business journalism is about providing access, over and above accountable public-interest style journalism: "You look at the people who have become prominent in business journalism and generally what they bring to the party is not sage analysis or rigorous attention to data, their unique ability to look at same story and divine a larger truth, it is their ability to talk their way in to the CEO's room. It's their ability to ingratiate themselves with investment bankers so they get the scoop on mergers and acquisitions."

Clearly, while some of the journalists see the merits of including members of the public, academics NGOs and charities as sources of information, the majority tend to agree that they simply do not provide market-relevant and timely information when compared to business sources. Evidently, academics would reach a much broader platform if they would provide more timely information, provide quotes in a language that a lay reader would understand, and make themselves more available to journalists who are operating in 24/7 instantaneous news cycle. Moreover, business sources cannot be matched in terms of resources and knowledge. The news agenda prefers scoops and insight, which means capture is a very real occupational hazard for journalists who are expected to gain access – and therefore risk their objectivity and integrity when they blindly accept what their sources tell them – and often to the detriment of "accountability reporting," as Starkman would describe it.

The question now is, does the expectation on journalists to gain access to get scoops, and preference for business and executive sources over others, affect the way everyday financial news is reported, the way the general public engages with this beat of news, and the way they are reported to as an audience? The evidence suggests that the business elites are the main audience even within the mainstream news media who place a wide section of society and the public interest at the core of their values: the general public is alienated as not just as a source of information, but as an audience.

The General Public as an Audience

By covering the world of business from the perspective of elites and in the context of the free-market status quo the financial press has arguably missed out the views of what Schiffrin and Fagan (2013, 152) call the "common man." Everyday practices that exclude the "voices" of everyday citizens misrepresent society and do not provide the public with a forum for democratic debate. This preoccupation with business sources above the general public and more "ordinary voices" has been a point of contention for academics and practitioners for decades (Bull 1998; Goodman 2011; Kitchener 1999; Kollmeyer 2004; Loeb 1966; Overholser 2001; Parsons 1989; Putnis 1997; Quirt 1993; Roush 2006; Schiffrin and Fagan 2013; Starkman et al. 2012; Welles 1973).

As early as the 1930s, after the stock market crash and the Great Depression, former US financial journalist, Carswell, lamented the lack of business news content that the average person could engage with (1938a, 191). He wanted to see business news presented in a way that a wide audience would understand:

> The fact is that business news could possess the most general human interest of any presented to men readers. Business affects everybody; everybody talks about it. It would be possible to present business news in such a manner that everybody would read it. (ibid.)

Three decades later, Gerald Loeb (1966, 38), a Wall Street financier, was complaining that "Nothing means anything in financial news unless the average reader of the newspaper understands it." (To encourage better business coverage he established the Gerald Loeb award for excellence in business journalism.)

US business journalist Jane Quinn (1998, 48) describes a type of "investment pornography" that abounded around the dot com period. She argues that business journalists "dine with the predators, [business managers, executives and CEOs] innocently, without even thinking about it." Quinn (ibid.) suggests that when business journalists start to embrace the predator's point of view the kind of reporting to come out of it is the top ten mutual funds to buy and "stock-touting pieces." More specifically, she points to the fact that business journalists choose to join in rather than simply observing and choose to worship business sources as secular gods.

By covering events through the prism of business and investment Quinn (ibid., 49) also underlines what the business press ignores – the people who need them: "Reporters are supposed to be tribunes of the people—not the rich people, who don't need tribunes."

Analysis of news content in the US identifies an extreme bias in favour of business sources over and above the more general public, which limits discussion on the interests of ordinary workers (Kollmeyer 2004, 432). Through a content analysis of 201 articles from the *Los Angeles Times*, the study shows that reports on the economy "privilege the interests of corporations and investors over the interests of the general workforce" (ibid.). Between 1997 and 1998 corporations and investors were enjoying robust profits but workers were suffering from stagnant wages and reduced full-time employment opportunities. However, less than 8% of the articles in his dataset used union leaders or workers as sources.

Therefore, because of the sources that were consulted for information and quotes, the problems affecting workers were not included in the frame of reporting. Also, when the articles discussed the general workforce, they "were relatively short … and rarely discussed policy alternatives to the status quo" (ibid.). The study was limited to articles appearing outside of the business section in order to harness those stories that had "the greatest chance of affecting public opinion" (ibid., 439). These results suggest that the general beats in newspaper coverage are also skewed towards corporate interests.

A similar picture is painted by Schiffrin and Fagan (2013) who analyse reportage of the 2009 US economic stimulus package. They included 718 articles from 16 specialist and non-specialist publications. They conclude with the following:

> US press coverage of the stimulus, by and large, confirms the existing critiques of business journalism. It mostly focused on day-by-day news events and the details of the proposed package, relied largely on mainstream sources and in many cases reflected a pro-business mindset. (ibid., 166)

The pro-business mindset includes mainly government and business sources that showed signs of bias. As a consequence, the financial press plays lapdog when it does not play a decisive role in shaping economic policy or setting the agenda. The authors recommend more scepticism about the sources' biased forecasts, more consultation with economists as sources of information, and more agenda-setting that discusses the long-term implications of economic restructuring (ibid., 168).

In the UK, an oft-cited study by Doyle (2006) argues that the mainstream financial press needs to communicate with the public through sources that they will understand and learn from. Doyle separates the news audience of elite publications, such as the *Financial Times*, from the more mainstream press, which she argues should be intent on engaging with a broad, lay readership through accessible and appealing content (ibid., 436). Therefore, one would expect that the kinds of sources used in the business sections of the mainstream financial press would be different from those used by the elite publications that cater to a highly specific investment community. Practitioners have attested to the fact that they tend to favour business sources above the ordinary public.

While attention has been paid to businesses and elites, with focus on profits and corporate growth, a "quiet crisis" has been playing out in the US for two decades and has affected "millions of ordinary Americans" (Goodman 2009, 94). *New York Times* journalist Peter Goodman (2011) describes ordinary people suffering from diminishing job opportunities, declining wages, with higher housing, healthcare, and education payments. He argues that "wages and incomes for working people are the crucial indicators of economic health" that are neglected when a new investment fad occurs (ibid., 121). This was his focus during the 2008 financial crisis as national economic reporter for the *New York Times*. To achieve this, he suggests that reporters should avoid partisan reporting, which relies on reputable establishment sources to the detriment of other points of views.

The evidence suggests that financial journalism has failed to live up to ideals of playing a watchdog role in the public interest and reflected the experience of all members of society. These criticisms were placed under the spotlight after the

GFC in 2008, but the examination of other booms and bubbles from the 1929 crash to the 2000 dot com boom show this has been the case elsewhere

The majority of the journalists interviewed think financial journalism in mainstream papers should be written for the average citizen. A number express their dissatisfaction with the current situation. Eduardo Porter, for instance, thinks "as whole journalism could do a better job. General market newspapers could explain financial activity, economic trends and dynamics, but we under explain a lot of stuff."

Rana Foroohar thinks mainstream financial news is still for business people, which is a problem, and raises issues about the business model of the media and the fact that the general lay public cannot afford to pay a premium: "If you look at a publication like the FT, for example, it is profitable in print before advertising, and we have a very robust online subscription business. But we charge over $400 for a one-year print edition and roughly the same for online. So you might be paying as an individual; close to a thousand dollars. That's not a lay person's price; that's a business person's price."

Starkman responds in a way that is reminiscent of Carswell writing in the 1930s, indicating the situation is little improved:

> Right now, it's [financial journalism in mainstream papers] riveted on markets and the interests of investors in the narrowest sense. That's going to marginalise business news further. To me it should be about explaining complex systems like the financial system, like the economy, like the corporate world, to the general public. Investor stuff is vital, and you have to have it, but if you're not also speaking to the general public you are going to marginalize yourself to the people who are already insiders.

Groupthink and the Financial Markets

In the last of our organisational and cultural pressures, here we discuss the tendency for financial journalists to take part in group-think. Mounting commercial and time pressures, particularly since the 1990s, have limited the opportunity for independent investigation and analysis, and affected the quality of financial reportage, subsequently impacting the extent to which financial journalists can access and challenge the financial world. These challenges have also exacerbated the tendency for financial journalists to hunt in packs, to emulate one another in an attempt to stay in the game, and to avoid straying from the established orthodoxy. Furthermore, groupthink is exaggerated when an economic bubble is present, as the human psyche tends to get swept up in the general excitement and euphoria

(Akerlof and Shiller 2009; Davis 2006; Kindleberger 2011; Schuster 2006; Shiller 2005; Wilby 2009).

In this environment, the financial press are far likelier to accept than to question and anybody that does will be viewed as a Cassandra. But the kind of reportage that is infected by groupthink is neither appropriately informative nor enlightening, nor fair and balanced. There is evidence that financial reportage affects price movements in the financial markets, creating distortions that can impact on the real economy and therefore society-at-large by fuelling bubbles and accentuating crashes (Akerlof and Shiller 2009; Davis 2006; Kleinnijenhuis, Schultz, Oegema and van Atteveldt 2013; Schuster 2006).

Observers have pointed out that the only type of criticism deemed to be acceptable during the dot com boom was "cautious optimism" (Schechter 2009, 19). Schechter recalls his experience witnessing the seductive display of wealth at the 2000 annual World Economic Forum in the Davos, Switzerland. He explains that the hype of that year was "about the promise of globalisation, and a capitalist system that could do no wrong" (p. 19). Furthermore, "many media outlets lacked the independence and critical judgment needed to investigate the financialisation of the economic system and warn of serious excesses and, sometimes, criminal conduct" (ibid., 20). Schechter (ibid.) says that his warnings about debt and credit problems in a film entitled, *In Debt We Trust: America before the Bubble Bursts* (2007), provided him with the labels of "doom and gloomer" and an "alarmist."

In addition to the criticism they might attract for challenging orthodoxy, journalists could find themselves chastised for potentially impacting on the financial markets. Schuster (2006) argues that the impact of the media on stock prices is minimal until the media begins to report in packs. He argues that the media can inflate prices "but that naïve investors are usually the ones that buy them" (ibid., 51–52). However, media does not have information that is not already reflected in the stock price and so the price soon reverses. Schuster (ibid., 52) cites the 1987 stock market crash and the "New Economy" dot com bubble as examples of "collective panic or euphoria." Also, the media selects information that it decides to focus on, which increases attention on the event and then legitimises it in the public sphere in a "feedback loop" (ibid., 69; see also George Soros' 2009 discussion along similar lines).

The risks of standing out as an outlier are illustrated by the case of Gillian Tett, assistant editor of the *Financial Times*. She was one of the few to question the realities of the credit and derivatives markets that prompted the GFC, but was heavily criticised at the World Economic Forum at Davos, in 2008 (Barton 2008). As capital markets editor Tett had been looking at credit and derivatives five years before the recession hit in 2008, while most journalists were focusing on equities, and mergers and acquisitions. She took an ethnographic approach to her research and learned the language of finance through objective eyes. But when Tett began to talk about what she called, "a revolution happening," and predicted the problems at the Northern Rock bank, her article was waved around on a podium at the Davos economic forum as an example of scaremongering. Tett paid attention to areas of finance that business journalists at the *Financial Times* ignored, such as credit derivatives, because they weren't part of the growth paradigm that so many were interesting in (Tett 2009). It's something respected *Financial Times* columnist Martin Wolf has admitted to missing (Schifferes 2012).

Any journalist that questioned any of the money-making activity before the 2008 recession was treated with the same disdain as a journalist that questioned the fact that Saddam Hussein had weapons of mass destruction (Wilby 2009). In addition to Tett, Wilby mentions Patrick Hosking at the *Times* as another journalist that predicted problems ahead. However, both Hosking and Tett were treated like "agents of leftist conspirators, intent on undermining capitalism" (ibid., 83). He argues that the GFC affected "people's livelihoods, homes, pensions and lifetime savings"; therefore, "if ever there was a case for journalistic whistleblowing, this was it" (ibid.).

On the contrary, financial journalists were talking up the stock market well into 2008:

> Even as the FTSE dipped below 6,000 – it would end the year at 4,343 – *The Times'* personal finance editor wrote that 'few serious economists are predicting a UK or worldwide recession. (Wilby 2009, 83)

Such optimistic overtones in reporting on a mass-scale leads Wilby (ibid.) to argue that "They [the journalists] may have deepened the crisis somewhat but, to a far greater extent, they helped to inflate the boom by encouraging readers to pile into what looked like an ever-rising stock market." It appears that financial journalists are more likely to report in packs than they are to report independently and along different lines. Thus, if the stock market is booming and the economy is growing, then there is also likely to be a bias towards optimistic reportage.

In 2007, the BBC's Robert Peston found himself at the center of a controversy when he was accused of causing the run on the Northern Rock bank (UK Treasury Select Committee 2009). The run began after Peston broke the news that Northern Rock was seeking emergency financial aid from the Bank of England. In 2009 Robert Peston, then BBC business editor, and others, were called before a UK Parliamentary select committee and asked to justify why they didn't suppress such news. *Financial Times* editor, Lionel Barber, also present at the Committee meeting, congratulated Peston on his Northern Rock scoop. He said there had been rumours for months about problems at the bank, but his newspaper did not report them because it was "not in the business of trying to drive Northern Rock out of business" (ibid.).

To establish the extent to which Robert Peston could have triggered a financial panic, Kleinnijenhuis and others (2013) conducted a study that revealed the long-term impact of financial news on the financial market. They were sceptical that individual journalists, such as Peston, "who lack financial expertise compared to their news sources," working with the "tardy BBC" against new automated High-Frequency Trading Algorithms, could cause such a panic (ibid., 272).[1] The study tracked, from 2007–2009, the mention of three Dutch banks, ING, AEGON, and Fortis, in the *New York Times*, the *Financial Times*, and *The International Herald* alongside the words "credit crisis," "financial crisis" and "credit crunch." It also tracks the values of the three banks on the Amsterdam Exchange Market (AEX) and the Dow Jones Industrial Index, as well as levels of consumer confidence.

They reveal that reports were "fear oriented" as early as July 2007 and news was soon framed in terms of a "crisis" (ibid., 285). They find a correlation between increased negative articles that frame financial events in terms of a "crisis" and drops in stock market values of the banks AEGON and Fortis. The authors recommend greater transparency concerning the interdependent relationships behind the market veil and the introduction of new policies on market regulation to support this.

Peston underscores his very different approach to his reporting on Northern Rock, which focuses on what the public deserve to know:

> In a curious way, of all of the stories I've done it's the one I am proud of. It was an important story and people deserved to know what was going on. I got a lot of criticism from politicians and regulators and economists – all through the autumn and in to the winter of 2008 that somehow I had been talking down the British economy, that it was unpatriotic and disloyal, and that I should be shut up. (Interview with author 2016)

The other journalists interviewed for this book tend to agree that media follow each other, and many cite the natural human psychology involved in following crowds; a phenomenon as old as markets and media, manifested in crises as early as the Dutch Tulip Mania in the 1630s. Ross Gittins, economics editor at the *Sydney Morning Herald*, refers to humans as "a social animal. We all tend to do and think the same things, which is how you get booms and busts. You get an optimistic mood, when people want to hear everything is on the up and up, and the media oblige." This is echoed by Ian King in the UK who describes human beings as "pack animals. That's how the fashion industry works; a trend leader is picked up on. That is true of everything, not just of journalists."

Elliott acknowledges the groupthink that existed around the dot com boom and the GFC, and underscores the difficulties of being a Cassandra: "It's quite difficult to write stories saying this is all going to go to custard in a big way when everything seems to be going really swimmingly."

Goodman provides an animated anecdote, which describes how he used to feel under pressure to compete: "When I was at the *Washington Post* in the 1990s, and covering Telecom, I did feel intense pressure to compete with the *New York Times* and the *Wall Street Journal*. I would wake up every morning in holy fear of whether the *Journal* had ruined my day."

The literature and the journalists themselves, therefore, suggest that there are limits on the extent to which financial journalists can question the status quo. There is institutional pressure to self-censor material and industry pressure to avoid upsetting the status quo. This, as the GFC illustrates, is not beneficial and can add to distortions in the market. Moreover, empirical studies have shown that financial reportage can influence the markets in both positive and negative directions. This would underscore the need for neutral, fair, balanced and critical reportage that is in the interests of everyone involved – not just investors in the markets, but the economy and the public at large.

Industry-Related Factors

Commercial Media Challenges

It is now clear that the traditional business model used by the press has been challenged in recent years as the Internet began to offer other options for readers and advertisers started to seek revenues off the news page. Quality has been the biggest casualty of this decline in resources, and now financial reporting, like reporting generally, increasingly resorts to entertainment and sensationalism to maintain commercial competitiveness in the face of declining revenues (Clark, Thrift and Tickell 2004, 304). As the process of the globalisation and the digitisation of news has continued, so social media, big media platforms like Google and Facebook, and now algorithms are increasingly acting as important mediators of news.

Never before have audiences been so connected, yet so polarised, as we see debates around fake news and a rise in populism. Some have referred to this as a "crisis" in journalism. We can view this narrative of a crisis in three parts: a lack of trust in news media (discussed in Chapter 1); a decline in the quality of news content (discussed in this section); and the associated implications for democracy when the public is increasingly ill-informed and disenfranchised – and turning to populist politics and nationalism (something we will discuss in the concluding Chapter).

Commercial pressures have undoubtedly impacted on the amount of watchdog-type investigations undertaken by a financial press that can no longer afford either the time or resources. Starkman (2009b) describes the newspaper scene in the US when he left the *Wall Street Journal* in 2004:

> The newsroom had gone through at least three rounds of layoffs, all white-knuckle, morale-crushing affairs. Benefits were cut to the point that the once-gung-ho staff took to picketing around a giant inflatable rat.

These changes placed more pressures on journalists to increase their productivity and risk losing their careers if an investigation did not work out. He underlines the main result, which is the diminished "appetite for confrontation and muckraking" (ibid.).

Tambini's (2010, 169) interviews with practitioners in the UK reveal decreasing resources and consequent time constraints that affect the quality of financial journalism. He also found that investigative stories were increasingly difficult to fund. In particular, Tambini (ibid.) highlights "accuracy" and "standards of verification and sourcing," and argues that few outlets are willing to commit to "two named sources for each story." On the other hand, some of the journalists maintained that they would engage in "higher verification standards if the story was likely to have an immediate market impact" (ibid., 170).

A recent case in the UK illustrated just how beholden some news outlets are to those who advertise on their pages. Peter Oborne, a well-respected senior writer at the *Telegraph*, quit his job in defiance when it appeared the paper's owners, the Barclay Brothers, wanted him to discard a story that challenged indicated aspects of fraud at HSBC, and particularly helping wealthy clients to evade paying tax, for fear of losing their valuable advertisement revenue. At the time Oborne wrote: "An editorial operation that is clearly influenced by advertising is classic appeasement. Once a very powerful body knows they can exert influence they know they can come back and threaten you. It totally changes the relationship you have with them."

Similarly, interviews with investigative journalists in Australia revealed that commercial pressures hinder their efforts to "undertake serious business investigations" (Kitchener 2005, 41). Kitchener interviewed journalists who conduct investigations most closely aligned with the concept of watchdog journalism. Therefore, they would be more likely to hold power to account and provide warnings of impending "market failure" or "corporate collapses" (ibid., 43). Yet, Kitchener (ibid., 46) describes a situation where "deskbound" journalists are coping with "stretched" resources "juggling daily news environments in addition to investigative work." The Internet, in this case, is actually seen as offering them a much-needed portal to the world outside the newsroom.

A study of corporate news content in Australian found that while crime investigations were on the rise, those that were investigating corporate crimes were on the decline – owing to advertisers who are put off by corporate advertisers and a rise in a trend toward tabloidization (Carson 2013, 297). Investigations in the public interest in Australian broadsheets have increased (quantitatively) decade-by-decade since the 1950s (Carson 2013). But Carson's results also indicate that investigative journalism, particularly targeting the corporate sector, started to decline in the 1980s at the same time as newspaper revenues began to fall. Also, since the 1980s, there has been a decline in reporting that places ordinary Australian citizens at the center of the news agenda. Her interviews with practitioners in Australia also revealed that owing to limited time and commercial pressures, follow-ups on investigative stories do not occur unless the story can be completed within a definite period.

Carson's interviews with practitioners reveal that news investigations still need the financial resources, credibility, and clout that traditional newspapers provide, underscoring the continued importance of established mainstream publications and the continuing value of investigative stories in the public interest.

So while the UK, the US, and Australia may have seen some excellent examples of, and a revival of, watchdog journalism in the 1960s, 1970s, and 1980s (particularly high-profile ones of a political nature coming out of the US, such as the Pentagon Papers and Watergate), and although numbers of investigations in broadsheets may have, in quantitative terms, been on the increase since the 1950s, the increasingly commercial nature of news has impacted on the practice of financial journalism and affected news quality. Overall, it has reduced the impact of stories in a fragmented media market, limited opportunity for investigation into abuses of power aimed at the ordinary citizen, and required journalists to pander to the corporate sector, which provides an important source of income.

Commercial Pressures on Journalists

The journalists interviewed for this book tend to agree that times are getting tougher for journalists – something they have witnessed first-hand. Many journalists are forced to compromise their craft skills and toil away with less money and more to do, while the public suffers from a dearth of information. The concept of "churnalism," as coined by Davies (2005) is clearly brought to life by journalists interviewed for this book. As Alan Kohler in Australia put it, "The staffing levels of media is going down so there's going to be more and more pressure. Journalists are going to have to work harder and get paid less." This is echoed quite vividly by senior financial reporter at the *Australian* newspaper, Glenda Korporaal, who refers specifically to a "crisis" in financial journalism. (When she was interviewed in 2016, journalists were protesting in the streets against more cuts by media company Fairfax.)

Colleen Ryan, also in Australia, describes a situation like that described by Elliott and Goodman when we discussed sources – that journalists do not have the time that they used to, to speak with members of the public. Goodman described a situation where journalists cannot "see the horizon." Ryan explains here that "you just don't have the time, to scout for information, and cultivate contacts; it's just a totally different world [compared to the 1980s and 90s]. So you have time pressures and staff-hour pressures because the number of journalists has declined. It just makes it extremely difficult to find the time to dig around, to find out the real stories, and really hold CEOs and market systems to account." "If you have a paper that is desperate for copy and the PR writes a really compelling press release, the temptations for plagiarism are intense."

Also in Australia, Paul Clearly says "You are seeing journalists writing three or four stories in a day in some newspapers. You look at those articles and think there's no way that journalists could be covering these issues in-depth, this is really just churning material out." This is a story told by Goodman in the US too. He explains that fewer eyeballs are checking the material, and there is much less time to proof generally. Meanwhile, there is now an emphasis on the number of clicks that a story produces online. This has an undesirable effect on the stories that journalists are choosing to cover in this commercial, or superficial environment: "Once you have people thinking about their stories as an editorial product, a commodity that is supposed to justify a return, you can talk yourself out of all sorts of important stories and work on the most obvious and easily executed stories."

Elliott expands on the theme that he started earlier when we discussed sources – that journalists do not have enough time to get out on the streets any more. But he explains fully the way the practice of reporting on the economy has changed over the past decade at the *Guardian*, and the very real and deflating consequences of a decline in resources and time for the quality of journalism:

> You're more prone to making mistakes, because you're doing things more quickly than you would have done 10–15 years ago.
>
> I want a little bit of time to think about what I'm writing about. Often the first thing you think of is not necessarily right. Now, in an instant immediate world you're expected to have an opinion very quickly. What we now do is amend our views; we have to because a lot of what we put out is not quite as rounded or full as it could be.

> So there is a trade-off between speed and quality. Inevitably, if you have a day writing a piece, and you write the introduction a few times, you read through it three or four times, it's going to be less of a rough diamond than if you bang something out.

One of the only journalists to give a positive outlook on the changes is Ian King, formerly at the *Times* UK and now at Sky. He describes a version of creative destruction and the streamlining of resources that minimises incompetence and poor performance. While he edited the city section of the *Times*, he explains that a third of the people there were fired. "If I look at my department, we've had enormous changes; we've got rid of a lot of deadwood – people that were underperforming. I've got in people who are much better. On our news section, I'm really happy with the quality, which I think has actually gone up. Commercial pressures can be positive and not always a negative."

We turn now to an industry that has grown rapidly in power and influence in the last few decades – public relations, or PR. Its power to shape the news agenda and turn a profit has had profound consequences for the role of financial journalists

The Power of Public Relations

In addition to its development within certain ideological and institutional constraints and ethical challenges, financial journalism has also developed alongside a PR industry with the principle aim of protecting the image of their business clients. The power of the PR machine has been growing, since its origin in the early 20th century, in tandem with big business (Bourne 2016; Roush 2006). This growth has accelerated during the past few decades, and it is now the source for a substantial part of media content. Globally, in 2016, the PR industry was worth $15 billion (see the Holmes Report 2017 https://www.holmesreport.com/footer-pages/about-the-holmes-report). In 2018, in his James Cameron Memorial lecture in London, Lionel Barber pointed out that there are now four PR professionals to every journalist. Since the 1980s, PR has played a major role in producing financial news, as Davis (2000b, 2006), Grunberg and Pallas (2013), and Lewis and others (2008) have demonstrated empirically. Therefore, PR not only challenges the watchdog nature of financial journalism, but it also mediates and influences the nature of the reportage.

The development of the PR industry has followed a similar trajectory in the US, the UK, and Australia. As early as 1963, Bart (1963, 32) describes the situation in the US where "A close-knit camaraderie has developed between the financial press and financial public-relations men—a camaraderie that works to the disadvantage of the ordinary newspaper reader." He describes a situation where financial journalists and PR practitioners work side-by-side and "cheat the proverbial widows and orphans out of their savings" (ibid.). Also, as early as 1966, Loeb (1966) was describing reliance on PR because of time restrictions; a pressure that has increased tenfold.

And one could go farther back to the decade before the Great Depression when stock exchanges were spending a hefty amount of their income on funding press relations. Journalists were found to be in cahoots with financial press relations professionals and were exposed in public for distorting the coverage that led to the 1929 market downturn, as part of the US Senate Pecora hearings which led to a tightening of US financial regulation and the creation of the SEC. (Lounsbury and Hirsch 2010, 231; Perino 2010.)

In the UK today, PR is overtaking financial journalism in terms of resources and personnel (Evans 2010, 31). PR companies grew alongside the financial products that culminated in the GFC: "Alongside the massive expansion in easy mortgages, credit derivatives, credit swaps, private equity companies in the big and seemingly endless boom before the crash, one industry benefited more than most: financial public relations." This occurred between the years 1987 and 2007 – described as the "golden years" for financial PR (Mair 2009b, 58). The growth of the industry has been matched by the expansion of its influence on financial journalists to report in favour of public relation companies' or their clients' interests. British companies spent GBP £37 million on financial PR in 1986, rising to GBP £250 million only a decade later. The profits gained from PR are being invested in the shaping of financial coverage (Tambini 2010, 167). Those resources are used to target elite audiences, which inevitably leads to the framing of content that excludes "non-elites" (Davis 2000, 283; see also, Miller and Mooney 2010).

The case of the merger between HBOS and Lloyds in the UK during the height of the financial crisis demonstrates just how uneven this playing field can be. The deal, brokered by Gordon Brown and welcomed by executives at HBOS and Lloyds, was announced in September 2008 as a way to rescue HBOS without involving a government bailout. But journalists and the public were deliberately kept in the dark about £20 billion of emergency loans provided by the Bank of England and the US Federal Reserve to keep HBOS afloat, and an additional £10 billion made directly from Lloyds as the deal was going through. The story went uncovered – not because journalists weren't on the ball, but because the information was deliberately hidden by Lloyds banking executives and their PR teams to ensure the merger went through.

In 2016, a case brought by shareholders in Lloyds against the bank revealed a number of ways in which Lloyds concealed and manipulated information to ensure that this merger got through and bad news about HBOS was concealed (report by expert witness Schifferes 2017). Lloyds executives, including former chairman Victor Blank, have defended their decision to merge with HBOS. In contrast, a group of Lloyds' shareholders have argued they were not fully briefed in a case heard in 2017–18 in the High Court of Chancery (Sharp v Blank). Evidence given by the expert witness, Professor of financial journalism Steve Schifferes, includes interviews with eminent financial editors and journalists that show just how seriously financial journalists would have taken this story. The BBC's business editor Simon Jack thinks "It would have been a massive story" and "We [the BBC] would have had to report it because for the same reasons we had to report the Northern Rock."

But, Lloyds' PR team did a good job of finessing the deal and obscuring some of the more crucial points to the public and shareholders. While the £10 billion loan made from Lloyds to HBOS at the time of the merger found its way to the pages of the *Sunday Times* – "Lloyds TSB's secret £10bn loan to HBOS" – the information could not be verified by the few journalists who had caught wind that something was amiss. The *Scotsman*'s financial editor Martin Flanagan was one of those journalists, but when he tried to follow-up the story he was knocked back by PR who denied the story's veracity.

And evidence from emails between communications advisors, executives and others at both HBOS and Lloyds show the length they would go to subvert journalists' attention. An email attachment from a communications executive for Lloyds to executives outlines the communications strategy around HBOS's circular says:

> HBOS releases its circular at 4pm on Friday 14 November. They have deliberately picked this time to give journalists only a short period to meet their print deadlines, although it is likely that there will still be significant interest in the document.

Further evidence shows they understood the implications of the deal. A communications director Mark Lidiard wrote to Lloyds' General Counsel, Kate Cheetham.

> *'One of the papers is asking why the £10 bn loan isn't in our circular. Seems like a good question.'*

More revealing yet is an email exchange between credit analyst Neil Bew and another analyst at Lloyds, Richard Welham.

> *'I dare say I am behind the times with this, but cat out of bag I assume? Neil'*

It could be argued that Brown and banking executives were averting the escalation of the crisis. The mutual payoff was clear: Brown saved his reputation which had been diminishing since the global financial crisis began (Schifferes and Knowles

2015), and executives oversaw the merger of two of the biggest banking behemoths in the UK and the consolidation of about a quarter of the UK mortgage market. But, the job of the journalist is not to serve the whims of political and financial interests, nor is it to save an n imploding system: it is to enlighten and inform the public and act as a check and balance to power.

Interviews with financial editors and journalists about the HBOS case show they are just as indignant about Peston was about Northern Rock. While this research says something about the way drivers of our economy can disable the crucial role of the media, it also says something about the serious implications of a power imbalance between the media, banking and the PR industry. The corollary of which is that we do not know just what else is lying beneath the surface.

And the extent to which PR has infiltrated the day-to-day news practices and quality of reportage within quality mainstream newspapers and broadcast news in the UK is alarming (Lewis et al. 2008, 2). PR, in the new media environment, can infiltrate the day-to-day practice of journalism since journalists are experiencing increasing pressures to produce more with less time. Independence is at the heart of journalistic autonomy and quality reporting, but the study finds that news content from quality broadsheet newspapers like the *Guardian* and the *Times*, and broadcast news from stations such as ITV and BBC is, more often than not, taken straight from PR. They included signs of content produced by news agencies into their study and found that if PR and news agencies are combined, then "60 per cent of press stories rely wholly or mainly on pre-packaged information" (ibid., 14).

The same trend can be found in Australia. A study of news content in the 1990s (Zawawi 1994) analysed several broadsheets in Australia and found that over half of the news comes directly from PR, while in finance reporting the result is higher, at around 90%. Her findings confirm Schultz's (1990) note that PR practitioners in Sydney "brag" about originating 50% of news coverage, and Tiffen's (1989) estimates that 90% of the business press' content comes from PR. A later study by Kitchener (2005, 52), involving interviews with practitioners, revealed that PR is more of an impediment to their reportage than legal constraints.

All journalists interviewed agreed they have witnessed the rise of this industry, with droves of PR personnel in comparison to numbers of journalists. Their perspectives, however, differ slightly on the influence PR can have on coverage. Some such as Starkman think it affects their daily practice more than it ever has in the past:

> There's a power imbalance between the financial sector and journalism that makes a big difference in terms of who has leverage in news organizations. This corporate empowerment naturally leads to PR empowerment.

Others such as Ian King think they have always been around and Gittins and Goodman who think it is the job of the reporter to maintain control of a story. Only Goodman says he has noticed a drop-off – but this is, he says, in comparison with the dot com bubble, when "The big companies were constantly pitching every incremental thing that they could because the market would trade on virtually anything. I look back on who was the most aggressive and they were by-and-large the companies who got themselves into the biggest trouble WorldCom, Nortel, Cisco and Enron." Now he thinks the situation is such that "people [in PR] have become very good at taking advantage of a relative lack of skill amongst the ranks of the new reporters."

Therefore, the PR industry has developed alongside financial journalism but has arguably surpassed it in resources. It now has the power to shape and dictate a lot of financial reportage if journalists are neophyte or do not approach press releases with caution, a trend that several studies have now proved empirically and the journalists themselves confirm. It has become a silent partner in financial journalism, thereby challenging the very notion and ideals that financial journalism can act as a watchdog that holds power to account.

Conclusion: What Is "Quality" Financial Journalism?

There is widespread agreement that the public is served best by financial journalism that serves a broad readership, not just business and investors' interests. Importantly, it should fulfil a watchdog role to ensure the public is informed in accordance with the democratic values of society. These values should be maintained by any media establishment reporting on business, economics, and finance, be they specialist or mainstream.

This review and discussion with journalists has produced criteria against which standards of financial reportage will be assessed in the case studies being analysed here. Based also on the core values of the publications being analysed – the *New York Times*, *Guardian*, and *Sydney Morning Herald* – objectivity, fairness, and impartiality, they are as follows:

- A variety of interpretations on an issue to promote discussion of alternative views;
- A variety of "voices" quoted directly to represent all sections of society;
- Everyday advice relating to finance and government spending for all sections of society, not just investors;
- Explanations that are unpacked with minimal jargon; and

- Sufficient scepticism and warnings that serve to signal an impending or potential crisis in the financial or economic systems.

The journalists interviewed here confirm the criticisms they have faced are warranted – they do use a narrow variety of sources for information, they were caught up in the market euphoria, and their reporting was shaped by dominant political narratives and the prevailing neo-liberal paradigm. However, a more complicated picture emerges, as those reporting on the economy are more attuned to an audience of the general public and write for a much broader audience. And while the majority do wish to report like watchdogs in the public's interest, they do so in an increasingly commercial environment with growing pressures on their workload, and less time and resources to do their jobs.

Roubini and Mihm (2010, 91) describe the moment of the financial crisis as the point when there is sudden aversion to risk and "sudden desire to dismantle the pyramids of leverage." This, they explain, was once known as "discredit" or "revulsion," but it is now better known as the "Minsky moment," which is named after Hyman Minsky, the post-Keynesian economist who believed in a balance of government regulation and the impact of financial markets on the real economy, and is known for his Financial Instability Theory (Minsky 1992). This concept is adopted here for media purposes and to illustrate the number of warnings the press provided pre-and-post with the "crisis" point. News stories are analysed a year before and two years after the crisis hits.

The 1990 Recession

November 1990 was chosen as the Minsky moment because it was the month that the recession was officially called in the US, and shortly after in Australia and the UK. There was no one single cause of the 1990 recession, so this was the most apparent indication and signalling of economic problems.

The Dot Com Boom

In the case of the dot com boom, March 2000 was the month that the NASDAQ, the market comprising all of the new Internet companies, peaked before starting its rapid decline from its phenomenal high. While the recession was not formally announced until the following year, from March 2000, the financial markets began a year-long nosedive, as new media companies that were listed on them fell one-by-one.

The GFC

The spring of 2007 has been identified as the Minsky moment for the GFC (Roubini and Mihm 2010). In August 2007 the French bank BNP Paribas halted trading and signalled its problems deriving from its links with the US subprime market. Two Bear Stearns hedge funds had also failed by August 2007 (Soros 2009, xx). It was, therefore, tangible that something was occurring happened in the financial markets. While the recession had not been called officially, from this date, the risk to the financial and economic systems was evident. (See Appendix for the full note on method.)

The Chapters that follow chart and just how far news standards have fallen from what can be regarded as "quality" from a normative and mainstream perspective, which places the public interest as central to its concern.

Note

1. Kleinnijenhuis and others (2013, 272) explain that High Frequency Trading algorithms 'had in 2007 replaced more than half of human equity trading.'

References

Akerlof, George, and Robert Shiller. 2009. *Animal Spirits: How Human Psychology Drives the Global Economy, and Why It Matters for Global Capitalism*. Princeton: Princeton University Press.

Bart, Peter. 1963. 'How to Read the Financial Pages without Going Broke.' *Harper's Magazine* 227 (1359): 31–35.

Barton, Laura. 2008. 'On the Money.' *The Guardian*, October 31. http://www.theguardian.com/business/2008/oct/31/creditcrunch-gillian-tett-financial-times.

Basu, Laura. 2018. *Media Amnesia: Rewriting the Economic Crisis*. London: Pluto Press.

Beecher, Eric. 2005. 'The End of Serious Journalism?' In *Barons to Bloggers: Confronting Media Power*, edited by Jonathan Mills, 65–75. Melbourne: The Miegunyah Press.

Berry, Mike. 2015. "No Alternative to Austerity: How BBC Broadcast News Reported the Deficit Debate.' *Media, Culture & Society* 38 (6): 844–863.

Berry, Mike. 2018. *The Media, the Public and the Great Financial Crisis*. London: Palgrave Macmillan.

Blyth, Mark. 2013. *Austerity: The History of a Dangerous Idea*. Oxford: Oxford University Press.

Bourne, Clea. 2016. *Trust, Power and Public Relations in Financial Markets*. London: Routledge.

Bryan, Dick. 2001. 'Reporting the 'Asian Financial Crisis': Australian Financial Journalists' Construction of a National Threat.' *Southern Review* 34 (2): 14–25.

Bull, George. 1998. 'A Peculiar Kind of Genius.' *British Journalism Review* 9 (1): 20–31.

Butterick, Keith J. 2015. *Collusion and Complacency: A Critical Introduction to Business and Financial Journalism*. London: Pluto Press.

Carson, Andrea. 2013. 'Investigative Journalism, the Public Sphere and Democracy: the Watchdog role of Australian broadsheets in the digital age.' PhD dissertation. University of Melbourne.

Carswell, Howard. 1938a. 'Business News and Reader Interest.' *Journalism Quarterly* 15: 191–195.

Chakravarrty, Paula, and Dan Schiller. 2010a. 'Neoliberal Newspeak and Digital Capitalism in Crisis.' *International Journal of Communication* 4: 670–692.

Clark, Gordon, Nigel Thrift, and Adam Tickell. 2004. 'Performing Finance: The Industry, the Media and Its Image.' *Review of International Political Economy* 11 (2): 289–310.

Craig, Geoffrey. 2001. 'The Global Financial News, Information & Technology Corporations.' *Southern Review: Communications, Politics & Culture* 34: 4–13.

Davis, Aeron. 2000. 'Public Relations, Business News and the Reproduction of Corporate Elite Power.' *Journalism* 1: 282–304.

Davis, Aeron. 2000b. 'Public Relations, News Production and Changing Patterns of Source Access in the British National Media.' *Media, Culture and Society* 22 (1): 39–59.

Davis, Aeron. 2006. 'Media Effects and the Question of the Rational Audience: Lessons from the Financial Markets.' *Media, Culture and Society* 28 (4): 603–625.

Davis, Aeron. 2011. 'Mediation, Financialization, and the Global Financial Crisis.' In *The Political Economies of Media: The Transformation of the Global Media*, edited by Dwayne Winseck, and Jin Dal Yong, 241–254. London: Bloomsbury Publishing.

Doyle, Gillian. 2006. 'Financial News Journalism: A Post-Enron Analysis of Approaches towards Economic and Financial News Production.' *Journalism* 7 (4): 433–452.

Evans, Trish. 2010. 'We Are All in PR now.' *British Journalism Review* 21 (2): 31–36.

Frank, Thomas. 2000. *One Market under God: Extreme Capitalism, Market Populism, and the End of Economic Democracy*. New York: Doubleday.

Giles, Robert, and Barry Sussman. 2011. 'What Would Good Reporting Look Like?' In *Bad News: How America's Business Press Missed the Story of the Century*, edited by Anya Schiffrin, 179–200. New York: The New Press.

Goodman, Peter S. 2009. *Past Due: The End of Easy Money and the Renewal of the American Economy*. New York: Times Books.

Goodman, Peter S. 2011. 'The Quiet Crisis.' In *Bad News: How America's Business Press Missed the Story of the Century*, edited by Anya Schiffrin, 94–121. New York: The New Press.

Greenfield, Cathy, and Peter Williams. 2002. 'The Politics of Finance Journalism: Approaches to the Field and a Rhetorical Instance.' Paper presented at the annual meeting for the *Australian & New Zealand Communication Association, Queensland, July 10–12, 2002*.

Greenfield, Cathy, and Peter Williams. 2007. 'Financialization, Finance Rationality and the Role of Media in Australia.' *Media, Culture & Society* 29 (3): 415–433.

Grunberg, Jaan, and Josef Pallas. 2013. 'Beyond the News Desk – The Embeddedness of Business News.' *Media, Culture and Society* 35 (2): 216–233.

Hamilton, Martha. 2009. 'What We Learned in the Meltdown: Financial Journalists Saw the Trees but Not the Forest.' *Columbia Journalism Review* 47 (5): 36–39.

Kindleberger, Charles, and Robert Aliber. 2011. *Manias, Panics and Crashes: A History of Financial Crises*. 6th ed. New York: Palgrave Macmillan. Original edition, 1978.

Kitchener, Jennifer. 1999. 'Business Journalism in the 1980s.' In *Journalism: Print, Politics and Popular Culture*, edited by Ann Curthoys, and Julianne Schultz, 229–244. St Lucia: University of Queensland Press.

Kitchener, Jennifer. 2005. 'Investigative Business Journalism in the Age of the Internet.' *Australian Journalism Review* 27 (1): 41–56.

Kleinnijenhuis, Jan, Friederike Schultz, Dirk Oegema, and Wouter van Atteveldt. 2013. 'Financial News and Market Panics in the Age of High-Frequency Sentiment Trading Algorithms.' *Journalism* 14 (2): 271–291.

Kollmeyer, Christopher. 2004. 'Corporate Interests: How the News Media Portray the Economy.' *Social Problems* 51 (3): 432–452.

Lacy, Stephen, and Frederick Fico. 1991b. 'Fairness and Balance in the Prestige Press.' *Journalism Quarterly* 68 (3): 363–370.

Lewis, Justin. 2010. 'Normal Viewing Will Be Resumed Shortly: News, Recession and the Politics of Growth.' *Popular Communication* 8 (3): 161–165.

Lewis, Justin, Andrew Williams, and Bob Franklin. 2008. 'A Compromised Fourth Estate? UK News Journalism, Public Relations and News Sources.' *Journalism Studies* 9 (1): 1–20.

Loeb, Gerald. 1966. 'Flaws in Financial Reporting.' *Columbia Journalism Review* 5 (1): 37–39.

Lounsbury, Michael, and Paul M. Hirsch, eds. 2010. *Markets on Trial: The Economic Sociology of the US Financial Crisis*. New York: Emerald Group Publishing.

Mair, John. 2009a. 'Top Journos Look behind the headlines.' In *Playing Footsie with the FTSE? The Great Crash of 2008 and the Crisis in Journalism*, edited by John Mair, and Richard L. Keeble, 23–34. Suffolk: Institute of Communication Ethics and Abramis Academic.

Mair, John. 2009b. 'Spinning Us All into Trouble?' In *Playing Footsie with the FTSE? The Great Crash of 2008 and the Crisis in Journalism*, edited by John Mair, and Richard L. Keeble, 57–58. Suffolk: Institute of Communication Ethics and Abramis Academic.

Mair, John, and Richard L. Keeble, eds. 2009. *Playing Footsie with the FTSE? The Great Crash of 2008 and the Crisis in Journalism*. Suffolk: Institute of Communication Ethics and Abramis Academic.

Mickler, Steve. 2012. 'Blame Liberals: Conservative Columnists and the GFC in Australia and Canada.' *Communication, Politics and Culture* 45: 5–23.

Miller, David, and Gerry Mooney. 2010. 'Introduction to the Themed Issue. Corporate Power: Agency, Communication, Influence and Social Policy.' *Critical Social Policy* 30 (4): 459–471.

Minsky, Hyman. 1992. 'The Financial Instability Hypothesis.' *The Jerome Levy Economics Institute* Working Paper 74.

Overholser, Geneva. 2001. 'Our Nose for News Fails Us When the Smell is Close to Home.' Columbia Journalism Review July/August: 56–57.

Page, Bruce. 2002. 'Pricking the Bubble: Financial Scandal and the Media.' *British Journalism Review* 13 (3): 49–57.

Parsons, Wayne. 1989. *The Power of the Financial Press: Journalism and Economic Opinion in Britain and America*. New Brunswick: Rutgers University.

Perino, Michael. 2010. *The Hellhound of Wall Street: How Ferdinand Pecora's Investigation of the Great Crash Forever Changed American Finance*. New York: Penguin Books.

Preston, Paschal, and Henry Silke. 2012. 'Market 'Realities': Decoding Economic Ideology in the Press.' *Critical Media Review*. http://criticalmediareview.wordpress.com/2012/08/05/market-realities-decoding-economic-ideology-in-the-press-paschal-preston-henry-silke-dcu/.

Putnis, Peter. 1997. 'The Business of Empire: Henry M. Collins and the Early Role of Reuters in Australia.' *Australian Journal of Communication* 24 (3): 11–26.

Quinn, Jane. 1998. 'When Business Writing becomes Soft Porn.' *Columbia Journalism Review* 36 (6): 48–49.

Quirt, John. 1993. *The Press and the World of Money: How the News Media Cover Business and Finance, Panic and Prosperity, and the Pursuit of the American Dream*. California: Anton/California-Courier.

Roubini, Nouriel, and Stephen Mihm. 2010. *Crisis Economics: A Crash Course in the Future of Finance*. London: Penguin Books.

Roush, Chris. 2006. *Profits and Losses: Business Journalism and Its Role in Society*. Illinois: Marion Street Press.

Schechter, Danny. 2009. 'Credit Crisis: How Did We Miss It?' *British Journalism Review* 20 (19): 19–26.

Schifferes, Steve. 2012. 'Trust-Meltdown for Business Journalism.' *British Journalism Review* 23 (2): 55–59.

Schifferes, Steve. 2017. Expert Witness Report prepared for Lloyds' shareholder, Sharp v Blank https://www.rpc.co.uk/perspectives/commercial-disputes/sharp-v-blank-and-others-2017-ewhc-3390-ch/ (Accessed May 1 2020).

Schifferes, Steve and Sophie Knowles. 2015. 'The Media and the First Crisis of Globalization.' In *Soothsayers of Doom: The Media and Financial Crises*, edited by Steve Schifferes and Richard Roberts. London: Routledge.

Schiffrin, Anya, and Ryan Fagan. 2013. 'Are We All Keynesians Now? The US Press and the American Recovery Act of 2009.' *Journalism* 14 (2): 151–172.

Schultz, Julianne. 1990. *Accuracy in Australian Newspapers*. Sydney: Australian Centre for Independent Journalism.

Schultz, Julianne and Zoltan Matolcsy. 1993. 'Business Boosters or Impartial Critics.' In *Reporting Business*, edited by Julianne Schultz, 9–31. Working Paper. Sydney: Australian Centre for Independent Journalism.

Schuster, Thomas. 2006. *Business News and Stock Market Movements*. Oxford: Lexington Books.

Shefrin, Hersh. 2002. *Beyond Greed and Fear: Understanding Behavioural Finance and the Psychology of Investing*. Oxford: Oxford University Press.

Shiller, Robert. 2005. *Irrational Exuberance*. 2nd ed. Princeton: Princeton University Press. Original edition, 1996.

Soros, George. 2009. *The Crash of 2008 and What It Means: The New Paradigm for Financial Markets*. New York: Public Affairs.

Starkman, Dean. 2015. *The Watchdog that Didn't Bark*. New York: Columbia University Press.

Starkman, Dean. 2009a. 'Power Problem: The Business Press Did Everything but Take on the Institutions that Brought Down the Financial System.' *Columbia Journalism Review* 48 (1): 22–30.

Starkman, Dean. 2009b. 'How Could 9,000 Business Reporters Blow It?' *Mother Jones*, January/February. http://www.motherjones.com/politics/2009/01/how-could-9000-business-reporters-blow-it.

Starkman, Dean, Martha Hamilton, Ryan Chittum, and Felix Salmon, eds. 2012. *The Best Business Writing 2012*. New York: Columbia University Press.

Tambini, Damian. 2010. 'What are Financial Journalists For?' *Journalism Studies* 11 (2): 158–174.

Tett, Gillian. 2009. 'Icebergs and Ideologies: How Information Flows Fuelled the Financial Crisis.' *Anthropology News*, 50: 6–7.

Tiffen, Rodney. 1989. *News and Power*. Sydney: Allen and Unwin.

Welles, Chris. 1973. 'The Bleak Wasteland of Financial Journalism.' *Columbia Journalism Review* July/August: 40–49.

Wilby, Peter. 2009. 'When Business Journalism Gets in Bed with the Financial Institutions.' In *Playing Footsie with the FTSE? The Great Crash of 2008 and the Crisis in Journalism*, edited by John Mair and Richard L. Keeble, 82–86. Suffolk: The Institute of Communication Ethics and Abramis Academic.

Zawawi, Clara. 1994. 'Sources of News – Who Feeds the Watchdogs?' *Australian Journalism Review* 16 (1): 67–71.

CHAPTER THREE

Case Study I: The Recession of the Early 1990s; the Recession We "Had to Have"?

> Nothing less than the highest ideals, the most scrupulous anxiety to do right, the most accurate knowledge of the problems it has to meet, and a sincere sense of moral responsibility will save journalism from a subservience to business interests ….
> (Pulitzer 1904, 655)

It is through the lens of over-consumption and inflating asset prices that one can understand former Australian Prime Minister Paul Keating's statement that the 1990 economic downturn was "the recession we had to have." But the 1990 recession was not confined to Australia. It was widespread and felt simultaneously across most developed economies. In 1990, the unemployment rate in all Organisation for Economic Co-operation and Development (OECD) countries was at a ten-year high. The countries hit hardest were Australia, the UK, the US, New Zealand, Canada, and Finland (OECD 1991, 1).

The liberalisation of exchange rates was driven by the collapse of the Bretton Woods system in the early 1970s. It was not just deregulation but privatisation of state-owned industries in the UK that drove neo-liberalism. In the US there was the savings and loan crisis in the late 1980s which was caused by the deregulation of building societies which over-invested in and collapsed after speculative investments went sour – and then had to be rescued by US government. Financial globalisation and investment across borders, especially by financial companies, was just beginning and given a boost by the Big Bang deregulation of the City of London in 1986.

In addition to a recession, the developed world economies had recently floated their exchange rates and seen the deregulation of the financial industry. This process was a part of the neo-liberal movement that favoured deregulation of industry, championed during the 1980s by influential politicians, such as US President Ronald Reagan and UK Prime Minister Margaret Thatcher. As a result, governments ceded control of some key industries with flow-on effects to ordinary households. There was first the global deregulation of the telecommunication industry during the 1990s and then the banking industry, through the repeal of the Glass-Steagall Act in the US in 1999. The financial press evolved in lockstep with the prevailing ideology of the time. Parsons (1989) and Matolcsy and Schultz (1994) document the extent to which the financial press accepted neo-liberal orthodoxy in the US, the UK, and Australia.

The Political Economy of the 1980–90s

> The Reagan era is over, but the ideology that animated it continues to hover, like a Cheshire cat's smile, above the landscape of American public policy. (Silk 1989, 1)

The decade of politics before the 1990 recession saw the stalwarts of neo-liberalism like Reagan and Thatcher enacting some pivotal economic and business-related policy changes. The neo-liberal undercurrent that characterised them would soon become the prevailing orthodoxy. This ideology supported deregulation of industry and privatisation that effectively supported the growing momentum of globalisation. But an increasing reliance on the market, which was exacerbating economic volatility (Hviding 1995, 30).

Some of the common reforms occurring across the OECD countries included freeing up the financial sector to set theirown rates on credit and interest rates, bank charges and restrictions on the movement of foreign exchange. All the changes that took place make it difficult to define the 1990 recession as an economic event, as there is still no one obvious cause for any of the countries that were affected (Hall 1993, 275). Instead, Hall attributes the recession to *contractions in all areas of investment* across the globe.

Hall compiled a list that illustrates the wide and varied factors that can be taken into consideration when assessing the 1990 global recession, with particular reference to the US (ibid., 278):

1. There was a price shock, and stabilisation policy depressed real output to limit inflation from shock.
2. Monetary policy switched to a lower target for nominal growth.
3. Government purchases of goods and services declined.
4. Tax rates increased.
5. There was a negative shock to aggregate technology.
6. Regulatory changes reduced the intermediation provided by banks.
7. Changes in the world economy had a negative effect on US output.
8. There was a spontaneous decline in consumption.

In the UK there were big effects from the sudden collapse of the house price boom. There was also the issue of too high an exchange rate which affected exports.

The United States

Politics in the 1980s in the US were defined by the burgeoning neo-liberal philosophy that favoured low interest rates to fight inflation instead of dealing with rising unemployment. There was the need for high interest rates to fight inflation that caused the 1982 recession – Reagan was highly critical of the head of the Federal Reserve for doing this and replaced him with the neo-liberal Alan Greenspan. The neo-liberal philosophy grew in popularity at a time when stagflation was dragging down the economy in the 1970s, and Keynesian remedies failed to work. It was during this period that market rhetoric started its reign and Keynesianism waned (Silk 1989, 1).

In its place, a new vision started to materialise that was "helped along by wealthy lions of the right" (Silk 1989, 1). Money was poured into conservative think-tanks and foundations that supported a version of capitalism that was unencumbered by regulation; with low taxes and a smaller role for the state in the economy. Indeed, Silk (ibid., 2) blames the new deregulatory stance and unfettered capitalism for the savings and loan crisis, which must have had a role to play in the 1990 recession.[1]

Other studies point to a consumption shock that caused a recession. There was a decline in consumer confidence that preceded official data indicating actual economic downturn (Blanchard 1993). Consumers were possibly anticipating a recession or negative factors in the economy, perhaps in part arising from the consequences of the invasion of Kuwait by Iraq in August 1990. These fears were justified, as the average net worth for families in the 1990s dropped by the US $181 billion (Davidson 1992, 11).

As the recession continued through 1991, President George H.W. Bush was unwilling to fight it – a rationale firmly backed up by a team of "do-nothing neoliberals" (ibid., 8). More importantly, the media employed the same rationale for the inertia, presenting it as "conventional wisdom" (ibid.). Referring to the upcoming 1992 US Presidential elections, Davidson discusses what he calls the "usual gang" of experts used by the media and Congress to explain the economic situation. And the "gang" are separated into five categories. Four espouse neo-liberalism, and just one provides support for Keynesianism, which at this time had been pushed out of favour by "deficit phobia" (ibid.).

Therefore, by the early 1990s, politicians in the US favoured a hands-off approach to directing the economy. This approach was manifested in deregulation of industry, notably the financial industry, and a preoccupation with letting the market solve any market fluctuations, with the view that the economy would regulate itself. This new status quo was supported by financial journalism, which used experts that favoured this approach to managing (or in this case not managing) the economy.

The United Kingdom

Prime Minister Margaret Thatcher's legacy will forever be associated with "the greatest period of deregulation in modern British history" (Bolick 1995, 527). Arguably the UK counterpart to Reagan across the Atlantic, she embraced and encouraged the neo-liberal economic approach that was taking off in the US. Soon after her inauguration in 1979, she promulgated a budget, which cut public spending by three per cent and reduced regulation. She also ended price, wage, dividend, and currency controls (ibid., 535). She oversaw the overhaul and restructure of the British economy, pushing individual entrepreneurship and empowerment through privatisation and deregulation. By 1991, 50 per cent of the industrial sector had been privatised and 20 per cent of the population were shareholders (ibid., 545).

Thatcher rejected the Keynesian approach and instead adopted an approach (not dissimilar to Reagan's) that promoted low inflation instead of low unemployment, also known as monetarism and a way a government can control the economy. Alongside this approach, rhetoric developed that favoured individual freedom and a version of "popular" capitalism (Rae and Drury 1993, 333). This rhetoric embodied a philosophy that the public understood. The "populist message" was patriotic and imbued the Conservative party with a cause that appealed even to working-class voters (Bolick 1995, 534). The lifting of morale and the sense of individual purpose that Thatcher inspired is perhaps best evoked in her speech at her first party conference as opposition leader, in 1975:

> Let me give you my vision: a man's right to work as he will, to spend what he earns, to own property, to have the state as servant and not as master: these are the British inheritance. They are the essence of a free country, and on that freedom all our other freedoms depend. (cited in ibid., 533)

The concept of "popular capitalism" was also defined by privatisation and the role the public played in buying shares: "Shares were marketed aggressively not to major investors but to 'Sid,' the prototypical average British share-purchaser featured in television promotions …" (ibid., 541). Thatcher contrasted the public's benefit from this system with the lack of opportunity offered in a stagnating economy and less prosperous times, or "dark" Marxism, as her election pitch made clear:

> This is a historic election. For the choice facing the nation is between two totally different ways of life. And what a prize we have to fight for: no less than the chance to banish from our land the dark, divisive clouds of Marxist socialism. (cited in ibid., 539)

Thatcher's policy changes, and the populist ideology that set them in motion, became the bedrock of British politics for the next two decades. And Thatcher's legacy left an indelible impression on Tony Blair's incoming Labour party, in 1997:

> … Socialism seems permanently vanquished, a new generation of Conservatives plans further advances against the welfare state, and even the opposition Labour Party now concedes basic premises about the virtues of markets and individualism.

This mandate to concede to the market as a power broker is best viewed by the Labour party's amendment of its charter from "common ownership of the means of production" in favour of equality of opportunity within "the enterprise of the market and the rigour of competition" (Barbash, cited in ibid., 546). The concepts of deregulation of industry, public share-ownership, and Thatcher's overall message were popularised in the media, through television programs like *Freedom to Choose* – which pushed Milton Friedman's free-market philosophies – and by the mainstream press (Bolick 1995, 541; Parsons 1989, 209).

Australia

The 1980s trend of deregulation was also taking off in Australia (Fitzgibbons 2006, 371). The financial sector had recently been deregulated and constituted a major reason for a speculative boom. Up until the 1980s, industries in Australia had been heavily regulated, especially the banking industry, which was controlled by the central bank – the Commonwealth Bank and then the Reserve Bank in 1959. Such regulatory powers and responsibilities of government were in keeping with Keynesian theory (ibid., 372).

It was during the 1970s that economic policies which favoured minimal regulation, or "economic rationalism" as it is known in Australia, overtook Keynesian theory in popularity. But unlike the US, where banks strongly supported internationalisation beyond local markets, the banking industry in Australia was initially more ambivalent and insular in its attitude towards deregulation of industry (ibid., 376). It was during the 1980s under the Hawke Labour government that Australian banks finally became interested in foreign expansion, the deregulation of labour markets, and floated the dollar (Henningham 1997, 46).

And the press provided a lot of support for the "rationalist" theory of market prevalence. Veteran political journalist Paul Kelly said, "… the Canberra press gallery in the 1980s, was essentially what I would describe as 'economic rationalist'" (cited in Toohey 1994, 214). Paul Keating, Treasurer in the 1980s and then Prime Minister from 1991–1996, pushed this line of thinking, and used the press for his own ends, as "ciphers for his view" (ibid., 221). The well-known financial journalist Alan Kohler (interviews with this author are cited in the previous Chapter) describes a financial press in the 1980s that was not perceptive enough to recognise that economic policy was being engineered by politics:

> When economic clothes are used to disguise ideology from either the right or left of politics and get it through the back door, because Australian journalists do not understand economics from dogma, then that needs to be exposed. The media has not exposed this enough. (cited in Schultz and Matolcsy, 1993, 7)

Financial Media and Business

In Chapters 1 and 2 we discussed financial news' rise in prominence throughout the 1970s and 1980s, as it was seen less and less as journalism's "ugly stepchild" (Lewin 2002, 19). The public had a new appetite for financial news in the 1970s. The new interest in the business news section came from a growing desire in the general public to understand how business and the economy were affecting their day-to-day-lives – a fact that is expressed well in a 1975 survey of business editors in the US. One of the business editors said, "Laymen realize that governmental policy decisions on the economy have a direct impact on them … They want to know why Joe was laid off from the local widget plant, and why the natural gas company is increasing its rates by yet another 25%" (Hubbard 1976, 489).

And the editors surveyed felt that the public needed the financial press to translate for them what was happening in business and the economy. As one business editor said, "The experts, political and economic, do not know the answers.

Hence more people are looking for their own explanations and relying more on their newspaper to help them understand" (ibid.). The survey demonstrated that the financial press was not only needed to act as a purveyor of business and economic information, but it was required to decode and decipher highly valuable information, which was being demanded from the public. It is interesting to note that the following year economics writer Brian Toohey (1994, xiii) was writing about the "inroads that economic jargon had achieved in Australian public life."

The results from this US survey also reveal the kinds of ethical problems faced by editors and journalists on the financial news desk in the 1970s: lack of time, lack of editorial identity, lack of front office support, the competence of reporters, and commercial pressure from advertisers (Hubbard 1976, 492). Increased spending on advertisements also had a direct effect on the topic chosen by financial journalists and the way the subject was presented. During this period Wall Street Week presenter, Louis Rukeyser, suggests that financial journalism, as a result of advertising interests, covers its subjects either superficially or "in an occasional mood of crusading." Rukeyser argues that as a consequence of superficial coverage the public is not being appropriately served, nor "are most newspapers doing the job they should be doing in helping the average citizen better understand the way in which the economic system really works" (Cited in Parsons 1989, 210).

Journalists' commitment to watchdog-style journalism, and the public's desire to understand business and economic developments was arguably further challenged by a business agenda to lobby for a positive image for business in the press and society. During the 1980s businesses employed a "five-pronged campaign" to influence society and produce discourse in its favour: it cultivated courses at major universities to provide education for the financial press, which it thought was lacking; it started to found think-tanks that would act on its behalf as "sources" and "experts"; it started awards for favourable coverage, such as the Loeb award in the US; it fostered meetings between business and media executives; and it produced advertising campaigns (Dreier 1982, 124–129). Dreier also underscores the challenges that were increasingly limiting journalists' autonomy from business. It was suffering from lack of time, limited staff and source access, and ideology that assumed "responsible capitalism" was the only way (ibid., 114).[2]

Another survey of business editors and journalists in the US (at 186 newspapers) in this period shows there was a split in half between journalists who wished to work autonomously from business as watchdogs, and those who wished to foster the development of the free enterprise system" (Barkin 1982, 299). And it was previously noted in Chapter 2 that, during the 1980s, the financial press used information and quotes from sources that supported deregulation of industry and a thriving stock market. Academics were disregarded in favour of "tipsters" who provided tips on the stock market (Parsons 1989, 8). This contrasts with the previous two or three decades, a time when leading economic gurus were in demand. Parsons (ibid., 213) prophesises, notably during the 1980s, that the move away from scholars indicates that the financial press will become "participants and 'puffers'" instead of "observers," as well as "extensions of PR companies" instead of "independent commentators."

There was a similar shift in approach to financial journalism in the UK, in the 1980s, alongside the emergence of "popular capitalism" that came with the privatisation of big companies, like British Telecom. This included coverage on television: "This growth of business coverage on British television in the wake of Mrs Thatcher's 'privatisation' programme is … a measure of significant cultural change in attitudes towards money and profits …" (ibid., 209). Parsons (ibid.) sees this as part of a shift towards more "popular financial journalism," which started with the personal finance column from the mid-1960s, but took off in the 1980s fuelled by the housing boom.

In Australia, the press was just as favourable toward economic orthodoxy and specifically neo-liberal government policies that included deregulation. The Treasury's stance has been cited as one reason why financial journalists approved the floating of the Australian dollar and the deregulation of the financial and labour markets (Henningham 1997; Matolcsy and Schultz 1994). An analysis of the Australian media's coverage of entrepreneurs, such as Christopher Skase, head of Quintex, which collapsed in 1991, and Alan Bond who did business with Chile's dictator Augusto Pinochet, demonstrates the uncritical nature of this reportage throughout the 1980s (Kitchener 1999, 229–230). The same study argues that deregulation in Australia in the 1980s was responsible for its newfound connection to the global economy, increased levels of business coverage, and growing public interest (ibid., 231).

How the Reporting of the 1990 Recession Has Been Measured Before

Previous studies on media coverage of the 1990 recession reveal a press that provided minimal forewarning of impending problems to the public and coverage that was too negative given the economic reality. There have been no studies of the sources used to frame the 1990 recession, but a study on the 1987 market crash that preceded the recession reveals coverage framed by elite sources of information that limited debate on the likely causes of the crash (Lasorsa and Reese 1990).

The 1990 recession was challenging to predict in the US because of deficiencies in the data at the time and the fact that it had different characteristics to previous recessions (Fintzen and Steckler 1999). The situation was not fully grasped by those telling the story, including the financial press. However, the recession could have been forecast if reports had looked at more varied data and had not included the forecasters' own biased assumptions. An analysis of the reports published in *Business Week*, the *Wall Street Journal*, and other more official economic forecast reports from the end of 1989 to the end of 1990, and the mean GNP predictions from every survey, show that a recession was not predicted (ibid., 310). In August 1990, after the Iraq invasion of Kuwait and a consequent rise in oil prices, forecasters started to predict a faster slowdown in economic growth, and by September a short recession in 1990 was finally predicted.

Looking at the evidence retrospectively the official economic data shows that a peak and drop in economic growth occurred in May 1990. However, data available at the time did not provide this clear picture, and the situation did not become clear until November, with the release of September figures. In addition, the GNP figures were wrong. Whereas data available to us now indicates that real GNP was in decline by the third quarter of 1990, data at the time, published by the Department of Commerce, indicated that it had grown by 1.8%. Despite this, Fintzen and Steckler maintain that the recession was predictable, but to do so, the data needed to be diverse and varied.

Wu and others' (2002) study of the 1990 recession, again in the US, found a correlation between the attitudes of the press, the public, and the movements in the economy. They examined content from the *New York Times* from January 1987 to January 1991, and then from January 1991 to 1996, which encompassed an upturn, downturn, and recovery period in economic growth. Peoples' perceptions were measured by the US Consumer Research Centre of the Conference Board. The state of the economy in the US was measured through the Economic Index (ibid., 25). They found that the public pay increased attention to the media during a downturn in the economy, and the media closely reflect the public perception in a downturn (ibid., 30).

Another US study of the 1990 recession argues that the tone of the coverage was more negative than was warranted by the actual economic situation (Goidel and Langley 1995). The authors compared the tone of articles from the *New York Times* (arguing that it is an agenda-setting publication) with economic factors in a regression equation, including the level of inflation, level of unemployment, change in inflation over 12 months, change in unemployment over 12 months, and GDP percentage change from the preceding quarter. The analysis reveals that the tone of the coverage of the economy in the years 1982, 1991, and 1992, which are affected by a recession, are different to coverage of the economy in years unaffected by recessionary characteristics.

A UK-based study examined the rhetoric used in the UK media to describe and define the recession unfolding at the end of 1990 (Rae and Drury 1993). The authors found that the economy in 1990, as part of a continuing trend identified by Emmison (1983), was presented as an independent agent, and reified through metaphorical analogies, or anthropomorphism (ibid., 352). They looked specifically at the last quarter of 1990 to examine the rhetoric about whether a recession had arrived and how the media discussed it. While a recession had officially been declared in the US and Australia, by this stage, it was not official in the UK because there had not yet been two consecutive months of negative growth, the technical definition of a recession. Therefore, there was still scope for debate about its existence. The authors collected 62 articles from the *Guardian* and 73 from the *Financial Times*.

The study shows that the *Guardian* first started to anticipate a recession midway through October 1990. A statement that a recession had arrived appeared on October 24. Rae and Drury (ibid., 344) note that the language used for the economy distinguishes between "it" and "us," and caused the authors to state that, "We will, therefore, refer to the main discourse inhabiting this text as people versus economy." In addition to the economy being seen as an independent agent through such active verbs as "hitting" and "biting," it was also presented as being under the command and influence of the government through words like "haul" and "steer" (ibid., 351). Once the presence of a recession had been established, the news media started to change its focus to questioning whether the economy and/or Britain were in a recession, and postulating as to its impact and severity (ibid., 352).

There are few studies on Australian media during the 1990 recession, but those that discuss financial reporting in the 1980s point to pro-business coverage (Kitchener 1999; Toohey 1994).

In summary, previous studies on the reportage of the 1990 recession conclude it was too negative given the economic circumstances, that negative reportage influenced the public's perceptions in a feedback loop that affected consumer's appetite to spend, that information was likely to be framed by elite sources, and that the economy was presented as separate from society and under the command of government.

Before now there have been no comparative studies; each focuses on one country and one period. What follows here is a comparison of the reportage of this recession in the US, the UK, and Australia. There is a comparison of the number, tone, and type of articles, and by identification of the primary sources of information that shaped the coverage of the 1990 recession. What it finds is far less dire than previous studies have described, and far more breadth of discussion and sources used for information than that which came to characterise the GFC.

Content Analysis Timeframe: November 1988–January 1992

There was so much going on, so many deals, so many infinitely complex deals, all with very tight deadlines. People just didn't have the time to understand what was going on. When you started asking "emperor without clothes" – type questions you were treated with disbelief (Ryan, Light and McGeough 1990).

This section analyses mainstream financial reportage from the US, the UK, and Australia, using quantitative and then qualitative methods, to measure and compare the amount, type, and nature of the coverage in each of the countries. The articles are measured against the criteria laid out in Chapter 2: the diversity of interpretations and sources used to frame the events, the advice given for non-investing members of the public – or a general audience – and the number of forewarnings and levels of scepticism shown before the crisis occurred. (See Appendix for a full chapter on the methodology.)

The Economic Context: What the Economic Data Tell Us

Following the Pew Research Center (2008) and Kollmeyer (2004), here we will look at some fundamental economic indicators – the GDP, and inflation and unemployment rates – to build an overall picture of the economic health in the countries before and during the 1990 recession.

The United States

According to GDP trends, the US economy started to slow down during the course of 1990. The year started with the GDP up by 2.7%, which then fell to 0.6% by the last quarter. At the start of 1991, growth slipped into negative territory and official recession.

The US inflation rate remained roughly between 4% and 6% through 1989 and 1990. It rises during 1990 to over 6%. It then reduces dramatically at the beginning of 1991 and continues to decrease to 3% by 1992. And the unemployment rate remained steady at between 5 and 5.5% through 1989. In mid-1990, it rises sharply and reaches 7% by 1992.

In the US, therefore, the data reveals that the economy was showing clear signs of inflation and rising levels of unemployment. While it might not have reached official recession status until the end of 1990-early 1991, the slowing GDP and increasing unemployment through 1990 should have been a cause for concern for journalists.

The United Kingdom

The UK economy, like that of the US, started to slow through 1990. However, it did not start to fall until mid-June 1990, descending from 2.8 per cent to just 0.4 per cent by the end of the year. From the end of 1990 and through 1992, the economy is in negative growth.

The inflation rate in the UK that starts from a low of 5 per cent at the start of 1989 and then climbs continuously through 1989 and 1990. By mid-1990, it is close to 7 per cent, and then remains between 7 per cent and 8 per cent in 1991 and 1992. Unemployment in the UK is higher than the US to begin with, as it stays around 7 per cent through 1989 and for the start of 1990. Mirroring the US, it rises steeply from mid-1990 to close to 8 per cent by the end of the year, and it continues to climb to well over 9 per cent by the end of 1991.

Overall, the UK economy experiences negative growth at the end of 1990 and through 1991. It has an unemployment rate that is already at 7 per cent in 1989 and increases steadily from July 1990 until it is close to 10 per cent by 1992. Inflation appears to be a constant problem through 1990, 1991, and 1992. Indeed, while the inflation rate in the US dropped in 1992 to 3 per cent, the UK inflation rate remained high at 8 per cent. Therefore, it can be expected that articles from the *Guardian* will be sceptical at least from mid-1990, and provide some warnings and explanations, especially with regards to persisting unemployment.

Australia

The economy in Australia slowed continuously from the end of 1989 until it went into negative growth at the start of 1991, where it remained through to 1992.

The inflation rate in Australia started higher than the US and the UK, at a peak of 8.6 per cent at the start of 1990. Unlike the UK, it started to decrease steadily through the rest of 1990 and 1991, to a low of 1.5 per cent at the start of 1992. The unemployment rate in Australia is higher than either the US or the UK. It remains close to 7 per cent through 1989 to mid-June. From mid-1990, it climbs steadily and reaches 9.5 per cent by mid-1991 where is remains through 1992.

Therefore, Australia slips into negative growth by 1990 and has a persistently high unemployment rate that reaches 9.5 per cent in 1991. The inflation rate, on the other hand, decreases throughout the period. This suggests that Australia must have been suffering from the effects of a recession and a stubbornly elevated unemployment rate at least from the start of 1990. These indicators should have rung alarm bells for financial journalists reporting on Australia.

Summary

According to the economic data from the US, the UK, and Australia, all three countries slipped into recession at the end of 1990. Unemployment was also high in each country. Inflation dropped in the US and Australia but remained high in the UK. The UK was the most affected of the three countries, with negative growth, high unemployment, and high inflation.

Therefore, according to the economic trend lines, the public could have expected that from at least mid-1990 onwards reportage would reflect negative economic conditions. However, the data shows early warning signs as early as the end of 1989, so that arguably there should have been some alert as to an impending downturn by early 1990. The level of unemployment was an obvious issue in each country, which also should have been reflected in the coverage.

The Reporting of the Recession?

Based on the key words specific to the economic boom and bust of 1990, a large proportion of the coverage appeared before the moment of crisis. This amount of coverage arguably presented the public with information they needed to anticipate a downturn in the economy. There were 226 articles in the two years preceding the Minsky moment, representing 60 per cent of the total data set. There were 158 articles in the year afterwards, or 40 per cent of the total data set. Figure 2 shows the distribution pre-and post-Minsky moment.

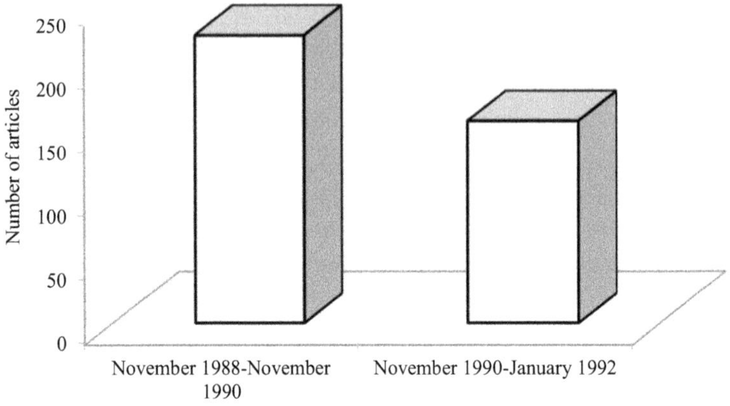

Figure 2. 1990 Recession: Number of articles pre-and post-Minsky moment

The Tone of the Reportage

In addition to the number of articles, the articles were assessed according to tone as sceptical, neutral, or optimistic. This method, developed by Griggs (1963), has been adopted by several studies since then (Bow 1980; Kollmeyer 2004; Schifferes and Coulter 2012). Articles were coded against a scale of 0 to 3, from most sceptical to most optimistic. The definition of sceptical, neutral, and optimistic is provided in Chapter 3.

To plot the trend across the entire timeline, totals were averaged for each quarter or three-monthly period (See Figure 3 below).

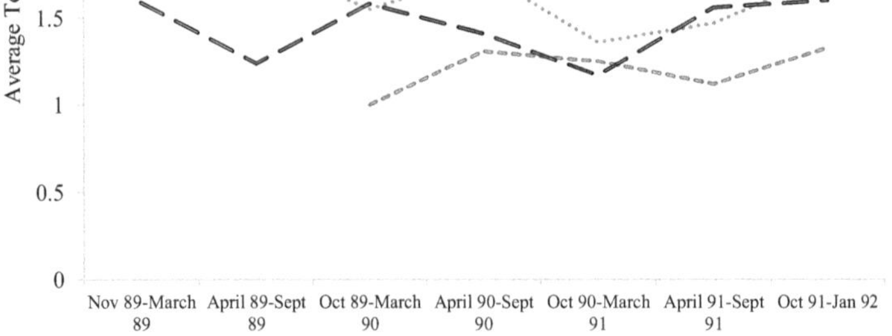

Figure 3. 1990 Recession: Tone Trend, November 1988 to January 1992

Key: 1=Sceptical 2=Neutral 3=Optimistic

*Note the *Guardian* did not produce any articles relevant to the key words until the end of 1989.

The tone trend indicates that all three publications remain below the neutral mark of two, indicating a uniformly neutral tone in their coverage. They follow the flow of economic events by edging more towards scepticism during the course of 1990, at around the time economic growth started to fall and unemployment started to grow. However, they all become more optimistic from early 1991 and into 1992.

The *Guardian* is the most sceptical of the publications, as it remains below 1.5 for the entire period. This aligns with the economic data, which showed that the UK had the worst economic figures and the crisis was felt most acutely there.

The Sources that Shaped the 1990 Recession

The mainstream financial press should arguably seek to represent society fairly, hold power to account, and promote a democratic society. It can strive to do so by speaking with and quoting a diversity of sources, an idea that arguably developed with the notion of the press as a Fourth Estate in the 19th century. The sources used were a relevant marker of quality for this study and the method adopted was to record the first two directly quoted sources from each article. Figure 4 below shows the directly quoted sources used across the timeline by each of the three publications, calculated as a percentage of each publication's total of sources quoted.

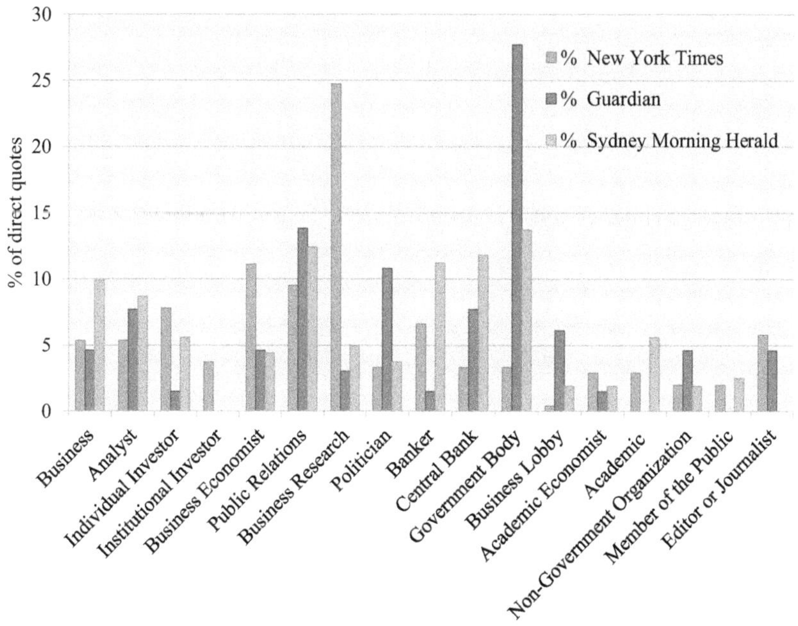

Figure 4. 1990 Recession: Number and type of directly quoted sources, as a percentage of publication's total quoted sources

Each publication used a variety of sources for direct quotes. The *Sydney Morning Herald* quotes from the most diverse range of source types. The majority of quotes from the *New York Times*, 25% of its data set, come from "business research" – referring here to research material relating to business or economic developments usually coming from corporate firms that have commissioned or requested it. This is distinct from "business" source, which refers directly to business executives, CEOs and managers. Business economists and PR are also high on the list, with close to 11 and 9.5%, respectively. Academics and academic economists comprise only 5% of the quotes from the *New York Times*. Conversely, members of the public and non-government organisations are low on the list. Only 2% of direct quotes are from members of the public and another 2 per cent are from non-government organisations.

In the *Guardian* the most quoted sources – close to 28% of total sources quoted – are from government bodies. Close to 14% are from PR and 11 per cent are from politicians. Only 1.5 per cent are from academic economists, and there are none from other academics or members of the public.

Sources in the *Sydney Morning Herald* are quite evenly spread. Close to 14 per cent are from government bodies, 12 per cent are from central government, and another 12 per cent are from PR. Close to 6 per cent are academics, 2 per cent are academic economists, 2 per cent are non-government organisations, and 2.5 per cent are members of the public. (See Figure 5 below.)

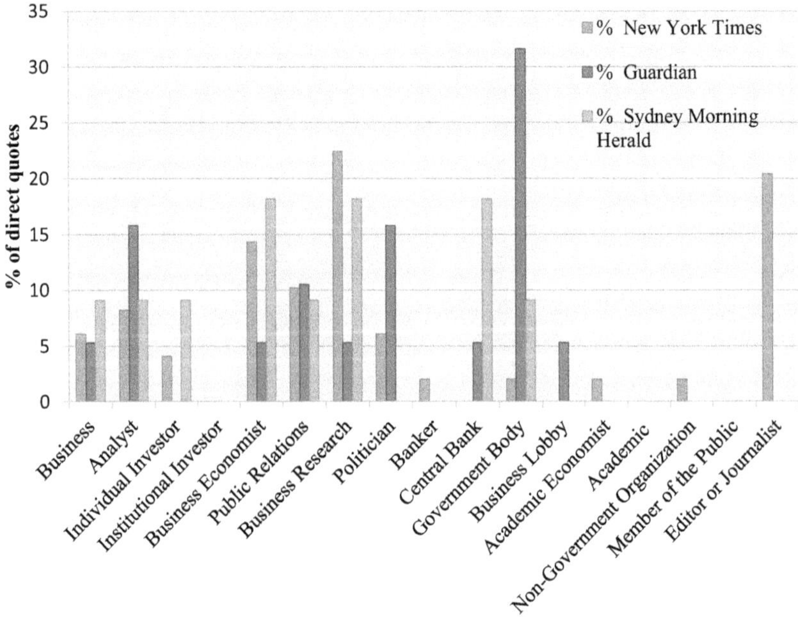

Figure 5. 1990 Recession: Sources quoted after the Minsky moment, November 1990 to March 1991

During the six months after the Minsky moment – November 1990-March 1991 – the types of sources quoted shift to the more elite. Although the publications adhere to a similar pattern overall, the pattern becomes more extreme and non-elite sources, such as members of the public, disappear altogether. Only 2% of the quotes from the *New York Times* are attributed to non-government organisations and 2% from academia. The *New York Times* stands out in this period with its reliance on media sources.

Conclusions from the Quantitative Analysis

The quantitative analysis has revealed that there was a lot of coverage before the Minsky moment – 60% of the total – on topics related to the key words. The coverage was broadly neutral, with the *Guardian* the most sceptical in tone when compared with the other publications. While the publications used a variety of source types for information and quotes, in particular the *Sydney Morning Herald*, there is a preponderance of quotes from elite sources in business and government, and a comparative paucity of quotes from academia and non-government sources, including the general public. PR already has a presence in the coverage of each publication.

The months after the Minsky moment, November 1990, reveal that each publication favours quotes from official source types, and the *New York Times* quotes directly from other media outlets. Also, the coverage in each publication turned a little more towards scepticism just after the Minsky moment. This suggests that the mainstream financial press adopts different reporting values in the aftermath of a financial and economic crisis.

News Framing and Discourse

The quality criteria were established based on the literature and the editorial codes from the publications being analysed (as discussed in Chapter 2). These qualitative measures are used to reveal different interpretations of events, whether explanations and advice were offered for the general public, and whether there were adequate warnings of looming financial or economic downturns, which could inform and spark democratic debate.

Main Topics of the 1990 Recession

Following the method used by the Pew Research Center in 2008, the main topics were identified.

Below we will deal with each topic in turn. A timeline illustrates the trend of the topic coverage for each publication and reveals when and where there was the most preoccupation with the topic, and how far the publications coincide in terms of media groupthink.

1. Interest Rates

The topic of "interest rates" occurred in 143 articles, 30% of the total data set.

The distribution amongst the three publications was as follows:

New York Times (38) 25.5% of publication's data set.
Guardian (39) 51% of publication's data set.
Sydney Morning Herald (66) 41.5% of publication's data set.

The *New York Times* had a consistent preoccupation with interest rates, while in the *Guardian* and the *Sydney Morning Herald* coverage on the topic peaked at the beginning of 1991 – the worst stage in the recession, as the economic data showed – see Figure 6 below.

The level of official interest rates was the most popular topic of concern during the 1990 recession in each publication. This is not surprising given that before 1988 interest rates were historically low, pre-empting a boom, and then rose quite significantly in each of the countries in this study. Also, the setting of

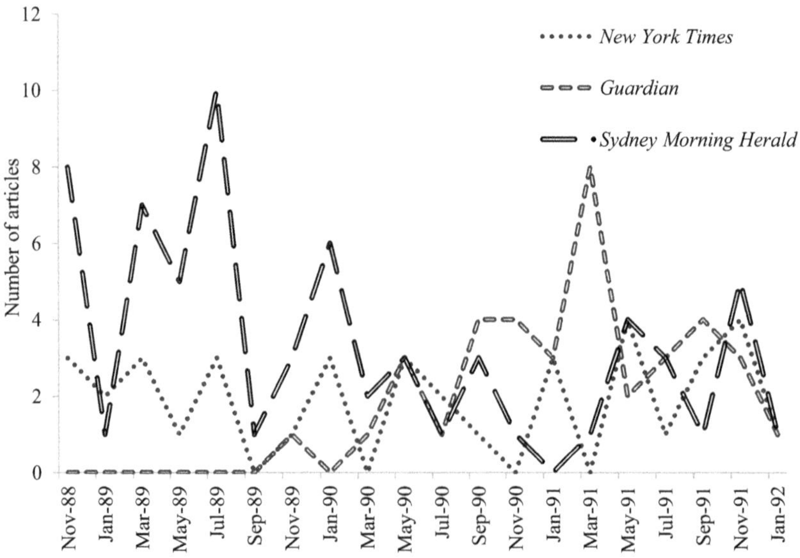

Figure 6. 1990 Recession: Distribution of articles on interest rates

official interest rates has significant implications for business as well as the micro and macro economy. However, the discourse about interest rates extends beyond reasonable concerns regarding their efficacy as an economic lever and was used by financial journalists to criticise the political economy that was directing the newly deregulated financial industry. Interest rate rises or falls, as set by the government, were presented as both the cause and the cure of economic and business woes.

Coverage of the interest rates topic first appears in 1988, characterised by comparatively high levels of scepticism. The *New York Times* and the *Sydney Morning Herald* begin to explain and define the topic as early as 1988, a year earlier than the *Guardian*. The *New York Times* is already discussing a recession and the *Sydney Morning Herald* is discussing pain in the mortgage market. For instance, on November 13, 1988, economics journalist Uchitelle argues that "Nearly every recession since World War II has been caused by the Fed pushing up interest rates." He claims that "higher rates might cause consumption to drop much more." Furthermore, he cites Nobel laureate in economics Paul A. Samuelson as saying "I know exactly what is going to cause the next recession – when there is one – and it is going to say on its bottom, 'Made in Washington'."

The *Guardian* and the *Sydney Morning Herald* are particularly sceptical in their reportage, while the *New York Times* switches more freely from scepticism to optimism. Overall then, there would have been sufficient scepticism and warning available in mainstream financial reportage.

The debate was framed politically, and it is certainly a lively one. In the *Guardian*, for instance, the main overall message is that the Conservative government under Margaret Thatcher stoked a consumer boom in the 1980s as rates were left too low for too long. They were then hiked too high and for too long in 1989 and 1990. For instance, on March 7, 1990, economics editor Hutton argues the following:

> Keynes would have spent the last decade warning of the blind alley where policy was leading; and he would have had a further warning still. Unless a firm grip was taken over the British financial system, the government and nation could be staring into an economic abyss.

But while the debate is particularly scathing of political management of the economy, there is little discussion of policy or non-Keynesian alternatives to promote democratic discussion. While more explanations were needed on the how/why/where and how of interest rate rises for a non-investing and ordinary public, the language is generally easy to understand in each of the publications.

Each publication does also provide views that consider the social impact of the rise of interest rates. In particular, economics writer Uchitelle at the *New York*

Times, economics editor Hutton and economics writer Elliott at the *Guardian*, and economics writers Cleary and Gittins at the *Sydney Morning Herald* express this view. The *Sydney Morning Herald* provides the most explanations, and they are unpacked with minimal jargon. However, unemployment was not mentioned by any of the publications as frequently as it might have been, given the economic evidence that the unemployment rate was stubbornly high.

In summary, there is comparatively little discussion about day-to-day finances, how interest rate rises or falls might impact the ordinary public and advice on how to make the most of the situation. Issues of public interest, such as jobs and personal finance are not dealt with consistently or systematically. Also, the articles were not necessarily geared for the more general public, who could have been more included in the debate. Each of the publications is, however, interested in the movement of interest rates in relation to the cost of housing. However, the coverage is too little and too late, with the general public generally a side issue compared to the tribulations of the economy and business. Therefore, it can be argued that the mainstream financial press provided some scepticism and offered debate on the efficacy of interest rate mechanisms. However, the debate was largely framed for business and investors and so failed to include the general public by neglecting its traditional watchdog duties to inform, educate, and hold power to account.

2. Recession

The topic of a "recession" occurred in 109 articles, 23% of the total data set.

The distribution amongst the three publications was as follows:

New York Times (42) 28% of publication's data set.
Guardian (30) 39% of publication's data set.
Sydney Morning Herald (37) 23% of publication's data set.

There was an increasing preoccupation with the topic of a recession. The economic data showed that each country was experiencing negative growth and growing unemployment at the end of 1990. The likelihood of a recession is debated vigorously from the start of the content analysis in November 1988 through to August 1990: 40 out of the 109 articles appear before the recession is officially called in the US, in November 1990. By September 1990, each of the publications has accepted its inevitability as well as the level of its severity. (See Figure 7 below.)

The *New York Times*, mainly through the economics journalist Uchitelle, provides the earliest warnings about a recession, in 1988. In particular, Uchitelle highlights some figures that indicate a recession in all states, contradicting the official figures being released. The *Guardian* also provides warnings that are contrary to

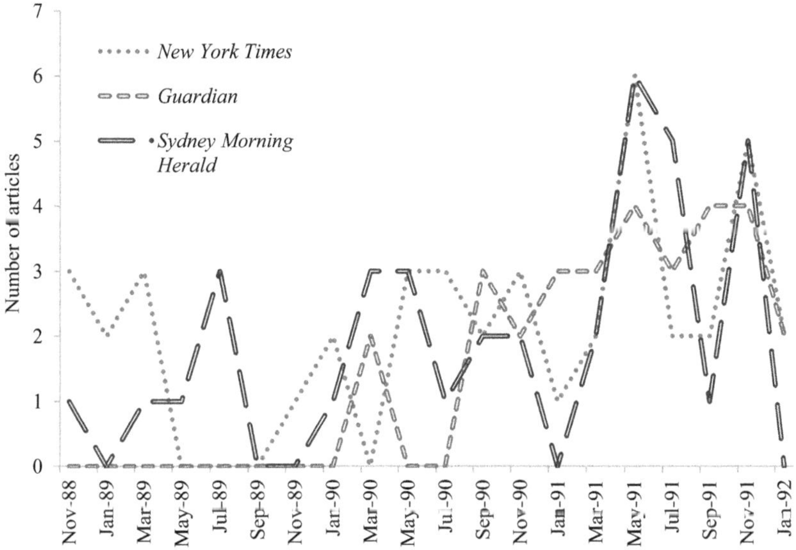

Figure 7. 1990 Recession: Distribution of articles on the topic of recession

the official line that there is no recession. It also maintains its scepticism, and suggests complacency in government, as it insists on the severity of the recession. The *Sydney Morning Herald* provides clear warnings by July 1989 from economics writers Cleary and Gittins. Quite soon afterwards it is more optimistic in its assessment, and by 1991 it already predicts recovery.

Also, before the recession is officially called in late 1990, various sources were consulted that provided the view that recession was on its way. Each publication used research from multiple bodies, which helped with their reporting. Uchitelle, in 1988, consulted data other than the official data released by the government, and predicted a recession. The *Guardian* questioned the official line that there was no recession, given in a government speech in early 1990. The *Sydney Morning Herald* consulted research released by the OECD in early 1989. Therefore, each publication was sceptical and probing in its reporting.

Like the interest rate topic, the language is easy to understand, with minimal jargon. However, there are few attempts at explaining what were, in fact, complex causes of the recession. Instead, the topic evolves in three stages: first, debate on whether there will be a recession; second, debate on its severity and chances of revival; and third, in the case of the *New York Times* and the *Sydney Morning Herald*, building a case for revival and lower interest rates, and in the case of the *Guardian*, highlighting the social cost of the recession caused by political incompetence.

What are missing from the reportage are thorough explanations of the causes and nature of the recession and everyday advice that could have helped the financial situations of many members of the public. The *Guardian* does stand out as it frames the debate in terms of lax policy-making and considers factors such as poll tax, which affect the public directly. Despite early warnings and scepticism, the reportage could have played more of a watchdog role for the general public, especially as the economic crisis deepened.

3. General Public and "Ordinary" Topics

The topic of the "ordinary" public occurred in 80 articles, 17% of the total data set. Articles were included in this section on the basis that they addressed an issue regarding jobs, personal finances, or government spending without jargon and geared towards "ordinary" people – for instance not just business people or investors but the more general and non-shareholding public too.

The distribution amongst the three publications was as follows:

New York Times (30) 20 per cent of publication's data set.
Guardian (17) 22 per cent of publication's data set.
Sydney Morning Herald (33) 21 per cent of publication's data set.

In numerical terms, the articles are spread quite evenly across the full three years surveyed: 23 in 1989, 16 in 1990, and 31 in 1991 (See Figure 8 below). However, the fact that the largest amount, 31, appears in 1991, indicates that there was a

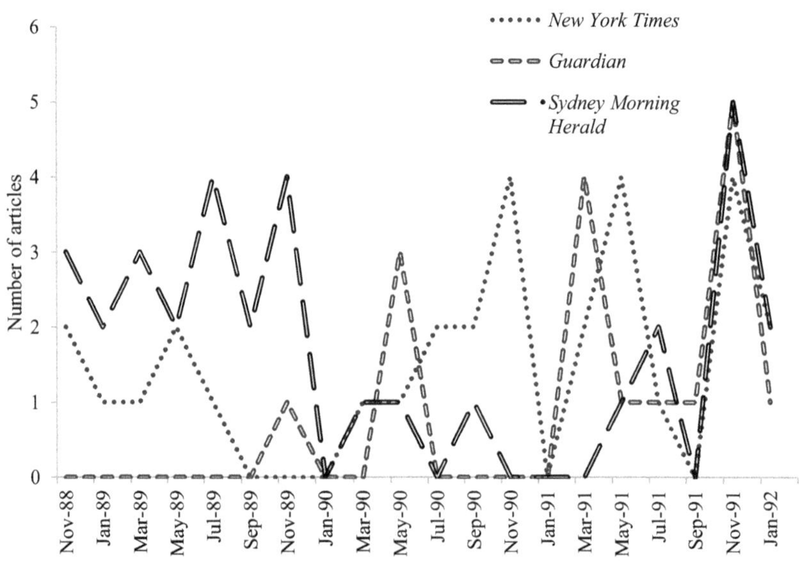

Figure 8. 1990 Recession: Distribution of articles for the "general public"

greater concern with communicating with the "ordinary" public in the aftermath of the recession than there was in the year preceding it when there were 16 articles, nearly half those in 1991.

This is a topic that sparked some varied interpretations. In each publication, sections of society are addressed that are not in other topics, such as working mothers, pensioners, and youths in education. It is revealed, and this is an emerging trend, that some of the earliest most prescient articles are those that draw on business and academic research and are usually written by economics writers. For instance, on May 12, 1989, economics writer Silk asks the question, "Why are the rich getting richer and the poor getting poorer in the United States – even as the long expansion in national income continues?" He cites a study by Sheldon Danziger, Peter Gottschalk and Eugene Smolensky, published in the May 1989 proceedings of the American Economic Association.

But compared with almost double the number of articles concerned with interest rates and a recession, it cannot be argued that the financial press prioritised public interest issues in their coverage of the 1990 recession.

Furthermore, the public is not being addressed as an audience but rather is treated as a player and influencer of business and the economy. The use of the collective noun shows the public as a force that can anticipate business and economic upturns or downturns, as well as one that can change the tide of events negatively or positively. The public is, therefore, represented in terms of: "consumers," "homeowners," "the unemployed," "first home buyers," "residents," "borrowers," "customers," "smart home seekers," "American families," "middle-high income earners," "the middle-class and low-income households," "private borrowers," "the labour market," "net borrowers," "voters," "household savings," "male workers," "buyers," "taxpayers," "workforce." Thus, a vast majority of the articles that were collected under the heading of "general public" were still quite skewed towards the business and investor audience.

The *New York Times* provides a range of views on government spending, jobs, and personal finance. For instance, some important societal issues like a widening gap between the rich and poor are raised, and average individual incomes are discussed – both interpretations are provided by economics writers. The *Guardian*, however, provides one dominant interpretation, which is that there has been a cultural shift that permits easy lending, and the public is addicted to credit as a consequence. It is seen a serious political faux pas as interest rates have been too low for too long. For instance, on November 18, 1989 (not by-lined), it laments the extent to which the public is effectively "hooked on credit." The debate has a political wedge, as Thatcher and the Conservative government's liberalism, namely in the form of the deregulation of banks, is described as creating and presiding over such a nation.

The *Sydney Morning Herald* provides interpretations for house owners, ordinary workers, and mothers. In fact, its coverage of topics that address "ordinary" concerns – jobs, government spending, and personal finance – arguably produces some of the more diverse interpretations from this publication so far. And more often than not, it distinguishes between benefits that are received by investors and by other members of the public, such as home-owners, pensioners, and youths. Toward the end of 1991, sound investment in housing is cited as the main reason that Australian consumers fared better than their US and UK counterparts.

With each publication, there is more concern with "ordinary" topics and a non-shareholding audience as the economic situation worsens at the end of 1990. The *New York Times*, through key economics writers, such as Silk and Uchitelle, probe widening wealth gaps and average individual incomes. There is a sense that the *Guardian* is representing the lower-to-middle end of the socio-economic groups in a fight against government neo-liberal attitudes that represented business over the people. The *Sydney Morning Herald* really highlights the social good that can be achieved in their framing of "ordinary" topics. They produce stark warnings, sage advice, and pressure on policy to factor in a non-investing public. Therefore, the articles in this topic arrived late on the timeline, but they would have been useful for the general public and, in this sense, the financial press played an effective watchdog role.

4. Blame Game

The topic of the "blame game" occurred in 72 articles, 15% of the total data set. Articles are included that blame something or someone for causing and/or prolonging the 1990 recession.

The distribution amongst the three publications was as follows:

New York Times (18) 12 per cent of publication's data set.
Guardian (26) 34 per cent of publication's data set.
Sydney Morning Herald (28) 18 per cent of publication's data set.

The blame game topic was an increasingly popular topic for each of the publications. Individuals and certain factors started to receive blame through 1990 and occurrences of this topic peaked from the end of 1990 onwards – the period that each of the US, the UK, and Australia felt the full impact of a global recession. (See Figure 9 below.)

This topic highlights the high level of criticism that each publication heaped on its respective government, as each is highly critical of economic policy and management. While the *New York Times* refers to Republican attitudes and Reagan

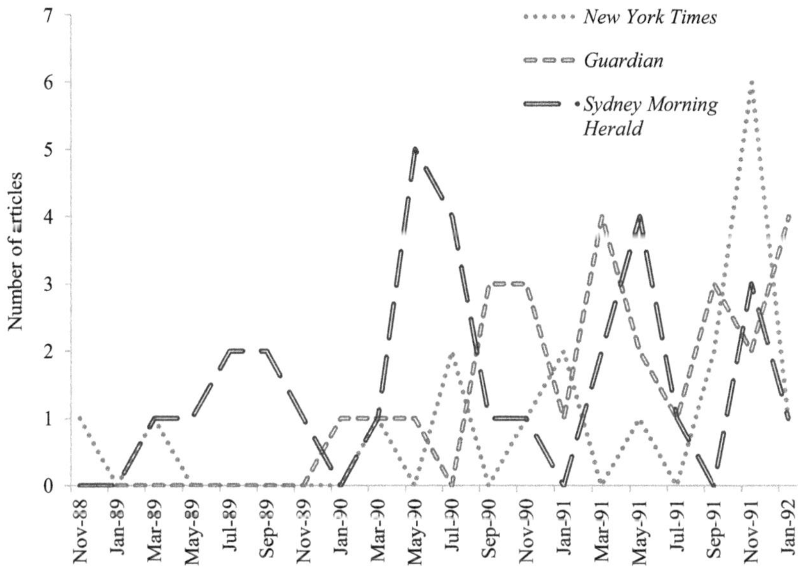

Figure 9. 1990 Recession: Distribution of articles on the blame game topic

policies, the *Guardian* and the *Sydney Morning Herald* stand out as especially critical. The *Guardian's* economics editor Will Hutton put the same criticism forward on many occasions and lay the blame mainly on Margaret Thatcher's shoulders. For instance, on November 22, 1990, he says:

> It was her [Margaret Thatcher's] refusal to put her revolution at risk that placed an effective veto on tax increases, thus exacerbating the consumer boom when it should have been reined back; her insistence on deregulation that fermented the gigantic growth of credit-financed spending ....

The *Guardian* continue to focus on the topic of deregulation and certain individuals, where the *New York Times* broadens its discussion to other areas of blame and causes for concern. Also, articles start to appear from early 1998 – two years before the world economies began to fall towards recession. Therefore, there would have been debate and discussion and sufficient scepticism for the public to weigh up the situation before the economy slowed down.

It also indicates that the public was offered a good amount of discussion on a topic that was arguably starting to impact their everyday lives. The issues are explained clearly, in terms appropriate for a lay audience. Therefore, the public would also have been informed about political economic mismanagement. The *New York Times* unpacks information for individuals in a few instances. For example, on November 29, Leonard Silk, an economics writer, directly quoting an academic, discusses the decreasing median wage. The blame game is aimed at criticising government economic management and, in this case, Ronald Reagan, Margaret Thatcher, and Australian Treasurer Paul Keating. For instance, on July 3, 1989, Walsh argues that financial deregulation has been used "to throw a national party. The rush to borrow abroad and expand credit to unsustainable levels was led by our own banking sector." He says Keating "may be called on to pay the ultimate price for a politician – loss of office. He certainly will be if he clings to the present model of deregulation as some icon of his economic courage."

That said, the focus on deregulation as a central object of blame is missing full explanations and alternatives that the public could act on. Furthermore, there is minimal everyday advice for ordinary non-shareholding citizens. Therefore, when reporting the 1990 recession, the blame game as a topic served the general public through scepticism, warnings, and debate.

5. Deregulation

The topic of "deregulation" occurred in 70 articles or 15% of the total data set. The majority of the articles from the publications reviewed here are particularly scathing of the new policies and debate the rationale, as well as the management of new economic direction. To some extent, this topic is an extension of the "blame game" topic, which framed the deregulation of the banking industry as the main culprit for causing the recession.

The distribution amongst the three publications was as follows:

New York Times (11) 7 per cent of publication's data set.
Guardian (30) 39 per cent of publication's data set.
Sydney Morning Herald (29) 18 per cent of publication's data set.

Deregulation was a popular topic for the financial press to discuss, a fact that is illustrated below. Coverage on the topic is constant in each publication throughout the period, as shown in Figure 10 below.

Both the *New York Times* and *Sydney Morning Herald* are sceptical of deregulation and its enactment by the government from 1988. The *Guardian* weighs in by late 1989. The *New York Times* is often contradictory, but is mainly critical; the *Guardian* reveals its left-wing tendencies as it attacks deregulation as an ideology and not based on its merits; and the *Sydney Morning Herald* sees it as a useful veil for the government.

For instance, the *Guardian* report (not by-lined) on November 18, 1989, sets the tone for the rest of the articles on deregulation from the *Guardian*. The journalist argues, "While Mrs Thatcher was allegedly chopping up her credit card in

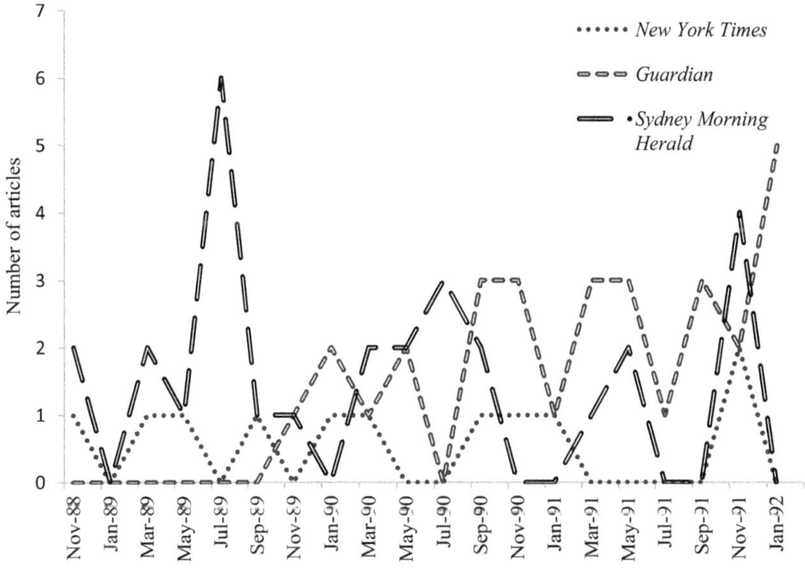

Figure 10. 1990 Recession: Distribution of articles on deregulation

disgust at her credit limit being raised without her consent, her Government was permitting deregulation to run rife." In the *Sydney Morning Herald*, Burton reports on November 11, 1988, that government are using deregulation as a veil to disguise their tightening of monetary policy: "thanks to deregulation the Government's conscience is not bothered by this type of white lie. Instead, as rates rise, the Government can luxuriate in the myth that the market sets the rates."

That said, the *Sydney Morning Herald* does provide the most explanations and considers the inevitability of deregulation based on global movements in that direction. An exposé of white-collar crime lays the blame on deregulation, and it also discusses its inevitability. Like the *Guardian*, it also reports critically about the government's role in managing deregulation and focuses on Keating's role as a Treasurer in particular.

Conversely, deregulation would have had enormous implications for every financial concern of ordinary members of the public, but they are arguably left out of the equation. Explanations are often complicated and filled with jargon – an issue the *Guardian* itself picks up on as it reports on January 2, 1990 (not by-lined), that deregulation is a "jargon" term. Each publication – the *New York Times* and the *Sydney Morning Herald* in particular – needs to unpack their explanations and the jargon terms that are used when defining deregulation.

Therefore, the topic of deregulation was highly contested at the time, and the financial press can be said to have fulfilled a watchdog role in terms of its scepticism and criticism of government deregulation policy. However, given the fact that deregulation represented such a massive shift in political economic management, it failed to provide satisfactory explanations to make it entirely understandable for an ordinary non-shareholding readership.

In general, governments in the 1980s were seen as economic actors who could influence and had to take responsibility for the economy more than in later periods, despite the rise of neo-liberalism.

Conclusion

Having presented the evidence what judgement can we make regarding the mainstream financial reportage of the 1990 recession in the US, the UK, and Australia?

There are a variety of interpretations presented in the publications on issues, which promote discussion of alternative views. In particular, the topic of deregulation of the financial industry elicits a variety of responses. Each publication also presents its unique take on events. For instance, the *New York Times* tends to provide a range of views and interpretations. The *Guardian* stands out as politically and economically left-wing, framing events to depict Conservative ideology as corrupt and a danger for society. The *Sydney Morning Herald* is also scathing of the government in power, but more so because of its management of the economy than its politics.

A variety of "voices" representing all sections of society are quoted directly and the data reveals that the *New York Times* favours business research, the *Guardian* favours government bodies, and the *Sydney Morning Herald* spread its quotes between government bodies, the central bank – the Reserve Bank – and PR. Contrastingly, none of the publications quoted much from non-government organisations, academia, or members of the public. The pattern of reportage shows how the "variety" contracts to the few most popular sources in the months immediately after the Minsky moment.

And in addition to various interpretations and "voices," there was room for discussion and debate as 60% of the data set appears in the two years before November 1990 – the Minsky moment. While there are a few warnings to signal an impending or potential crisis in the financial or economic systems, the economic data suggests in this case crystal ball-gazing would have been difficult. Adverse economic effects were not felt in the US, the UK, and Australian economies until mid-1990 and even then previous studies reveal that the economic downturn was blamed on several different factors that would have been difficult to predict (Fintzen and Steckler 1999).

Another trend that is identified is that economics editors and writers tend to be more sceptical than those who focus on the financial markets, as well as more prescient, mostly through consultation with non-biased sources like academics and members of the public. Overall, reporting remains uniformly neutral on the three-point scale. Of the publications, the *Guardian* is the most sceptical. This scepticism is confirmed in the discourse analysis that revealed disdain for the pervading neo-liberal ideology favoured by the government.

With regards to information geared towards the general public, there is some everyday advice relating to finance and government spending, directed at all sections of society, not just investors. However, during a period of significant economic and financial change, one might have expected more advice to be directed to members of the public on managing their everyday finances. The majority of the coverage features clear explanations about interest rates and deregulation but contains a large amount of jargon that could have been unpacked further. There is also a preoccupation with topics that relate to the "ordinary" public, such as jobs and personal finance, are noted when the economy starts to move downwards.

Quantitative analysis reveals that the 1990 recession was reported in a fairly neutral way and included several "voices." There were a large number of articles before the Minsky moment, providing room for democratic discussion and debate. Also, even though the general public was not always included in the debate as much as it could have been, there are some illuminating articles that lobby on behalf of the general public, criticise power, provide stark warnings, and ultimately address a large section of society as opposed to a specialist business audience. On this evidence, it appears that the financial press played a watchdog role.

We turn now to the dot com boom of 2000–2001, the next case study in the next decade, and track quality in the same way. This case study is characterised by a spectacular boom, with a heady belief in the new Internet companies as the wave of the future even if they were not profitable. But many investors, as well as much of the press, were caught flat-footed when their shares came crashing down and the tarnished reality became clear.

Notes

1. The savings and loan crisis affected most savings and loan institutions in the US from 1985 onwards. The institutions were liberalised during the early 1980s, and in particular in 1980, by the Carter administration, and in 1982, by the Reagan administrations, giving the institutions powers to act as banks—accepting and using depositor money—with minimal regulation. They proved to be fraudulent both in their accounting practices and the unethical way they attracted investors. The Federal Deposit Insurance Corporation provide a comprehensive bibliography

of books and articles relating to the nature and consequences of the savings and loan crisis (see: http://www.fdic.gov/bank/Historical/s&l/).

2. Dreier (1982, 116) explains that having a limited assumption about the world is a symptom that is mostly suffered by mainstream media, as smaller publications like *Mother Jones* and *The Nation* look at issues that the mainstream media tend to ignore until the story has been broken. The unspoken worldview is 'responsible capitalism' (Gans, cited in ibid.).

References

Barkin, Steve. 1982. 'Changes in Business Sections, 1931–1979.' *Journalism Quarterly* 59 (3): 435–439.

Blanchard, Olivier. 1993. 'Consumption and the Recession of 1990–1991.' *The American Economic Review* 83: 270–274.

Bolick, Clint. 1995. 'Thatcher's Revolution: Deregulation and Political Transformation.' *Yale Journal on Regulation* 12: 527–548.

Bow, James. 1980. "The Times' Financial Markets Column in the Period around the 1929 Crash." *Journalism Quarterly* 57 (3): 447–450.

Davidson, Paul. 1992. 'How to Avoid Another Great Depression: The Curse of Unemployment.' *The New Leader* 72 (2): 8–13.

Dreier, Peter. 1982. 'Capitalism vs. the Media: An Analysis of an Ideological Mobilization among Business Leaders.' *Media, Culture and Society* 4 (2): 111–132.

Emmison, Mike. 1983. *The Economy: Its Emergence in Media Discourse*. London: Blackwell.

Fintzen, David, and Herman O. Steckler. 1999. 'Why Did Forecasters Fail to Predict the 1990 Recession?' *International Journal of Forecasting* 15: 309–323.

Fitzgibbons, Amanda. 2006. 'The Financial Sector and Deregulation in Australia: Drivers of Reform or Reluctant Followers?' *Accounting, Business and Financial History* 16 (3): 371–387.

Goidel, Robert, and Ronald Langley. 1995. 'Media Coverage of the Economy and Aggregate Economic Evaluations: Uncovering Evidence of Indirect Media Effects.' *Political Research Quarterly* 48 (2): 313–328.

Griggs, Harry. 1963. "Newspaper Performance in Recesion Coverage." *Journalism and Mass Communication Quarterly* 40(4): 559–564.

Hall, Robert E. 1993. 'Macro Theory and the Recession of 1990–1991.' *The American Economic Review* 83 (2): 275–279.

Henningham, John. 1997. 'Characteristics and Attitudes of Australia's Finance Journalists.' *Economic Analysis and Policy* 27 (1): 45–58.

Hubbard, J. T. W. 1976. 'Business News in Post-Watergate Era.' *Journalism and Mass Communication Quarterly* 53 (3): 488–493.

Hviding, Ketil. 1995. 'Organisation for Economic Co-operation and Development.' *The OECD Observer* 194: 30–33.

Kitchener, Jennifer. 1999. 'Business Journalism in the 1980s.' In *Journalism: Print, Politics and Popular Culture*, edited by Ann Curthoys, and Julianne Schultz, 229–244. St Lucia: University of Queensland Press.

Kollmeyer, Christopher. 2004. 'Corporate Interests: How the News Media Portray the Economy.' *Social Problems* 51 (3): 432–452.

Lasorsa, Dominic, and Stephen Reese. 1990. 'News Source Use in the Crash of 1987: A Study of Four National Media.' *Journalism Quarterly* 67 (1): 60–71.

Lewin, Glenn. 2002. 'The Watchdog Role Business Reporters Need to Play.' *Nieman Reports* Summer: 19–21.

Matolcsy, Zoltan, and Julianne Schultz. 1994. 'Errors in Financial Journalism.' *Australian Studies in Journalism* 3: 335–355.

OECD (Organisation for Economic Co-operation and Development). 1991. 'OECD Employment Outlook: Highlights' *OECD Observer* October, 172.

Parsons, Wayne. 1989. *The Power of the Financial Press: Journalism and Economic Opinion in Britain and America*. New Brunswick: Rutgers University.

Pew Research Center. 2008. 'The Changing Narrative: How the News Media Have Covered the Slowing Economy.' http://www.journalism.org/files/legacy/Economy%20report.pdf.

Pulitzer, Joseph. 1904. 'The College of Journalism.' *North American Review* 178 (570): 641–680.

Rae, John, and John Drury. 1993. 'Reification and Evidence in Rhetoric on Economic Recession: Some Methods Used in the UK Press, Final Quarter 1990.' *Discourse Society* 4 (3): 329–356.

Ryan, Colleen, Deborah Light, and Paul McGeough. 1990. 'How Banks Bartered Us Into Trouble.' *Sydney Morning Herald*, July 31, from Factiva.

Schifferes, Steve, and Stephen Coulter. 2012. "Trust-Meltdown for Business Journalism." *British Journalism Review* 23 (2): 55–59. doi: 10.1177/0956474812450671

Schultz, Julianne, and Zoltan Matolcsy. 1993. "Business Boosters or Impartial Critics." *Reporting Business*: 9–31.

Silk, Mark. 1989. 'Reagan's Legacy: A Deregulation Fad Pushed too far.' *Atlanta Journal and Constitution*, February 19, from Factiva.

Toohey, Brian. 1994. *Tumbling Dice: Economists Are Our Gods, but Do They Live in the Twentieth Century?* Port Melbourne: William Heinemann.

Wu, Denis, Robert Stevenson, Hsiao-Chi Chen, and Nuray Z. Guner. 2002. 'The Conditioned Impact of Recession Headline News: A Time-Series Analysis of Economic Communication in the United States, 1987–1996.' *International Journal of Public Opinion Research* 14: 19–33.

CHAPTER FOUR

Case Study II: The "Irrationally Exuberant" Dot Com Boom of 2000–1

> The men and women who scrambled to explain the economic turmoil of the 1970s – the gas lines and the shuttered factories and the apparent erosion of American competence – were not writing for consumers or investors. They were writing for citizens, for people who cared deeply about how this nation turned out … I don't know about you, but I'd rather be writing for those people again. (Henriques 2000b, 21)

The late 1990s and early 2000s were characterised by, and are now infamous for, a fascination with Internet stocks and new Internet companies. Globalisation had hastened and advances in technology, specifically the Internet, saw online companies spring up in large numbers and command huge market valuations. The Internet was a recent phenomenon, and the public was taking part in the speculation, specifically on the NASDAQ that hosted Internet stocks. And in a neo-liberal political and economic climate, deregulation was the common mantra.

One prescient warning, and one that now stands out as one of the most famous quotes by a US Federal chairman, was given by Alan Greenspan in 1996. In a televised speech he warned about the threat of "irrational exuberance" on an overheated stock market. His warning had an immediate impact on the markets, which plummeted in response but only in the short-term. The boom that he was referring to continued soon after unabated and did not burst for another few years. In just two years, from early 1998 to February 2000, the Internet sector earned over 1,000% returns on its public equity. But when the mania was over, by the end of 2000, these returns had all but disappeared (Ofek and Richardson 2003, 1113).

Despite Greenspan's warning and the constant threat of inflation in 1996, during the late 1990s, Greenspan and his Federal Open Market Committee (FOMC) did nothing to stop the growth of the stock market until the very end (Schiller 2000, 40). The official interest rate in the US increased for the last time in 1995 and remained at this level until August 1999 (ibid.).

As well as warning of "irrational exuberance" during his December 1996 speech, Alan Greenspan described the prevailing view of central bankers, whom he thought should only concern themselves with the "real economy":

> We as central bankers need not be concerned if a collapsing financial asset bubble does not threaten to impair the real economy, its production, jobs, and price stability. Indeed, the sharp stock market break of 1987 had few negative consequences for the economy. But we should not underestimate or become complacent about the complexity of the interactions of asset markets and the economy. (The Federal Reserve Board 1996)

He highlighted an indifference towards the relationship between real economic fundamentals and the stock market at the time. It is also typical of the prevailing view that financial markets are self-correcting, an ideology better known as market-fundamentalism.[1] Market-fundamentalism and neo-liberalism came to dominate political policy in the US, the UK, and Australia in the late 1990s.

The Political Economy of the Dot Com Boom

Neo-liberalism developed into something more than a free-market ideology in the 1990s because it was shaped by policy (Akram-Lodhi 2006). Globalisation, based on the principle of a world without financial borders, meant companies could merge and interact without any national obstructions to the flow of capital. It represented classic neo-liberalist thinking, which favoured little or no regulation, as well as privatisation. The principles of neo-liberalism, neo-conservatism, and globalisation defined this epoch. There was also the development of something that came to be known as the "new economy," which was dominated by a conviction that a world connected by money and markets heralded a new age – an unparalleled rich and advanced modern era.

The United States

The US economy had been in positive growth for more than nine years. This growth lulled investors and consumers into a false sense of security, and it was one that politicians – particularly Alan Greenspan – were promoting (Soros 2010, 42). They presented the idea that a new economic and business cycle was underway, one that benefitted from positive growth and low inflation with few downturns.

Deregulation was its hallmarks and, in the late 1990s, the deregulation of the telecommunications industry was particularly important to new Internet-related industries. The telecommunications Act of 1996, signed by then-President Bill Clinton, opened and overhauled telecommunications law for the first time in 60 years (Federal Communications Commission 1996).

The United Kingdom

A similar movement occurred in the telecommunications industry in the UK, to create more competition for British Telecoms, privatised in the 1980s. The trend began in 1991 with the government white paper *Competition and Choice: Telecommunications Policy for the 1990s*, and in 2001, a paper by the Department of Trade, which argues that deregulation of the sector encouraged progressive and sustained competition (OECD 2002, 9). The paper sees the UK as leading the way in encouraging the growth and expansion of the telecommunications market: "Liberalisation and competition have been the keys to dramatic reductions in prices and the much greater choice now available to consumers as other countries have followed the UK's lead and opened up their markets" (ibid.).

In the UK, deregulation and the embracing of the new economy were closely associated with New Labour. Prime Minister Tony Blair and his Chancellor of the Exchequer, Gordon Brown, were eager to bring Britain into the 21st century and wanted to make sure that it was not left behind in Europe's shadow. They wanted the UK to be fully engaged with what they saw as a technological revolution, and even leading it. In February 2000, Gordon Brown was recorded in New York as saying, "We are determined that Britain will lead in the next stage of the Internet revolution. Our target is within three years to become the world's best environment for electronic commerce" (cited in Denny 2000).

Australia

Australia also wanted to be in the game and, according to Australian technology journalist Stuart Fist (1997), made its first move in 1990 when the then Labour government decided to compete for a share of the market alongside the US: "I particularly relish memories of the announcement in December 1990 by Communications Minister Beazley that a merged Telecom and OTC (Megacom) was necessary for Australia to have an international player in telecommunications to compete with the Americans."

Fist describes Howard's conservative coalition government, which replaced the Labour government in 1996, as slow-moving and "shown up" by Tony Blair's New Labour, which he thinks "hit the ground running" (ibid.). The buzz, lure, and excitement that surrounded New Labour were evident: "No-one can be sure where New Labour will leave Britain. But Tony Blair, his senior ministers and closest advisers are intent on change. Now" (ibid.).

These thoughts were echoed in 2000 by Kevin Rudd, then a Labour MP who would go on to become Prime Minister of Australia in 2007. He made his thoughts clear in an opinion piece he wrote in the *Sydney Morning Herald*, arguing that Australia must join the global economy for better prosperity and an inclusive democracy (Rudd 2000). His support for globalisation went so far as to associate what he termed "globophobia" with xenophobia:

> ... we are committed to the development of an internationally competitive knowledge economy in part by bridging the emerging digital divide within Australia, by democratising people's access to the tools of the new economy.
>
> The recipe for avoiding the rise of globophobia and its near relative on the Right, xenophobia, is not another bout of capitalist triumphalism. It lies in providing all peoples, at home and abroad, with a tangible stake in the globalisation project. (ibid.)

But there was an underside to the growth of market fundamentalism and what was becoming a global competition. Australian economist Ross Garnaut (2009) argues that the boom which prevailed in these years were directly related to the cause of the GFC: "By the middle of the first decade of the twenty-first century the psychology of the boom was well established" (ibid., 21). In the US and the UK, "credit standards" were in decline, and new mortgage products were being created. This, he says, was also happening in Australia, where "non-conforming" or unregulated loans arrived at the turn of the century and were being used by even the most conservative of the banks (ibid.).

The Relationship between Financial Media and Business

The stock market in the 1990s came to symbolise wealth creation and opportunity. Furthermore, it became symbolic of something beyond anybody's control, even Alan Greenspan's. Cheney (1998) called the stock market one of the most celebrated ideas in economic life in industrialised society. He describes consumerism, and the prevalence of financial markets, as a means for the public to create wealth, as a force that is accepted in daily discourses, in the media, and therefore in society.

Also, his reference to "The Market" as a "social actor" produces the image of a reified being: "The Market is a supreme social actor and a motivator of human action, and that consumer choice, particularly in its mundane forms, represents a high form of democratic expression and participation" (ibid., 26).

The press joined the chorus of enthusiasm. There were, however, pressures felt by financial journalists to report positively. Schuster (2006, 75) quotes one dot com reporter in the US as saying, "There was enormous pressure to report positively about what was going on at the stock market." As the financial markets grew, so did the amounts paid by for advertisements in the financial media.

It has also been argued that the media's pro-business attitude was encouraged primarily because of the general public's investment and involvement in the stock market (Simons 1999). Investment in the stock market had expanded, particularly in the US, and touched everyone from micro to macro level investment: "Today, virtually everyone out there (journalists among them) is a business 'player' – if not a direct investor then by dint of their company pensions or 401ks or employee stock ownership plans" (ibid., 56). Therefore, the media were taking direction from the audience they wrote for, as Simons phrases it, "Taking a cue from their readers, newspapers have enthusiastically climbed aboard the business bandwagon" (ibid.).

Venal Journalism

As the enthusiasm for individual investment and get-rich-quick schemes grew, so did the public images of the icons of the new economy: young technically savvy entrepreneurs who amassed millions on the stock market. Within the media, according to Simons (ibid., 56), "The feature about the nouveau riche twenty-something exchanging his battered Hyundai for a Porsche when his company goes public has become such a newspaper staple it's already a cliché."

But finance journalists were not just under the spell of the young entrepreneurs – they were dazzled by opportunities for their financial gain. Unsurprising "in a world where the go-go entrepreneurs and the reporters covering them both tend to be young and ambitious, opportunity and its attendant temptation are rearing their heads" (Simons ibid., 57). Venal journalism soon became standard practice. Henriques (2000b, 20), a journalist at the *New York Times*, wrote that journalists covering the "new economy" in "new media" did not consider accepting cheap insider stock or investment in industries they cover to be a problem. The same can be said for analysts and advisors who were convicted for insider dealing when the dot com bubble burst.

And a picture is painted of a press benefitting financially from the dot com bubble through increased and expensive advertising space and subsequently higher salaries. There was a jump in salaries beyond $100,000, and stocks potentially worth millions, if business journalists made the transition from traditional print media to writing online about high-technology companies and stocks – something he calls "the leap from print-on-paper to print-on-glass" (Simons 1999, 67) – and a trend we now know would eventually "kill" the dominant business model of the print media.

The dazzling financial lures of the "new economy" paved the way for biased and unquestioning reporting. It also produced a shift in news values, as journalists were captured by their sources. Stories shifted focus from ordinary citizens to responding to the beat of the market. For instance, Quinn (1998, 48) referred to rich business sources as "predators" who journalists tended to dine with "innocently, without even thinking about it." They are the story, she writes, "not average folks."

shNews values were soon moving away from economic stories that covered social welfare and placed more of a premium on the economic strength of competitors (Parker 1998, 129). There was an increase in budgetary pressures imposed by a new generation of producers and managers. And as a consequence, Parker argues that the format of economic stories changed and became more like political competition "horse race" narratives (ibid.).

Groupthink

Lack of objectivity and too close a relationship with business sources of information resulted in groupthink journalism. Groupthink, as discussed in Chapter 2, and as described by Schuster (2006, 70), is the manner in which the media "conditions" individual perceptions through positive and biased reporting, creating homogenous mass behaviour. James Surowiecki of the *New Yorker* argues that "CNBC style" coverage precipitates a herd mentality and does not encourage independent decision-making and "you end up with a mob instead of a market" (cited in ibid., 75).

Others point to new financial news channels like CNBC and Bloomberg, the rise of new financial journals, and the Internet as significant factors that fed the dot com boom (Davis 2006, 619). Davis argues that these outlets provided a "speculative forum" with which to hype Internet stocks and promote the cult of the "new internet entrepreneur" and the ideology of the "new economy" (ibid.). Schiller (2000, 76) similarly credits new financial channels and publications, and specifically their business models that push deadlines, for a reportage at the time "devoid of genuine thought." According to Schiller, these new outlets were platforms for promoting business, and they were not useful for "rational, critical, sensible, differentiated and diversified investor behaviour."

Davis (2006) also alludes to a feedback loop that existed between media and consumers of media during the dot com boom. The self-reflexive nature of communications is prompted by the investment process, which encourages participants to observe and react as their rivals would. One of Davis' interviewees, Paul Woolley, chairman of fund management company GMO, resisted temptations to follow groupthink but he saw clients promptly withdraw their funds. He said the following about the telecommunications, media and technology (TMT) bubble:

> The TMT bubble offered a classic example of the bandwagon effect. Unrealistic expectations were the main culprit, but the share price explosion was undoubtedly fuelled by demand from managers concerned to protect their portfolios against benchmark risk by staying close to index weights in the sector. (ibid., 620)

How the Reporting of the Dot Com Boom has been Measured Before

Earlier studies show the media helped to sustain some of the common myths that were popular at the time of the dot com boom, such as that of a "new economy" – which meant high growth and minimal inflation, and get-rich-quick schemes. They also spruiked the benefits of the Initial Public Offering (IPO) activity of new Internet companies, and pandered to analysts, institutional investors, and a new investing public, with sensational reporting.

The closeness of the finance journalists to their sources and the personal benefits they derived from the dot com boom led them to perpetuate the myths around the bubble. Howcroft (2001) enumerates four of these myths. The first myth is the myth of the "new economy": the move from old industry to a new digital economy. The example of the merger between Time Warner and America Online, which happened in January 2000, is described as a prime example of a "new era" company (ibid., 196).

The second myth is of the entrepreneurial geek, who achieves success and riches (see also Goozner and Janis 2000): "Much of the dot.com publicity focuses on 'rags to riches' tales, thereby engendering feelings that large-scale success is not only possible but there for the taking (particularly for the young and technologically competent)" (Howcroft 2001, 196).

The third myth, the myth of innovation, arose because the Internet was promoted as technological innovation and a "new way of doing business" – this legitimised the euphoria around high-technology shares (ibid., 200). But e-commerce has been an established part of business vocabulary for decades before the Internet promised so much in the way of e-commerce – first originating with the EDI and

VAN concepts in the early 1970s (ibid.).[2] Also, over-optimism about new technologies has been witnessed before with both the telegraph and television:

> Just as the telegraph would bring democracy and television would educate the masses, the Internet and with it, the new dot.coms are heralded as the technology that has the potential to profoundly affect many industries and the entire retail experience. (ibid., 202; see also Best 2005; Schiller 2000)

The fourth myth is that of virtual and mass-scale success. Success during the boom is not success in the traditional sense of profit-making but in the virtual sense and false predictions of future profits based on the rate of growth of sales (Howcroft 2001, 197). Stock market analysts, it is argued, replaced traditional profit-making measures with empty promises about potential success on a massive scale. The fact that most new dot com companies fail within the first few years was ignored. Similarly, the fact that the people running these businesses were new, inexperienced, and working in a new industry was also ignored.

The role of the media in sustaining these myths has been researched empirically (Pollock and Rindova 2003). Analysis of 225 IPOs and the media attention they received showed the media, and especially the tenor of the coverage played a significant role in exaggerating their potential for success and profitability. The authors show that publicly available information not only legitimises IPOs but also, by making them appear legitimate, influences investor behaviour. They emphasise the vital role played by the media in sustaining the cult of the Internet.

The amount of media coverage about deals and the framing of this information, either positively or negatively, is one key to influencing public and investor behaviour (ibid., 631). Therefore, any Internet companies that did appear in the media stood a higher chance of increasing their market valuations on the first day the shares were sold.

The frenzy that surrounded the dot com bubble, sustained by the media, is also aptly compared by to the frenzy that surrounds celebrities: "… at the turn of the millennium, we were relating to the Internet in much the same way as we relate to a celebrity." Best (ibid., 362) identifies two strands of an argument or narrative, that told the story about the Internet before and after its implosion: first, that the Internet was a key element in an unstoppable, exciting, and extremely profitable wiring of the world; and second, after the implosion, that the Internet was an important technology which should be judged against old economic fundamentals.

Several important factors contributed to the popularity of Internet company stock. First, there was the media, who were crucial for the promotion of an investment culture (ibid., 371). Second, there were the "celebrity agents," who promoted the cult, such as stock analysts and investment bankers (ibid.). This promotion was exacerbated by the rise of financial journalism and the contemporary sensationalism of media, which has become more "entertaining and personal" (ibid., 372). Third, there was the environment of the time, which saw the rise of the individual investor, the increase in mutual funds, and the increasing use of stock options for employees, which reduced fears in risk. Last, the Internet added fuel to the fire, as it offered new possibilities like online trading and stimulation of interest through newsgroups and message boards (ibid., 372).

The role of the media in perpetuating the myths of the new dot com economy is well established by previous studies. There is a heavy focus on the US, with minimal studies on the UK and Australia. What is missing is a more comprehensive empirical survey of the coverage and the extent to which the financial press played a watchdog role and served the interests of the general public during this period. The next section shows just how positive and narrow news content was during this crisis, in terms of sources used for information, and the range of topics that were discussed.

The Reporting of the Dot Com Boom: March 1998–May 2001

In the last few years of the 1990s, the idea of a "New Economy" gained wide currency, almost rivalling "globalization" as a neologism that characterizes our era (McChesney 2008, 291).

Here we look at the mainstream financial coverage of the dot com boom using the same method that was applied to the reporting of the 1990 recession.

What the Economic Data Tell Us

The economic indicators show that high growth and low inflation throughout 1998 and 1999, and part of 2000 – the indicators of the "new economy." By 2000, each country was feeling the impact of lower economic growth and higher inflation. But unemployment was declining in each country. In Australia, it is higher than in the US or the UK, but it was declining nonetheless. Official data shows that each economy was showing signs of slowing, while inflation was getting higher, and this information should arguably have been available by mid-2000. This is later than the NASDAQ peak and fall. Therefore, the economic picture is clear, when looked at retrospectively, but the real economic conditions might not have been clear and available to financial journalists until mid-2000.

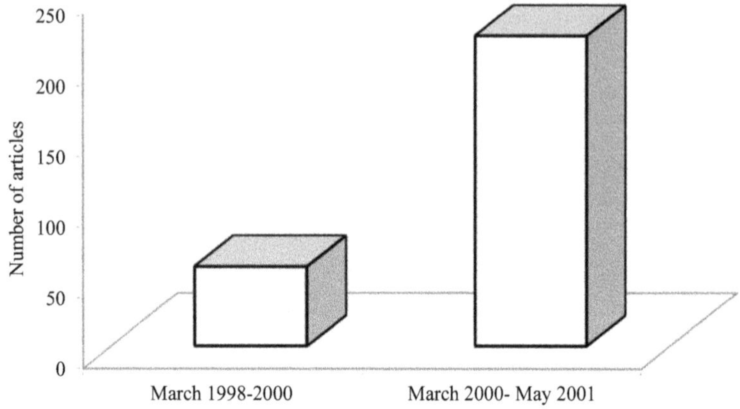

Figure 11. Dot Com Boom: Number of articles pre- and post-Minsky moment

Soothsayers?

Articles were collected for two years before the markets began to crash. In the last case study, there was a relatively large number of articles before the recession, which would have given the public an element of forewarning. The data show that number of articles that appear *before* the crisis has diminished when compared to the 1990 recession. Before the 1990 recession, more articles were available in the two years leading to the recession (See Figure 11 below). In the case of the dot com boom, there is a dramatic decline in articles offering an element of forewarning about a downturn or signs of weakness and slowdown compared to our first case study.

The Tone of the Reportage

Each of the publications reports with an average tone between neutral and optimistic until around March 2000, at which point each publication heads towards more considerablescepticism. (See Figure 12 above.) Therefore, each of the publications also reflects the economic situation discussed in the section above, as the economies slowed and inflation grew from mid-2000. The level of optimism maintained by each publication is quite high until the NASDAQ fell from its peak in March 2000 – the Minsky moment for this case study – when the switch to scepticism is dramatic.

The Sources that Shaped the Dot Com Boom

Business sources, analysts, and institutional investors were the most quoted sources for each of the publications. An overwhelming percentage of direct quotes come from business sources like CEOs and executives: 38.3% in the *New York Times*, 40.3% in the *Guardian*, and 31.7% in the *Sydney Morning Herald*. In second place are analysts, with institutional investors not far behind. (See Figure 13 below.)

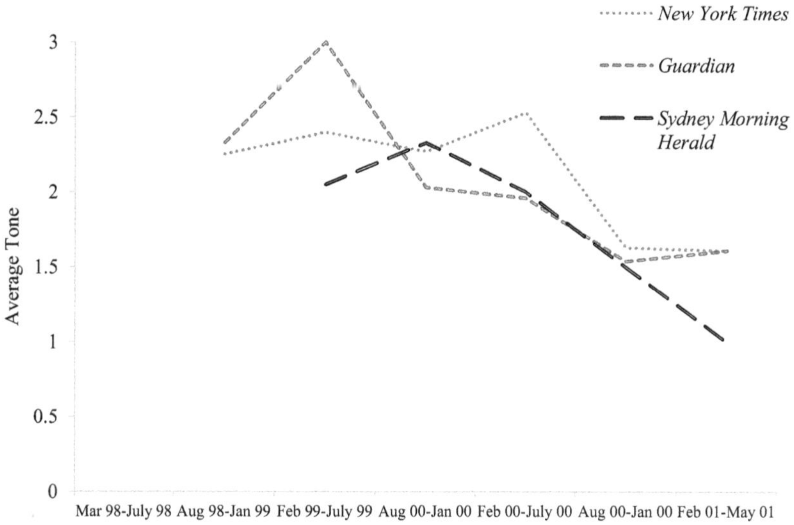

Figure 12. Dot Com Boom: Tone Trend, March 1998 to May 2001
1=Sceptical 2=Neutral 3=Optimistic

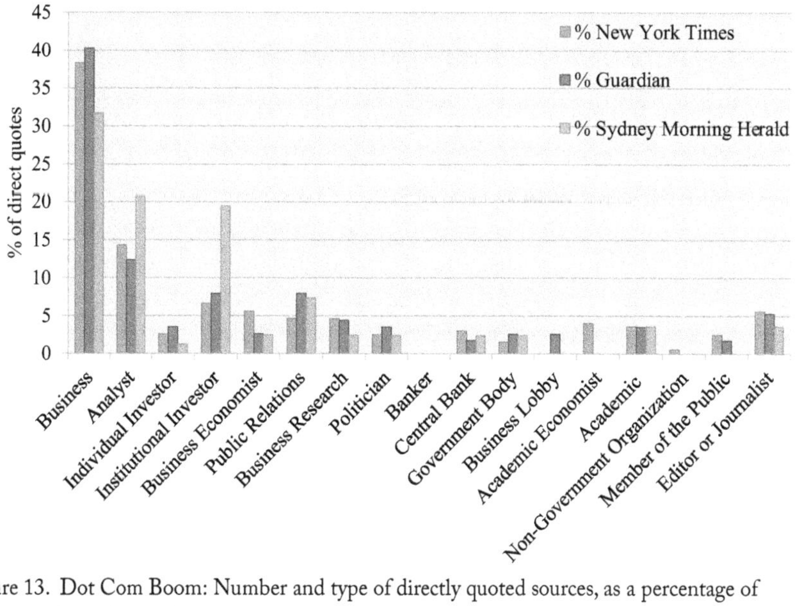

Figure 13. Dot Com Boom: Number and type of directly quoted sources, as a percentage of publication's total quoted sources

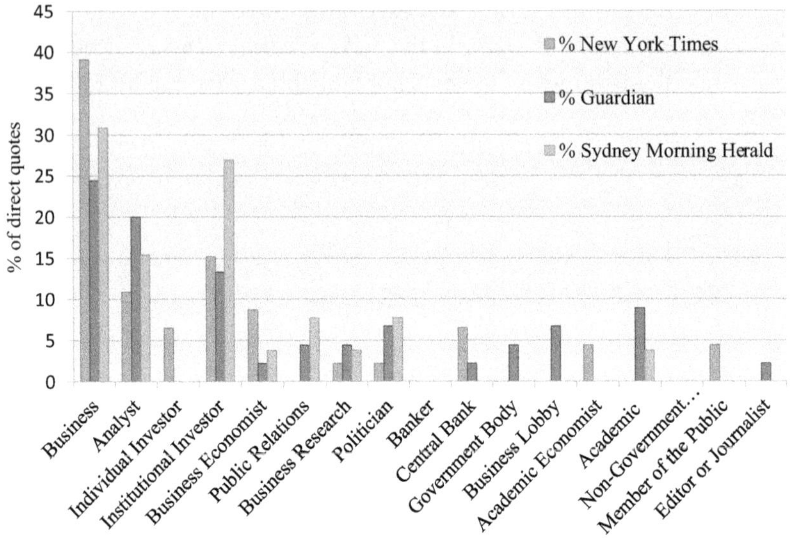

Figure 14. Dot Com Boom: Sources quoted after the Minsky moment, March 2000 to July 2000

The general public and non-government organisations are grossly underrepresented by each of the publications. Only 0.5% of quotes from the *New York Times* are from non-government organisations, and 2.5% are from members of the public. Similarly, under-represented, 4% are from academic economists, and 3.6% are from academics.

Of the quotes from the *Guardian*, only 1.7% are from members of the public, 3.5% are from academics, and there are none from academic economists or non-government sources. The *Sydney Morning Herald* is similar, but with no quotes from members of the public, academic economists, or non-government sources, and only 3.6% from academics.

And in the months immediately after the Minsky moment – March 2000, the month the NASDAQ peaked and started to deflate – similar sources are used by each publication. The majority of direct quotes in each publication come from business sources, analysts, and institutional investors (See Figure 14 below). Non-government sources are not quoted directly by any of the publications, while only the *New York Times* quotes members of the public, and this is only 4.4 per cent of its total quotes. Also, only the *New York Times* quotes academic economists, at 4.4 per cent. Only the *Guardian* and *Sydney Morning Herald* quote academics, at 8.9 per cent and 3.8 per cent respectively.

The economic situation in each country took a turn for the worse in mid-2000. The economies slowed and inflation grew. However, unemployment was in decline. Therefore, while there might have been room for some optimism in financial reportage, the tone was arguably overly optimistic in each publication. As a result, there was quite a dramatic switch to scepticism after the March 2000 Minsky moment.

The reportage was dominated and shaped by business sources, analysts, and institutional investors who supplied the bulk of information and direct quotes for each publication. Use of the same types of sources means that there is far less representation of other sources, including academics, non-government organisations, and members of the public. This is in contrast with the previous case study on the 1990 recession, which provided a much fairer representation through its direct quotes.

As was the case with the 1990 recession, after the Minsky moment, the reliance on business, analysts, and institutional investors is even more extreme. This suggests that alternative voices were not being sought even at a time of crisis when the public is arguably most tuned in to financial news.[3] News values do not shift, but rather they are magnified.

Main Topics of the Dot Com Boom

Bursting of the Bubble

The topic "bursting the bubble" occurred in 103 articles, 28% of the total data set. This theme brought together a collection of articles that mention the bursting of a bubble and its consequences, and ultimately builds the narrative that shaped the public's understanding of the bursting of the Internet bubble.

Figure 15 plots the coverage against the study timeline. It shows the preoccupation with the bursting of the dot com bubble in the US, the UK, and Australia from March 2000, after the March 2000 peak on the NASDAQ. Only four articles appear before March 2000, two in the *Guardian* and two in the *Sydney Morning Herald*, and they are curiously prophetic in predicting the bursting of the dot com bubble.

This theme brings out the reactive nature of the financial press, as most articles reflect investor behaviour and do not criticise it until late 2000-early 2001 when there are huge losses on the stock market, and company reports begin to appear. Each publication presents their version of the bursting of the dot com bubble. The *New York Times* was cautious and reported optimistically in places and compared the US favourably against Europe's dot com success. The *Guardian* does present some early scepticism, but mostly it reports with optimism and little criticism of stock market speculation. There is little evidence of its political leanings and the

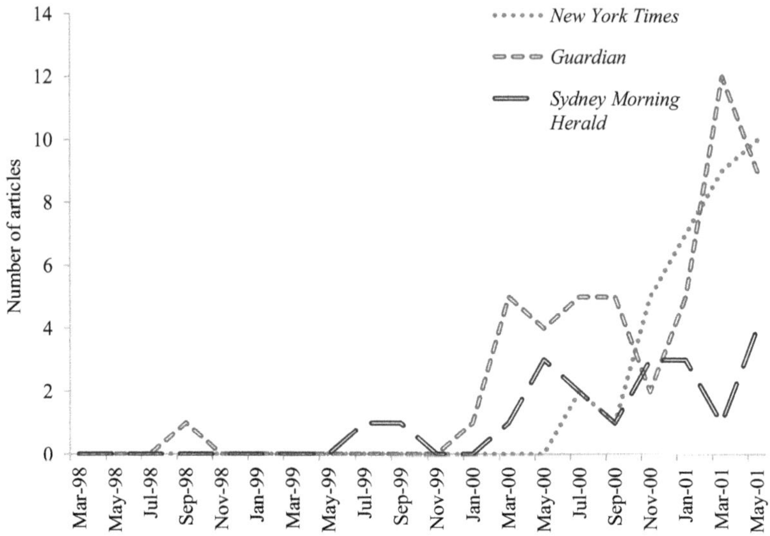

Figure 15. Dot Com Boom: Distribution of articles on the bursting of the Dot Com Bubble

criticism of political management and ideology, which characterised its reporting during the 1990 case study. The *Sydney Morning Herald* sees Australia in favourable contrast to the US. It reports on the events of the bursting of the bubble with relish.

There is little critical examination of the pitfalls of the stock market investments and movements of the real economy. There is also little coverage about why the "new" technology stocks were popular with investors or any discussion about their non-sustainability, given they were often based on unsustainable business models with little or no real profits. Journalists let investors dictate the timing of the bursting of the bubble when arguably they should have investigated the nature and sustainability of the bubble long beforehand.

Therefore, there were some warnings and scepticism, but the articles were not always geared for the general public. This is also evidenced by the minimal everyday advice on finance and government spending as the bubble burst. Furthermore, there are only a few examples – for instance, one in the *Guardian* by Atkinson (March 24, 2000) and one in the *Sydney Morning Herald* by Eakin (January 1, 2001) – that discuss the significance or potential impact of the falling stock market for the real economy and therefore society-at-large.

In summary, the issue is understated, and the public is largely not alerted to the magnitude of the crisis ahead. Moreover, articles are geared mainly to investors. Therefore, it can be argued with some certainty that the publications – concerning the "bursting of the dot com boom" – were not playing an effective watchdog role on behalf of the more general public.

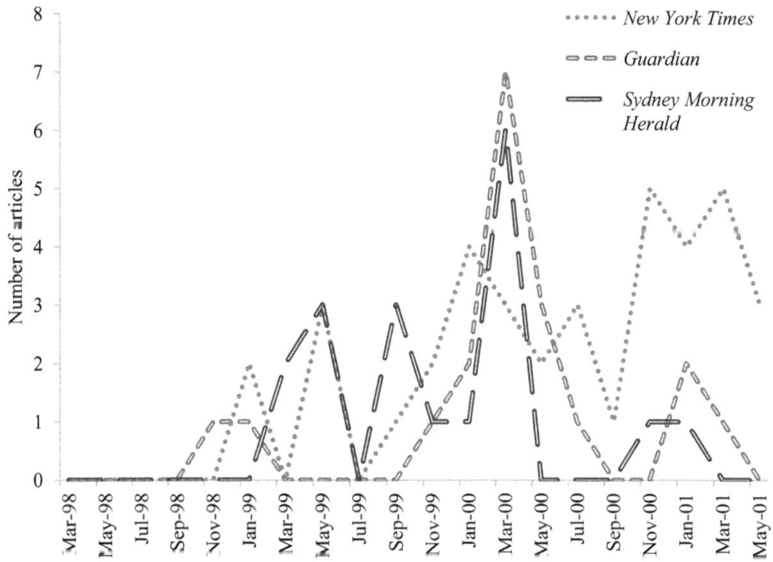

Figure 16. Dot Com Boom: Distribution of articles that refer to the "new economy"

2. The "New Economy"

The topic of debate on the "new economy" occurred in 75 articles, 20.5% of the total data set. As a concept, the "new economy" had various meanings as it was used in reportage throughout the late 1990s. For instance, it could be used to describe certain types of stocks or could refer to something more substantial, a movement toward a new way of thinking and a new way of living, a cultural shift that was more modern and enabled by high-technology advancements. It was also about how the internet revolution would permanently boost productivity and allow the economy to expand much faster without the danger of a slowdown or crash.

Figure 16 plots the coverage against the study timeline. It shows discussion and debate of what constituted a "new economy" continued through the case study period, but was particularly popular with the *Guardian* and the *Sydney Morning Herald* in March 2000 – the period that the NASDAQ peaked and then fell.

In addition to technological advances, the new economy symbolised a more liberal way of thinking and doing business in open and globalised markets. The premise of economic growth simultaneously fuelled the hype surrounding new Internet companies that went public through IPOs and inflated the financial markets. By 1998, the concept had started to take on the meaning of technological revolution. The variations in definitions did not always provide an accurate overall picture of what the "new economy" was and contributed to the mystique that maintained the allure of the new Internet companies and ventures.

Most importantly, each publication told its own story and was concerned with its own unique placement within this "new economy." The US wanted to be ahead in the game as an exponent of high economic growth with low inflation. The UK tried to establish itself as its own center of creativity, led fervently by New Labour. Meanwhile, Australia attempted to emulate the US. All three publications were taken with the idea of a "new economy" and were primarily concerned with new ways of doing business in a newly freed-up economic system that would grow without inflation.

As much as the new economy is discussed, along with the shifts in the economic paradigm that it appears to bring in its wake, few articles dwell on the significance and long-term impact this might have for the general public. Also, the few alternative interpretations that exist, which consist of economics writers using academic research (such as Gittins on March 22, 2000, and Elliott on July 2, 2000), highlight social inequality. The topic of the "new economy" and its associated social and economic changes do not include advice for everyday finances. There is minimal jargon. However – except for a full explanation of the "new economy" in the *Sydney Morning Herald* on March 22, 2000, by economics editor Gittins – there are only brief references and varying definitions as to what constitutes the "new economy."

In summary, two narrative strands emerge: first, the "new economy" is hyped with the focus on events in the US; and second, reality crashes through with the US rather than business attracting the criticism. Overall, each publication was taken with the concept. This representation of a "new economy" as a panacea for business and the economy was not useful for the public, and certainly not in the interests of the individual mum-and-dad investors who were drawn into the bubble. In this sense, the financial press, arguably infected by the market euphoria, was not playing an effective watchdog role for the public.

3. "Old versus New"

This topic was discussed in 71 articles, 19.5% of the total data set. The "old versus new" topic is an extension of the debate around the emergence of a "new economy." As the "new economy" started to symbolise a cultural shift to a new more modern way of living, so a narrative emerged that viewed anything that was not "new" or related the "new economy" as old and out-of-date.

Figure 17 plots the coverage against the study timeline. It shows that the "old versus new" frame increased in popularity throughout the case study. The debate was most popular with the financial press during the late 1990s, and well into 2000. The *Guardian* and the *Sydney Morning Herald* use it for the first half of 2000 and particularly in March – again, the month the NASDAQ market peaked and

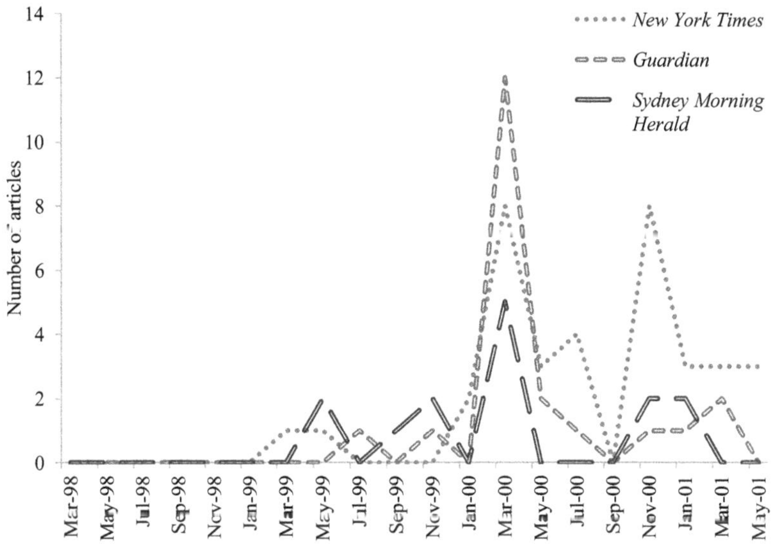

Figure 17. Dot Com Boom: Distribution of articles on the "old versus new" topic

fell. By 2001, opinion had shifted and the old economy had regained favour in the financial press.

Each publication shapes the reportage of the dot com bubble and its subsequent burst into a relatively simplistic narrative of "old versus new." Analysis of this topic shows the extent to which all three publications adhered to a similar narrative that failed to expose the weaknesses inherent in the dot com bubble.

The *New York Times* focused most of its reporting on the replacement of the "old" with the "new" economy, directing itself mainly at an audience of investors and more often than not, and especially through the year 2000, reflecting and condoning investor behaviour. It does become more sceptical as time goes on, so that by November 2000 the validity of the "new" is questioned, and "traditional" business values, even including labour concerns, creep in.

The *Guardian* is mostly sceptical about the merits of a new way of doing business. However, it does favour the "old versus new" narrative. What constitutes "old" is clear, as it represents the old, traditional, stable, and profits-based way of doing business. However, what constitutes "new" is more elusive, as it encompasses many elements, such as gender equality, speed, and technological advances.

The *Sydney Morning Herald* provides a more sceptical analysis about what the change from "old" to "new" entails. It also makes an effort to explain the merits of technology that benefit the old way of doing business. While it also uses the oppositional narrative, it tries to minimise the division between "old" and "new." This perspective would be useful for a non-shareholding public that might otherwise feel compelled to keep up with the times, as well as for investors tempted to shun the "old" in favour of the "new."

In summary, the narrative of "old versus new" would be the overriding message to a non-investing public, with the "new" presented as having greater appeal. Of the publications, the *Sydney Morning Herald* played the most effective watchdog – through its attempts to explain the real conditions of the "new" economy. However, through their adherence to this narrative all the publications lent further weight to the "new economy" thesis, supporting what would turn out to be unsustainable new Internet companies and the high growth low inflation economy stimulated by them. Thus, some of the main requirements of a watchdog press were not met: they did not provide independent and informative reportage, which would subsequently give a fair evaluation of the real economic situation to a non-shareholding public.

4. Warnings

The topic of "warnings" occurred in 66 articles, 18% of the total data set. This topic included all articles that provided any semblance of warning about potential repercussions from the dot com bubble.

Figure 18 plots the coverage against the study timeline. It shows that warnings gained momentum and peaked in March 2000 – arguably too little and far too late. However, there were some early warnings and signals that will be discussed below.

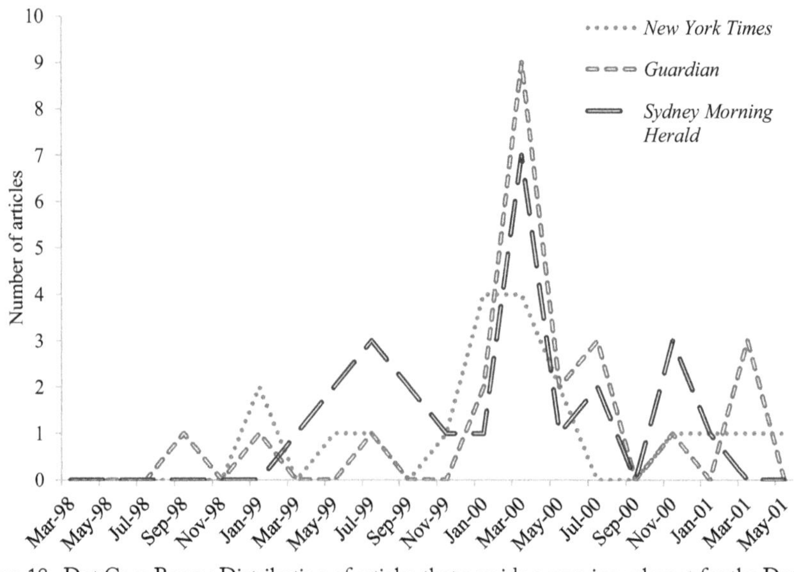

Figure 18. Dot Com Boom: Distribution of articles that provide a warning relevant for the Dot Com Bubble

The *Sydney Morning Herald* produced the most warnings. In the two years leading up to March 2000, 24 articles within this data set include a clear warning of imminent financial or economic danger. In contrast, 20 articles appeared in March 2000, the month that the NASDAQ, the market that caters to technology stocks, peaked and then dropped substantially. In the context of the entire 275 article data set, 66 warnings are arguably not a substantial amount. They certainly were not enough to offset the positive framing of the majority of articles during the boom.

The majority of the warnings that are present run contrary to coverage of the "new economy" and the "old versus new" narrative. They provide some of the best examples of reporting against the grain. It is interesting that there was still inbuilt optimism and continued support for the new economy, given the type of warnings that existed. The warnings that are given are clear and easy to understand, with minimal jargon. Arguably, the explanations needed to be longer and sustained through repetition. Clearly, the warnings did not generate enough attention until economic events turned sour from March 2000.

The *New York Times* provides the lowest number of warnings, at only 17% of its data set. Also, the warnings are not always explicit and mainly pertain to stock market movements. They are also frequently balanced with optimism. Only a few warnings appear from the *Guardian*. Of the data set from the *Guardian*, 23% provide warnings. They are directed mainly at investors, and relate to movements on the stock market.

Furthermore, the warnings do not come from sceptical reporting or investigation but come mainly from top officials. Of the data set from the *Sydney Morning Herald*, 24% provide warnings. It also produces the earliest warnings. Although the economic data in the quantitative analysis shows that the economies did not slow until around mid-2000, the *Sydney Morning Herald* refers to the threat of a slowdown in 1999.

The *Sydney Morning Herald* also produces one of the only pieces of advice for a general public, on July 21, 1999, Nicholas warns Joe Bloggs against investing in Internet stocks. This – considering the subsequent fall in stock prices – is arguably the best everyday advice for the general public from the data set. Early on, it also starts to consider the ramifications for the real economy from the stock market implosion, something that would have been useful for a non-shareholding public, as well as investors. Therefore, with regards to scepticism and warning, and appeal to the general public, the *Sydney Morning Herald* plays a significant watchdog role. The other two publications fare less well, as the *New York Times* and the *Guardian* produce fewer warnings, less scepticism, and less information geared to the general public.

5. "Ordinary" Topics

This topic captured articles that contained information on government spending, jobs, and personal finance, that were geared to a non-shareholding audience, and that contained minimal jargon. The topic occurred in 50 articles, 14% of the total data set.

Figure 19 plots the coverage against the study timeline. It shows that the publications increasingly reported on these "ordinary" topics for non-shareholders as time went on and the recession deepened. There is a peak in coverage in each publication in March 2000, and then increased coverage by the *New York Times* and the *Guardian* at the end of the year – the *Sydney Morning Herald* comparatively provides more constant coverage.

The articles placed within this topic had specific requirements, to begin with: thcy had to have minimal jargon and report on topics like government spending, jobs, and personal finance for non-shareholders. There is evidence that this data – unemployment and wage data – can provide early alerts as to an economic downturn. There is a lot of scepticism in the articles that report on "ordinary" topics for an ordinary audience. Some stark warnings come from reporting on jobs data.

However, the majority of warnings and scepticism appear only as economic data shows a sign of slowing, and the recession is being felt by society-at-large.

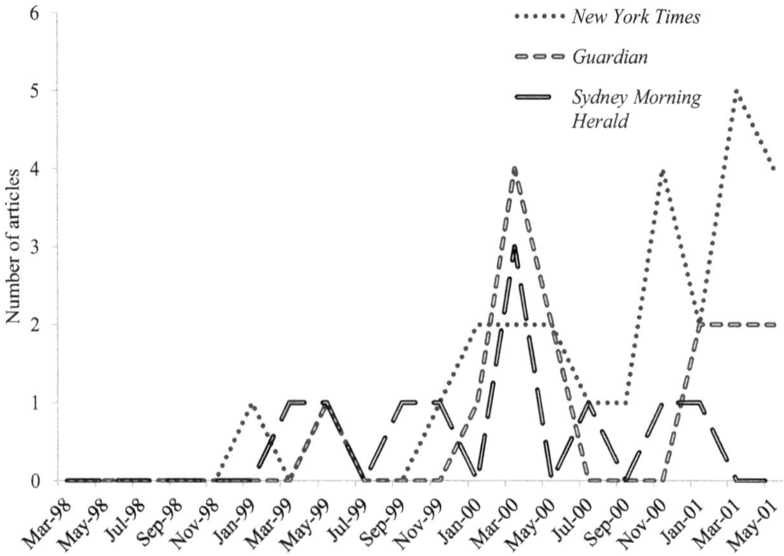

Figure 19. Dot Com Boom: Distribution of articles for the "general public"

This trend is more pronounced than it was in the 1990 recession. As the economy falters, each publication engages with the general public and produces articles that really highlight the social cost of the "new economy" that was being felt by members of the public. There is an increasing concern with individual households as the economy took a turn for the worse. Figure 19 shows that this is the case for all publications as the preoccupation with "ordinary" topics peaks around March 2000.

The *New York Times* uses jobs data to support, then debunk, and highlight the social cost of the "new economy" myth. It reports on individuals' circumstances through individual-level analysis, something the *Sydney Morning Herald* also does and the *Guardian* does less often. The *Guardian* reports directly to a general non-shareholding audience once, and on this occasion, it describes another face of the "new economy" and predicts recession in its wake. Overall, however, it does not often consider the human or social costs of the "new economy," and reports quite matter-of-factly about unemployment and the jobs market.

There are only a few articles from the *Sydney Morning Herald*, but these demonstrate a style of financial reporting geared to a more general audience, tackling issues, such as jobs data and personal finances, from a societal as well as an economic vantage point. These articles also tend to be written in laymen's terms and also provide everyday advice (such as warning the public to avoid get-rich-quick schemes), as well as some of the starkest warnings. However, there were also minimal explanations. Jobs data was used to discuss broad economic movements, and wages data was used to illustrate some inequalities. The issues that are discussed are easy to understand. However, there are missing links between this data and every day working and living situations that the general public could use to understand their position in the financial world.

As with the 1990 case study, this topic reveals a similar trend towards an increasing concern with the "ordinary" public as the economy worsens. This topic demonstrates that each publication plays a watchdog role for the general public when it considers "ordinary" topics – jobs, government spending, and personal finance – notably the *New York Times* and the *Sydney Morning Herald*. However, it is also the topic that provides the most scope for publications to take on this watchdog role.

Conclusion

Unlike the 1990 recession, the reportage during the dot com boom fits less well with the quality criteria that we established in Chapters 2 and 3: diversity of interpretations and voices, articles a non-investing public might understand, and a degree of scepticism. The articles mainly reflect investor movements that served to justify the sky-high value of Internet stock prices. Each of the topics and narratives uphold the "new economy" thesis, which is arguably a political construct built on high economic growth, low inflation, and steady employment. This thesis suited the needs of business, but it certainly did not satisfy the needs of the ordinary public that was adversely affected when the economy plunged.

While during the 1990 recession there was a diverse range of "voices" included in the reportage, there is now a narrower range of sources, and these come mainly from within business. Institutional investors and analysts make up the majority of the direct quotes in each publication and feature more prominently than in the previous case study. Now, the quotes are concentrated in these few areas, with less distribution amongst other source types.

The under-representation of non-biased and non-elite source noted in the previous case study continues here. Members of the public, academia, and non-government organisations are grossly underrepresented. For each publication, only around 2–3 per cent of quotes come from non-government organisations and only the *New York Times* uses members of the public for quotes, approximately 2 per cent of total sources quoted. This case study illustrates well the notions discussed in Chapter 2, that journalists were "captured" by the business elites promoting dotcom companies and also subject to group think about the boom.

As was also the case in the 1990 recession, the pattern is exaggerated in the months immediately after the Minsky moment, with even less representation of non-elite sources. This is an emerging pattern. The same sources that shape the coverage before the crisis have a monopoly on the framing of the events when the crisis is finally revealed to the public.

The public was provided with optimistic reporting, minimal warnings, and minimal discussion of issues most relevant to the dot com boom before it was too late in March 2000. The tenor of the reportage is more optimistic in each publication than during the 1990 recession. The data reveals how reportage changed quite quickly to scepticism during March 2000 (the Minsky moment). This is also the period that warnings start to gather in each of the publications. Compared to the 1990 recession, where 60 per cent of articles that related to the keywords appear in the two years before the Minsky moment, in the dot com boom, only 20 per cent of the articles appear before March 2000.

As with the 1990 recession, the economics editors and writers provide the most sceptical and prescient reportage, another emerging pattern across the case studies. The *New York Times* highlights the social cost of the dot com boom on a few occasions, mainly from economics writers like Uchitelle. Similarly, in the *Guardian*, it is the economics editor Elliott who expresses the most sceptical views.

The *Sydney Morning Herald* does produce some criticism of what was construed as "new" in the "new economy" and provides more practical explanations that put the "new economy" in a more realistic context. These criticisms mainly came from economics writers, such as Gittins and Mitchell.

It is fair to conclude that, on the whole, the reporting of the dot com boom was framed for the markets and not for the more general and non-shareholding public. In each publication in each country, there is a sharp deviation from the watchdog function it played for the general public during the 1990 recession.

This deviation and departure from the number of warnings and breadth of sources used for information during the 1990 case study continues for close to a decade after the dot com boom and is seen most profoundly in our next case study: the crisis that brought the world economy to its knees in 2008, the Global Financial Crisis.

Notes

1. Soros (2010, 38–39) defines market-fundamentalism as, 'The prevailing misconception … that financial markets are self-correcting and should be left to their own devices.'
2. EDI (electronic data interchange) and VAN (value-added network) were the precursors of web-based e-commerce, and were the original systems used on computers to support commerce, mainly between businesses. See Harreld, Krill and Schwartz (2002) for a discussion of the merits of web-based commerce over that provided by EDI and VAN technology.
3. See: Thurman and Schifferes (2012), Pew Research Center (2008), and Blood and Phillips (1995), which provide evidence of increased public attention during periods of financial and economic crisis.

References

Akram-Lodhi, A. Haroon. 2006. 'What's in a Name? Neo-Conservative Ideology, Neoliberalism and Globalisation.' In *The Neoliberal Revolution: Forging the Market State*, edited by R. Robison. London: Palgrave Macmillan. pp. 156–172.

Best, Kirsty. 2005. 'Celebrity.com: Internet Finance and Frenzy at the Millennium Consumption.' *Markets and Culture* 8: 361–378.

Blood, Deborah, and Peter Phillips. 1995. 'Recession Headline News, Consumer Sentiment, the State of the Economy and Presidential Popularity: A Time Series Analysis.' *International Journal of Public Opinion* 7 (1): 2–22.

Cheney, George. 1998. "'It's the Economy, Stupid!': A Rhetorical-Communicative Perspective on Today's Market.' *Australian Journal of Communication* 25: 25–44.

Davis, Aeron. 2006. 'Media Effects and the Question of the Rational Audience: Lessons from the Financial Markets.' *Media, Culture and Society* 28 (4): 603–625.

Denny, Charlotte. 2000. 'Brown Targets Red Tape that Strangles Start-Ups.' *The Guardian*, February 23. http://www.theguardian.com/money/2000/feb/23/personalfinancenews.efinance (Accessed May 1 2020).

Federal Communications Commission. 1996. 'Conference Report, Telecommunications Act of 1996.' House of Representatives, 104th Congress, 2d Session, H.Rept. 104–458.

Fist, Stuart. 1997. 'Dawn of a Deregulated Australian Telecommunications Market.' *The Australian*, July 1.

Garnaut, Ross. 2009. *The Great Crash of 2008*. Melbourne: Melbourne University Press.

Goozner, Merill, and Lauren Janis. 2000. 'Blinded by the Boom: What's Missing in the Coverage of the New Economy.' *Columbia Journalism Review* 39 (4): 23–35.

Harreld, Heather, Paul Krill, and Ephraim Schwartz. 2002. 'Vans Shift EDI Layer.' *InfoWorld* 24 (29): 31–32.

Henriques, Diana B. 2000b. 'Business Reporting: Behind the Curve.' *Columbia Journalism Review* 39: 18–21.

Howcroft, Deborah. 2001. 'After the Goldrush: Deconstructing the Myths of the Dot.com Market.' *Journal of Information Technology* 16: 195–204.

McChesney, Robert W. 2008. *The Political Economy of Media: Enduring Issues, Emerging Dilemmas*. New York: Monthly Review Press.

OECD (Organisation for Economic Co-operation and Development). 2002. 'Regulatory Reform in the UK.' In *OECD Reviews of Regulatory Reform*. http://www.oecd.org/regreform/2766201.pdf (Accessed May 1 2020).

Ofek, Eli, and Matthew Richardson. 2003. 'DotCom Mania: The Rise and Fall of Internet Stock Prices.' *Journal of Finance* 58 (3): 1113–1138.

Parker, Richard. 1998. 'The Public, the Press, and Economic News.' *Harvard International Journal of Press/Politics* 2 (2): 127–131.

Pew Research Center. 2008. 'The Changing Narrative: How the News Media Have Covered the Slowing Economy.' https://www.pewresearch.org/wp-content/uploads/sites/8/legacy/Economy-report.pdf (Accessed Feb 20 2020).

Pollock, Timothy G., and Violina Rindova. 2003. 'Media Legitimation Effects in the Market for Initial Public Offerings.' *Academy of Management* 46 (5): 631–642.

Quinn, Jane. 1998. 'When Business Writing Becomes Soft Porn.' *Columbia Journalism Review* 36 (6): 48–49.

Rudd, Kevin. 2000. 'Global Good not Global Greed.' *The Sydney Morning Herald*, July 27, from Factiva.

Schiller, Dan. 2000. *Digital Capitalism: Networking the Global Market System*. Massachusetts: MIT Press.

Schuster, Thomas. 2006. *Business News and Stock Market Movements*. Oxford: Lexington Books.

Simons, Lewis. 1999. 'Follow the Money.' *American Journalism Review* 21 (9): 54–68.

Soros, George. 2010. 'The Soros Lectures at the Central European University.' *Central European University Lecture Series*. New York: Public Affairs.

The Federal Reserve Board. 1996. 'Remarks by Chairman Alan Greenspan: The Challenges of Central Banking in a Democratic Society.' Remarks presented for the annual dinner and Francis Boyer Lecture of the *American Enterprise Institute of Public Policy Research, Washington, D.C., December 5, 1996*. http://www.federalreserve.gov/boarddocs/speeches/1996/19961205.htm

Thurman, Neil, and Steve Schifferes. 2012. 'The Future of Personalization at News Websites: Lessons from a Longitudinal Study.' *Journal Studies* 13 (5): 775–790.

CHAPTER FIVE

The Global Financial Crisis: "Why Did Nobody See It Coming?"

> The who-what-why-where-when of the story we've been trying to tell is impossible to define. Some of us have been treading the canyons of capitalism for years, and still, we don't know. It's as if all we see are … reflections and shadows, and from these, we compose our myths and fables. (Wilson 2008, 57)

We are now some ten years on from when the Global Financial Crisis began in 2008, and we are still feeling its ramifications and trying to understand its roots and implications. As described in Chapter 1, we have seen how the financial crisis eventually meant recession for many countries, and austerity has become the common policy response by governments. There has, consequently, been a widening of economic inequality, a rise in relative poverty, and a clawing back of the welfare state. This moment in 2008 also signalled a turning point in the global political economy – that the world is no longer formed and lead by one superpower, or by a dichotomy between East and West. The GFC had emphasised the global nature of our political and economic systems, and the Washington Consensus of economic power that had ruled for decades, was over (Tooze 2018, 3).

From the 1990 recession to the dot com boom, the Chapters have chronicled a decline in the reporting standards we have been tracking. There has been a narrowing in the framing of the discussion, with fewer voices being represented and less warning of potential risks to the economy. This case study shows that the discourse has continued to narrow, along with the narratives that are offered by each publication, which chime together with the same version and interpretation of events. Voices used to explain the situation have narrowed further, and the public relations industry has a strong hold on the interpretation of the crisis once it hits.

The GFC: An Overview

The challenges and underlying problems in finance journalism were magnified by the 2007 events and recession that followed. Financial journalists received blame for not predicting the crisis and for getting too close to the sources that they should have been holding to account (Mair and Keeble 2009). They also attracted blame for exacerbating the crisis as it unravelled – the UK government even explored the idea of financial journalists practising self-censorship to reduce public panic (UK Treasury Select Committee 2009). While some business journalists are baffled about their industry's lack of foresight, others can pinpoint exactly where problems occurred.

Howard Kurtz (2008), then a media writer for the *Washington Post*, was grappling with the sensational financial overhauls and bailouts of 2007 and 2008 that left journalists wondering how they did not see this coming. In October 2008, in one of his blogs, he commented that the business media might have raised a few issues by whistleblowing before 2008. Instead, they were "A day late and several dollars short" (ibid.). In the same blog, Kurtz cites David Brancaccio from PBS, "We journalists have had a long history with accepting what the smart people hand down to us, especially on complicated stuff." And Dean Starkman (2009b), former financial writer for the *Wall Street Journal*, and author of the *Watchdogs that didn't Bark* (2015), argues that the business press missed the story and then provided "excellent retrospective work," which he likens to "kicking the wreckage after the plane has crashed."

The Political Economy during the GFC

> Democratically elected governments have, over the past three decades, willingly ceded control of the world economy to a new elite of freebooting super-rich free-market operatives and their colleagues in national and international institutions. We call these people the New Olympians. (Elliott and Atkinson 2009, 4)

The United States

The GFC had roots in the bursting of the dot com bubble, during which time the US Federal Reserve cut rates from 6.5% to 3.5% (Soros 2009). The 2001 terrorist attacks on the World Trade Centre prompted even lower rates to bolster the economy so that they were down to 1% by mid-2003 (ibid., xv). Such low rates, according to Soros, precipitated a housing bubble in the US. Federal Reserve Chairman Alan Greenspan, the same Chairman that warned of "irrational exuberance" in 1996, attracted particular criticism for facilitating access to easy money. Other politicians, more widely, have been charged with encouraging deregulation that prompted easy lending practices and encouraged speculation (Taibbi 2010).

In 1999, the Glass-Steagall Act, created in 1933 after the stock market crash of 1929, was repealed and replaced by the Financial Services Modernization Act. The original Act had banned commercial banks from underwriting securities, which saw the split of banks, such as the House of Morgan into the commercial bank JP Morgan and the broker-dealer Morgan Stanley (Davies 2010, 79). But the move towards the repeal of the Glass-Steagall Act began as early as 1987 with the appointment of Greenspan who oversaw a "softening" of the Act (ibid.). This move, which effectively freed up commercial banks to get involved in the same activities as investment banks, along with the low-interest rates that ensued after the dot com boom and 9/11 terrorist attacks in 2001, paved the way for the growth of unregulated institutions that acted as banks such as Goldman Sachs, proffering credit across the globe, while the regulated banks engaged in unregulated activities like credit default swaps.

Previous crises usually led to stricter regulation, but the two decades following the dot com boom and bust have benefitted from the influence of market-fundamentalism. Banks in the US were granted greater freedom to make money as the restrictions that had been imposed on them since the Great Depression – namely the separation of banking and commercial banking – were removed through the repeal of the Glass-Steagall Act. And another notable policy change freed securitisation from regulation by credit rating agencies (Garnaut 2009, 78). The Commodity Trading Futures Commission was prevented from regulating the new derivative products such as CDOs, which were based on securitized assets. Credit agencies were not regulated or regulators, however, they were widely criticized for giving high AAA ratings to these products and not realising how dangerous and insecure they could be.

A further loosening up occurred again in 2004 when the Securities and Exchange Commission allowed the big five Wall Street investment banks to raise leverage ratios threefold from 12-to-1 to 35-to-1 (ibid.). The Federal Deposit Insurance Corporation's (FDIC) unwavering faith in "a new age of banking perfection" was evidenced by its suspension of banking premiums, which had been collected as collateral to insure deposits, as part of its role to supervise financial institutions (ibid., 79–80). Overall, the easy lending practices and deregulation that characterised the 1990s were bolstered by further policy changes at the turn of the century.

The United Kingdom

In the UK, the financial sector emerged as a force to be reckoned with from Greenspan's "irrational exuberance" speech in 1996 onwards. According to Elliott and Atkinson (2009, 16), "the fastest-growing parts of the finance sector expanded at around 7 per cent a year between 1996 and 2006." The authors place the roots of the GFC in the "aggressive marketing of Britain as an offshore financial sector with a light-touch regulatory regime" (ibid., 44). They say this spawned the easy credit culture that ultimately provoked the spectacular failure of the UK-based Northern Rock bank. The Northern Rock was one of the UK's largest mortgage providers, and it had been speculating its mortgage products on securitisation. When the credit market started to dry up in 2007, it did not have enough money on its books to cover its debts. At the time Robert Peston, the business editor for the BBC (and interviewed for this book), had written about its precarious position on his blog, which instigated the first run-on-a-bank in over a century. It was not long before this narrative was forgotten, and simplistic explanations and blame culture took over tabloid headlines. Berry's focus groups in the UK showed that only one person from the 16 groups he facilitated pinpointed and understood banks' overdependence on the wholesale money markets (Berry 2018, 103).

The move to laissez-faire finance had strong political support, specifically from New Labour. During this period, the UK enjoyed a "golden age of mortgage innovation" (Garnaut 2009, 21). Credit standards were declining and, after 2000, banks were offering mortgages worth more than 100 per cent of the property. By 2005 this had risen to 125 per cent. So in the years after the dot com boom, an asset boom grew without being reined in and a shadow banking industry was free to flourish.[1] The UK story is, however, less about shadow banking than reckless existing banks like RBS. The US shadow banks also operated in the UK and were often attracted by the sometimes even weaker regulation in the UK.

Australia

Politicians in Australia were less wedded to neo-liberalism and more inclined towards regulatory policy (Garnaut 2009). Australian banks had begun to seek risk elsewhere, in offshore borrowing, and had constructed their own version of a shadow banking industry, which did effectively prompt an asset bubble. The banking industry was also taking risks with securitisation and shadow banking activities were emerging, notably at National Australia Bank. Garnaut (ibid., 142) argues somewhat ironically that while this indicated that Australia might have been heading down the same path as the US and the UK, it was saved by the GFC, which stopped it in its tracks. An inherent conservatism in Australia was its potential salvation.

Financial Media and Business

The criticism that financial journalists did not forewarn the public arises out of the fact that the media either ignored or failed to understand the significance of the debt market and products, such as CDOs, being sold around the globe, and their relationship with the subprime housing bubble in the US. The debt market had, in fact, been growing for two decades. Writing about the US, Phillips (2008, viii) states that, "between 1987 and 2007, debt—in all flavours, from credit card and mortgage debt to staid U.S. treasury and exotic Wall Street—became one of the nation's largest, fastest-growing businesses." Indeed, the global credit market debt quadrupled during this time, from $11 trillion to $48 trillion to create a kind of super-bubble (ibid.).

From the 1980s onwards, the financial sector blossomed into a full-scale super bubble thanks to the expansion of financial credit and the extension of mortgage lending to subprime borrowers who were unable to pay them back (ibid., 39). This super bubble is evidenced by data that was collected by the Bank for International Settlements that reveals the total amount of credit households held internationally (up to 2010), including loans from non-banks and foreign lenders (Dembiermont, Drehmann and Muksakunratana 2013). It shows the phenomenal levels of credit provided to households and non-government institutions by unregulated financial institutions since the 1980s. According to the authors, households in Australia and the US owe more than the corporate sector (ibid., 79). They also point to a link between decreasing regulation of the financial industry and the "emergence of a shadow banking industry" (ibid., 78). Therefore, what was happening in 2007 was not a recent phenomenon, but one that had been slowly gathering steam for almost two decades. The repeal of the Glass-Steagall Act in 1999 – discussed above – gave extra licence to a sector that was already growing exponentially.

As the credit market grew and regulation faded, finance companies targeted vulnerable borrowers. Two of the largest perpetrators are Fannie Mae and Freddie Mac, for-profit and government-sponsored bodies, which were responsible for providing home loans to the Latino and African-American communities. The two enterprises became involved in subprime packages, which were essentially the repackaging of mortgages into financial instruments that were sold-on.

They were not allowed initially to make subprime loans and had strict underwriting conditions. Consequently,y the commercial banks created "subprime" categories that did not conform to fed standards. But since the GSE lent two-thirds of all mortgages they were eventually swept up in the crash of the housing market and had to be nationalised by the government – they were not well managed. The extent to which the newly packaged loans were disseminated to the Latino and African-American communities is alarming: "Home loan figures from 2006 show that 53.3% of loans issued to Black borrowers were high-cost subprime, along with 46.2% of loans to Latinos, compared to 17.7% to white borrowers" (Chakravartty and Schiller 2010a, 681).

The bundling together of toxic mortgage loans into packages involves a process known as securitisation. Securitisation was not new. What was particularly toxic was the re-bundling of the securitised assets in to artificial financial instruments known as collateralised debt obligations, which were then sold to other financial institutions such as pension funds. As Phillips (2008, viii) describes it, "To oversimplify somewhat, sophisticated financial institutions discovered gold in tying together five hundred or five thousand loans, mortgages, or whatever, and then selling fresh securities based and valued on the new assemblance." The processes involved in securing assets were, as such, quite complex and sinister. To have actually put the pieces together, it has been argued, would have been beyond the feat of a "humble" journalist:

> Expecting humble scribes to put all these complex concepts together, as well as name the day and form in which the whole thing will all come tumbling down – and run a decade-long campaign for regulatory change and oversight – is probably asking a bit too much. (Caplen 2009, 32)

Hamilton (2009), former reporter at the *Washington Post*, also touches on the intricacies of the products that underwrote the subprime market. They were, undoubtedly, difficult to understand even for some of the most eminent financial journalists. Hamilton cites Floyd Norris of the *New York Times*, who admits that he did not understand the full extent of CDOs and collateralised mortgage obligations, or the fact that rating agencies might not be assessing risk accurately. Hamilton also explains that predicting a disaster is not as sexy as covering one.

Hamilton (ibid., 36) sees this as evolving out of structural and cultural biases, which include the bias that speculative "this trend could be dangerous" stories should be avoided. The idea that the financial press was caught up in a larger process is suggested by other academics. Davies (2010, 201) calls this "climate" the "culture of the moment." He also argues that the press does not have any statutory responsibility to guard against financial excess, although he does pose the pertinent question: "were there no sceptics who questioned the sustainability of the dramatic growth in credit and asset prices that were under way?" (ibid.). Therefore, there are two different, but intrinsically related, reasons as to why financial journalists were handicapped: first, the GFC was complicated; and second, pointing out tentative dangers went against cultural biases that favour optimism within financial news practices.

The closeness of the financial journalists to their sources also induced a certain level of self-censorship. Brummer (2009, 20), city editor at the UK *Daily Mail*, admits that in some cases during the crisis top officials asked the business press to censor themselves – " and we have" he writes. He gives the example of Lionel Barber, editor of the *Financial Times*, who argued during a UK Treasury Select Committee (2009) meeting with financial journalists that it is not the job of his paper to bring the banking system down. Brummer (2009, 20) then goes as far as to describe the *Financial Times* as "the cheerleader for capitalism. The paper's income is highly dependent on full-page ads from the masters of the universe."

Gillian Tett of the *Financial Times* was one journalist who did, in fact, understand the financial products, having covered this shady area for years, but when she connected the dots, she was ignored by the industry and practically ridiculed. She tried to voice her concerns at the Davos economic forum in 2006, but she was not heard. Tett told a journalist at the *Guardian*:

> One of the most powerful people in the US government at the time stood up on the podium and waved my article, the article that predicted the problems at Northern Rock, as an example of scaremongering. (cited in Barton 2008)

Tett also argues that she benefitted from a PhD in anthropology, which had trained her to see the bigger picture (Fuller 2009, 88).

Mair (2009a, 23) touches on the various reasons as to why financial journalism failed to spot the impending crisis, making the argument that there is a larger systemic problem with financial journalism, as well as the financial industry, and the capitalist system generally. He lists various viewpoints from the academics and journalists who contributed to the collection of essays in, *Playing Footsie with the FTSE? The Great Crash of 2008 and the Crisis in Journalism* (Mair and Keeble 2009). Brian Caplen, editor of the *Banker*, says he "sunk" his doubts about securitisation; Hugh Pym of the BBC says "we were all deluded"; Matthew Fraser of the INSEAD business school in Paris blames poor training of financial journalists; and Howard Davies, the director of the London School of Economics, blames all institutions (Mair 2009a, 23). The different viewpoints suggest there is more at issue than the simple case of an industry that has lost its way. It points rather to systemic failure in both financial journalism and the financial industry at large for the absence of public forewarnings.

How the Reporting of the GFC Has Been Measured Before

Various methodologies have been employed to assess the reportage of the 2007–2008 financial crisis, ranging from studies on the main frames and narratives used to represent the crisis, through to investigations into the modus operandi of the financial journalists themselves (Mair and Keeble 2009; Pew Research Center 2008; Roush 2009; Schifferes and Coulter 2012; Starkman 2014; Tambini 2010). Cumulatively, the studies on the 2007–2008 financial crisis that exist portray a mainstream financial media that is limited by a narrow frame of reality, and dependent on a small coterie of PR operators, analysts, and business sources who are treated uncritically. Moreover, there is a sense that the financial press, which is faced with increasing time and commercial pressures, has generally lost its desire and capacity to report in the public interest. However, there is still a need for more thorough, comprehensive, and empirical research into financial journalism. Schiffrin and Fagan (2013, 153) acknowledge that "Despite the wide anecdotal criticism there is not much academic research on business/economic journalism."

The study "Power Problem," which was conducted by Dean Starkman (2009a) for the *Columbia Journalism Review*, was particularly influential in relation to the research design for this study. It focused on the US business media and analysed articles from 2001–2007. It searched Factiva for the names of important institutions, like Bear Stearns, and matched them with search terms, such as "predatory lending" and "securitization" (ibid., 26). Also, news outlets were asked to volunteer their best work during the period. The study was scathing of the business media and concluded with the following:

> CJR's study … provides strong support for the idea that sometime after 2003, as federal regulation folded like a cheap suitcase, the business press institutionally lost whatever taste it had for head-on investigations of core practices of powerful institutions. (ibid., 30)

The most significant and interesting finding of the Starkman study is that the most useful warnings and journalistic analysis of the subprime housing market, and its links with synthetic products on Wall Street, occurred from 2000–2003. As Starkman (ibid., 27) states: "business journalism during this period comes close to reaching the holy grail – the critical Wall Street/subprime connection." Had investigations continued along these lines they might have mitigated the subprime mess. From 1999–2004, some anti-predatory lending laws were passed in the US, and there were some large litigation cases as a consequence. For instance, Citigroup had to sign a US $240 million settlement with the Federal Trade Commission to cover two million customers. The business press pushed the issue and put pressure on officials, such as Elliott Spitzer, New York Attorney General from 2002–2007 and then Governor until 2008, resulting in what Starkman (ibid., 28) terms a "virtuous cycle of reform." Eventually, however, the business press developed "collective amnesia" and officials like Spitzer were ousted (ibid.).

Starkman enumerates a few of the issues he sees as causes for poor business reporting in the lead up to the GFC. First, he touches on the capture of business journalists by sources. This is something he calls "a form of Stockholm Syndrome" (ibid.). Second, he comments on superficial under-researched reporting, "nothing about boiler rooms and CDO factories were there, no matter how carefully you read" (ibid.). Third, he blames the public that did not listen, and a business press that did not manage to get through to the public, or what he calls the "thick skulls of a Pick-a-Pay Nation" (ibid.). Toward the end of the study, Starkman also blames Bush-era deregulation and business media's financial travails. He highlights the close connection between regulation and great journalism, as well as editorial leadership and news ownership that clear a space for financial journalism (ibid., 30).

Roush (2009, 36) comes to a different conclusion in his study, arguing that the business press did "yeoman's work during the past decade-plus to expose wrongdoing." However, government regulators and the public chose to ignore them, caught up in the moment of a "populist bull market" (ibid., 39). He did what he refers to as an "examination" of coverage before 2007, and found "ample coverage of the dangers that lay ahead" (ibid., 37). However, Roush's study does not elaborate on how he examined the coverage, making it difficult to gauge whether his results are quantifiable or reliable.

Roush does produce solitary examples of good quality reporting. The articles he refers to, such as Morgenson's *New York Times* story in 2007, "Mortgages may be messier than you think," are indeed some of the best examples of reporting before the crisis (ibid.). He argues that journalists like Morgenson and Pearlstein of the *Washington Post*, cut out the jargon that the public does not understand and "made it clear that trouble was brewing in the economy" (ibid.). However, the examples he provides focus heavily on mortgages and the lending institutions Fannie Mae and Freddie Mac. They do not connect-the-dots to paint the picture of a much larger interconnection between a subprime market and a shadow banking industry that had global reach.

The Pew Research Center (2008) discusses the narratives that various media in the US used to tell the financial crisis story. They collected 5,000 news stories from January 2007 to January 2008, which included 48 news outlets in total (ibid., 1). They discovered that the financial crisis story was the number two story, with the Iraq war as a close number three. However, the main story was unsurprisingly the presidential election (ibid., 2). They discovered that the coverage often lagged behind economic events. For instance, the recession received coverage in early 2008, a period the Pew Research Center argues would be a strengthening economy. Yet, the media moved away from the topic at a time when it warranted attention in the second quarter of 2008. The media also produced fewer stories on the slowing economy, even as there was increased public interest in the economy and the GFC. They also tracked the different topics favoured by various media. For instance, they found banking and housing are big issues in print media, gas prices are more popular with TV, and the press still covers the economy more than any other medium (ibid., 14).

A study conducted just before the 2008 financial crisis, at the London School of Economics and Political Science by Tambini (2008), produced similar results to Starkman (2009a), highlighting the serious inadequacies it found in a period it calls "a crisis for financial journalism." Tambini used interviews with business journalists, editors, and their lawyers, as well as some of the sources and stakeholders used for stories, to reach his conclusions. Tambini sums up by saying that financial journalism faces challenges, including "pressure of speed due to 24-hour news cycle; increasing complexity; PR strategies; sustainability; and the challenges of globalisation" (ibid., 4). He also adds a more recent challenge, which is the identification of precisely who is a financial journalist, with the entrance of new media mediums and platforms.

In Australia, there has been minimal study on the financial press before, during, or after the GFC. Mickler (2012) produced an interesting study that assesses the writings from opinion writers in Australia and Canada. It finds that they diverted blame from conservative free-market thinking to liberal attitudes towards spending and obtaining credit among the public. The Australian media, owned predominantly by Rupert Murdoch, is notoriously conservative (Muller 2017). Therefore, the reporting of finance in some mainstream newspapers in Australia promoted conservative views above all else, failing to bring in healthy criticism and democratic debate for citizens.

The studies done separately in the US, the UK, and Australia indicate that during the GFC the financial press did not devote enough attention to the potential problems in the economy, did not provide forewarning, and framed the debate in a way that supported market fundamentalism. In essence, reporting in the public interest was not of primary importance. There is a need for a transnational comparative study, which could bring all of the criticisms and concerns about financial reporting standards together in one place. Of the three case studies in this research project, it is the reporting of the GFC that has attracted the most critical attention. However, the academic studies, a review of the literature, and the political, economic climate that existed indicate that the financial press was also dealing with considerable institutional pressures. First, there was the cultural pressure to report within certain pro-business and free-market ideological parameters. Second, there were the commercial and time pressures, which gave less time for investigation into an increasingly complicated financial system that was growing in wealth and power.

The Reporting of the GFC: August 2005–October 2008

This section analyses the amount and quality of content that was available to the public before and after the GFC. It is the last of the three case studies, and follows the same pattern as the two that have gone before; the collected articles will be analysed first quantitatively and then qualitatively. The aim is to answer some of the key criticisms that have been levelled at financial journalism – that it is too close to its sources, is too optimistic in its reportage, and is, therefore, lacking the scepticism needed to hold power to account and produce timely warnings of impending disaster for the public. While pre-existing studies have already focused on these criticisms, it is anticipated that this research design – employing a longitudinal, transnational, and mixed-methods approach – will provide a more comprehensive snapshot not just of the GFC, but of the trends as they have developed across three decades of financial reporting.

What the Economic Data Tell Us

> We are in the midst of the worst financial crisis since the 1930s. In some ways it resembles other crises that have occurred in the last twenty-five years, but there is a profound difference … the current crisis is the culmination of a super-boom that has lasted for more than twenty-five years. (Soros 2009, vii)

This case study deals with arguably the most serious of the economic crises examined in this research project. As noted in the quote above, Soros describes it as a "super-boom" that has been gaining momentum for the past 25 years.

According to the key economic data for the period of study, the US and the UK experienced a period of economic growth and low inflation from 2002 to 2005. However, both experience slower growth toward the end of 2007. By 2008, both the US and the UK are in a recession. By way of contrast, Australia's economy does not dip into negative growth, although it does slow from mid-2007 onwards. The inflation rates in the US, the UK, and Australia also climb from early 2008.

The US and the UK have similar unemployment trends that head upwards to around 6%, especially through 2008. Conversely, Australia's unemployment reduces from 5 to 4.5% and remains there for much of 2008.

Therefore, Australia's economy stands out during this period. Although it did experience slower growth and some increased inflation, the levels are modest when compared with the US or the UK. Furthermore, the official data would not have provided any indications of a slowdown, as it did not happen in each country until mid-2007. At this point, growth slowed, inflation grew, and in the US and the UK at least, unemployment increased, all at dramatic rates.

Soothsayers?

The search produced a data set of 546 articles, comprising 279 articles from the *New York Times*, 147 from the *Guardian*, and 120 from the *Sydney Morning Herald* (see Figure 20 below).

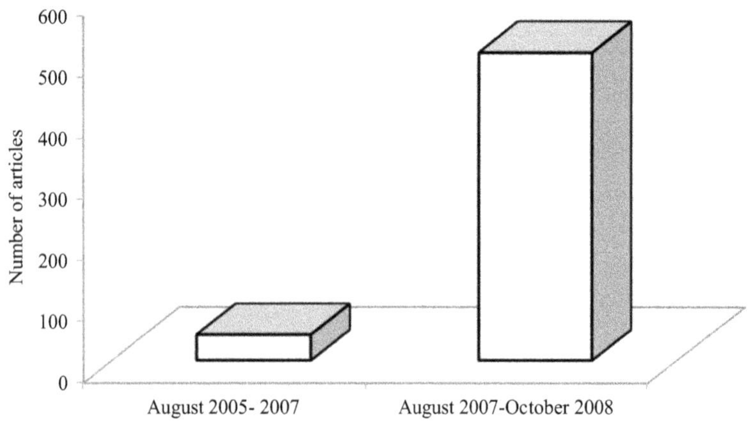

Figure 20. GFC: Number of articles pre- and post-Minsky moment

In this case study, the Minsky moment was August 2007 – the moment that the crisis was revealed by the French bank BNP Paribas and became a story available widely for the public (Kleinnijenhuis et al. 2013; Pew Research Center 2008). To ascertain the number of articles available to the public before the crisis was revealed, and therefore the opportunity for warning and debate among citizens, articles were collected two years before the Minsky moment. Based on the keywords, 42 articles appeared in the two years before August 2007 (8 per cent of total coverage), and 504 afterwards (92 per cent of coverage). This suggests a minimal amount of coverage on topics pertinent to the subprime housing bubble before it imploded. In comparison, 504 articles in a little over a year afterwards suggests that the public was inundated with articles after the story broke.

The Tone of the Reportage

As with the other case studies, and as described in Chapter 4, the articles were coded along a three-point scale as sceptical, neutral, or optimistic. To plot the trend across the entire timeline, totals were averaged for each quarter, or three-monthly period (see Figure 21 below).

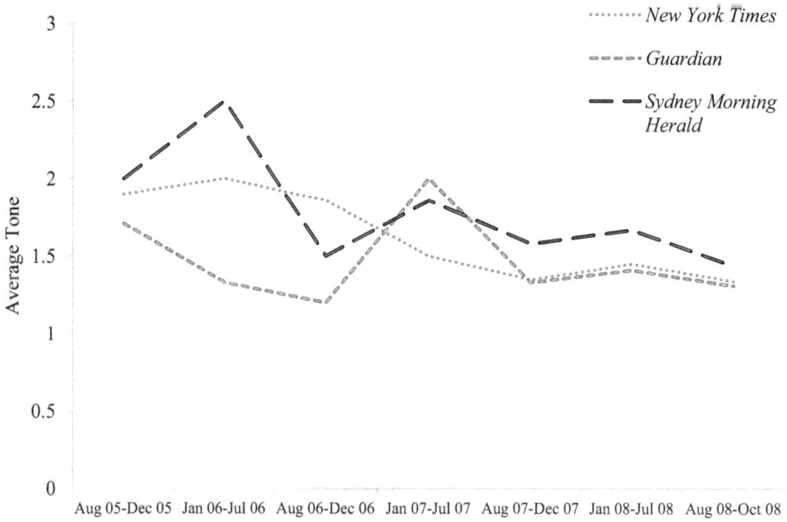

Figure 21. GFC: Tone Trend, August 2005 to October 2008
1=Sceptical 2=Neutral 3=Optimistic

Figure 21 illustrates that all publications reflect the economic events quite closely in the tone of their coverage. The *New York Times* starts on a neutral tone in 2005 and heads downwards towards scepticism for the period. The *Guardian* has a spike of optimism in mid-2007, which is interesting considering the subprime revelations in August 2007, but not so surprising given the higher economic growth around the same time. The *Sydney Morning Herald* coverage is between neutral and optimistic at the start of 2006. Still, it then remains close to neutral for most of the period, which is likely a reflection of Australia's more favourable economic conditions.

The Sources that Shaped the GFC

To ascertain the level of diversity and representation of society, the first two direct quotes were coded for each article. It was hoped that this would also ascertain the extent to which PR spokespeople and press releases were quoted directly.

Additionally, the direct quotes that were available in the months directly after the Minsky moment, in August 2007, were coded and represented in a separate bar graph. This approach was used to guage whether journalists used the same sources for information and quotes that they used before the crisis, or whether there was an Emperor's clothes moment of revelation when they sought alternative sources (see Lewis 2010). The results are represented in Figure 22.

According to Figure 22, business sources are the most quoted source by each publication. Of the direct quotes used by the *New York Times*, 19 per cent are from business, while 27 per cent for the *Guardian* and 21 per cent for the *Sydney Morning Herald* are also from business.

Analysts and PR are also popular sources for information and quotes. Of the quotes from the *New York Times*, 13 per cent are from analysts, and 11 per cent are from PR. The *Sydney Morning Herald* is similar, with 18 per cent from PR and 12 per cent from analysts. By way of contrast, the *Guardian* uses 19 per cent from politicians and 11 per cent from the UK's central bank, the Bank of England, for the majority of its direct quotes.

Members of the public and non-government associations are not used often for direct quotes. Of the quotes from the *New York Times*, 3.1 per cent are from members of the public, and 1.1 per cent comes from non-government organisations.

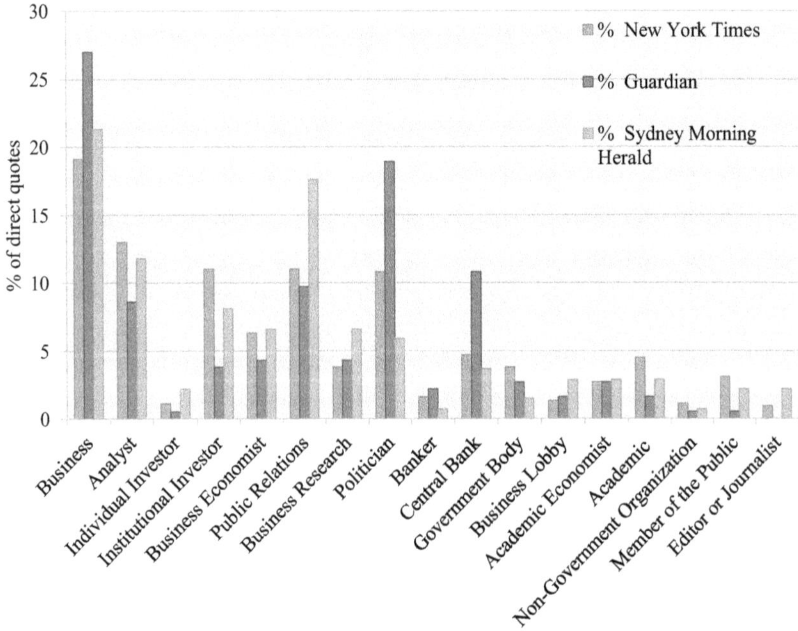

Figure 22. GFC: Number and type of directly quoted sources, as a percentage of publication's total quoted sources

In the *Guardian*, 0.5 per cent are from members of the public and 0.5 per cent are from non-government organisations. In the *Sydney Morning Herald*, 2.2 per cent are from the public and 0.7 per cent are from non-government organisations. Slightly more quotes are used from academia. Of the quotes from each publication, around 3 per cent are from economists. Similarly, from other academics, the *New York Times* uses 4.5 per cent, the *Guardian* uses 1.6 per cent, and the *Sydney Morning Herald* uses 3 per cent.

During August 2007, and in the months that followed, as Figure 23 indicates, the quoted sources remain similar, but PR sources increase, while fewer members of the public and academics are quoted.

Sources, Tone and Warnings

The tone is close to neutral in each publication and is, therefore, a far cry from the optimistic reporting of the dot com boom. There is a slight turn to scepticism in August 2007. This was when the subprime market was exposed, and it is also, according to the economic data when the economies started to take a turn for the worse. Therefore, while the publications were not sceptical beforehand, they were quick to shift the tone of their coverage once the economic situation showed signs of deterioration.

As is seen in Figures 22 and 23, members of the public, non-government organisations, and academia are far less popular as sources for information and

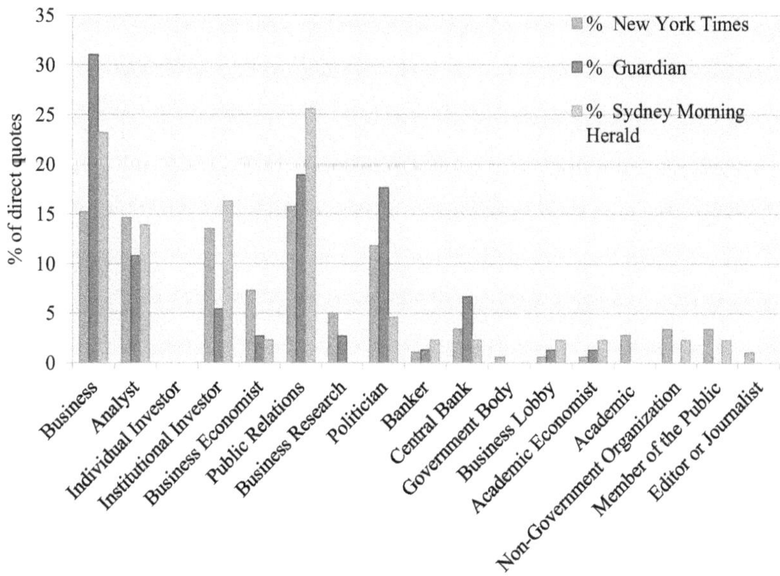

Figure 23. GFC: Sources quoted after the Minsky moment, August 2007 to December 2007

quotes compared to business, PR, and analysts. Indeed, we can see from the data the extent to which each publication actively favours direct quotes from business, PR, and analysts. In the case of the *Guardian*, there is a trend emerging that sees politicians and central bank sources used most for quotes.

As is seen in Figure 23, in the months after the Minsky moment, in August 2007, PR and business sources predominate – an emerging trend common to all the case studies. The selection pattern for sources post-crisis becomes exaggerated, and sources like non-government organisations and even government bodies are now rarely quoted. This leaves the field clear to the elite sources that are implicitly connected to the business world and its reputation to define the aftermath of the crisis.

These results make it possible to form a view on two of the quality measures: the diversity of "voice" and levels of scepticism. However, to assess the articles against the remaining criteria – relating to the accessibility of content for the general public and the extent to which it provided appropriate warnings, and held government and business to account – it was necessary to employ qualitative methods.

News Framing and Discourse

This section examines the frames and language used by journalists in their reportage of the GFC.

Main Topics of the GFC

As with the other case studies, the most salient topics of discussion were identified and worked out as a percentage of the total data set (see Figure 24 below). The top five most referred to topics – connected dots, crisis talk, the blame game, bailouts and general audience – are then analysed qualitatively, the key narratives are discussed, and the publications are measured against the quality criteria and compared.

1. Explanations and Connected Dots

The topic of "explanations and connected dots" occurred in 219 articles, 25.5% of the total data set. The topic includes all of the explanations that relayed the complicated situation that was unfolding to the public. Almost half of the data set is included in this category, which suggests that a lot of explanations were available to the public. There was a dramatic peak in August 2007, and only ten articles appear before this date. After this month, the coverage remains high and constant in each publication (See Figure 24 below). The spread of the data verifies August

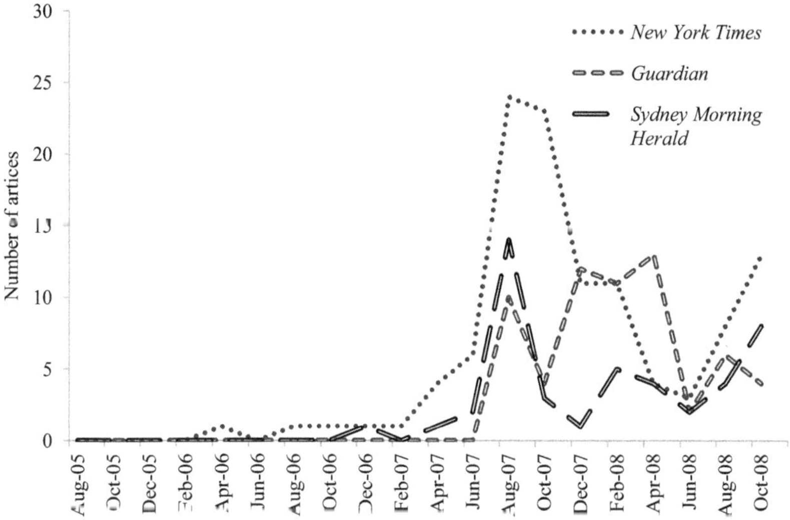

Figure 24. GFC: Distribution of articles that provide clear explanations

2007 as a month when the lid on Pandora's Box was indeed lifted, and it can be considered a revelatory moment.

Three features are tracked in the analysis: the nascent warnings, the use of a US-focused narrative, and the use of short-hand jargon.

The majority of articles arrive in August 2007 when it is too late for any forewarning. Instead, an avalanche of articles inundated the public with the same message – a crisis has arrived, and it was born in the US. There are few interpretations to learn from: similar explanations and narratives are adhered to by each publication. The GFC emanated from the US and was caused by financial products that spread like a virus. There is little movement away from this version and account of the GFC. Therefore, each publication contributed directly to the shaping of the GFC using the same dominant narrative of a US-born disaster that was catching like the plague.

Indeed, the fact that 48 of the 220 articles, or 22 per cent, appear in August 2007 also illustrates that this must have been a moment of revelation for the financial press, as well as the public. It also highlights groupthink and the financial press' collective reactive response to the events. Furthermore, it suggests that complicated financial products, their connection to the subprime market in the US, and the interconnectivity between the financial markets across the globe, were not fully scoped by financial journalists until August 2007.

Two accounts of the GFC that provide warnings come from financial writer Norris at the *New York Times* and economics editor Gittins at the *Sydney Morning*

Herald. These are two writers with decades of experience in writing about finance and economics respectively. Their reporting tends to be sceptical in tone and contains warnings for the public, here, as well as in the other case studies. The *Guardian* is the tardiest of all the publications, with no warnings at all before it begins reporting on the GFC in August 2007.

Eventually, full explanations faded out of the reportage and, by April 2008, they were replaced with short-hand accounts that assumed public knowledge of complicated financial products like CDOs. Thus, the terms that were clearly defined and explained in 2007 became part of the financial press' vernacular. Where explanations did appear, they started to focus on broader questions and broader contexts. For instance, journalists began to look beyond the events of the GFC to question their domestic economy's position in the global system, the unsustainable nature of free-market doctrine, and the deficiencies of the regulatory oversight system.

Therefore, according to the qualitative analysis of this topic, the financial press arrived quite late in the genesis of the GFC. In this sense, they did not play a watchdog role with regards to scepticism, warnings, and holding power to account. However, from August 2007 onwards, through the provision of information and explanations, they certainly played a watchdog role for the public. They did a comprehensive job of connecting the seemingly nebulous dots as the situation unfolded in August 2007. Indeed, August 2007 is full of lengthy and detailed explanations of the events and products at the heart of the crisis. The explanations are detailed, mostly free of jargon, and attempt to explain the inner workings of some of the complex financial products and their links to the real economic events.

2. Crisis Talk

The topic of "crisis talk" occurred in 196 articles, 23 per cent of the total data set.

Nearly half of the data set uses the emotive description of a "crisis" to define the GFC as it unfolded. This is illustrated in Figure 25, which shows the extent to which each publication refers to a "crisis" after August 2007.

Only five of the articles appear before August 2007. Figure 25 also shows that the GFC was defined as a crisis until early 2008 when the theme trailed off and then peaked again by August 2008, especially in the *New York Times*. This trend relates strongly to the events surrounding Lehman Brothers during this period.

There are only a few mentions of a "crisis" before August 2007. The general public was not forewarned or informed about the GFC in its totality at any time before August 2007. Until August 2007, there was little scepticism or forewarning. From this point onwards, there is an avalanche of articles and reportage that is critical.

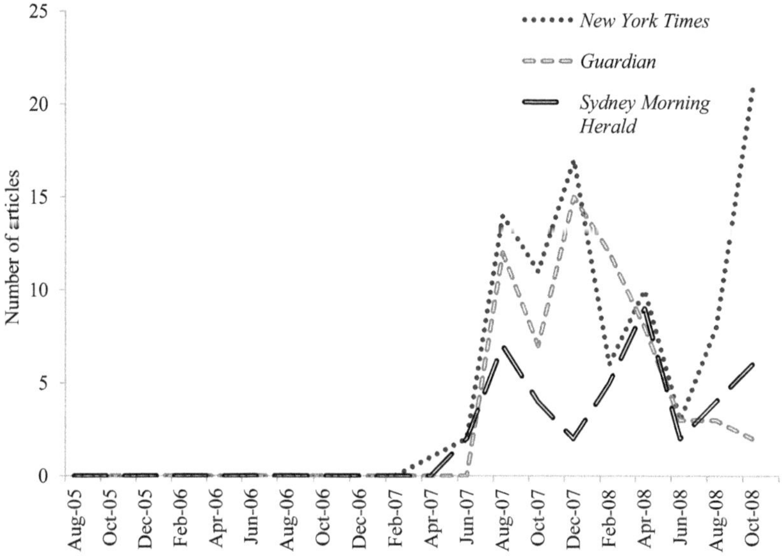

Figure 25. GFC: Distribution of articles that refer to a "crisis"

The discussion of events framed in terms of a "crisis" often acted as an extension of the narrative that formed from August 2007 – that of a disaster spreading from the epicenter of the US, and one that was contagious like a disease. This analogy of a disease removed blame away from financial institutions and the financial markets. The "crisis" was framed in terms of problems relating to financial institutions, investors and bankers, and jobs in the finance sector, rather than in terms of the impact on ordinary households or ordinary job losses, or losses in individual savings accounts. This is despite the fact that the "crisis" had reached the "real" economy and was affecting all sectors, both public and private.

Also, the word "crisis" was used to denote various types of crises – including credit, debt, economic, financial, global, housing, national, lending, liquidity, subprime, market, international, mortgage, insolvency, mortgage fraud, current, today's, and the US. This frequent and indiscriminate use of the word would have made it more difficult for the "ordinary" public trying its best to understand a situation, especially as explanations for complicated terms fell away in 2008.

The explanations that were offered did not pull the elements together to define the GFC in ways the general public could easily understand. The way that the crisis, or the crises, is framed is often full of jargon. The simple references to debt, housing, or liquidity crises, for instance, assume knowledge. Moreover, the references were rarely teamed with full explanations, which is why the GFC itself might have been difficult for the general public to grasp. There are some examples of clear explanations of specific crises, such as the one offered on August 17, 2007, by economics editor Elliott from the *Guardian*. There is also one offered by journalist Washington in the *Sydney Morning Herald*, when quoting academic economist Nouriel Roubini on June 16, 2007.

Therefore, the "crisis" topic reveals that the publications were not playing a watchdog role with regards to fair and informative reportage for the general public. The reporting initially failed to take advantage of the opportunity this topic offered to bring everything together to help the public understand the nature of the GFC, the extent of the crisis, and its actual and potential impact.

3. Blame Game

The topic of "blame game" occurred in 190 articles, 22% of the total data set. Articles within this topic, blame something or someone for causing or stoking the GFC. This defined a majority of the coverage of the GFC, and the issues are represented in highly political terms.

Figure 26 below plots the coverage against the study timeline. It shows that articles within this theme peak in August 2007.

There was not one particular person or institution to blame, and the financial press did disseminate the blame among various parties. Fourteen areas of blame

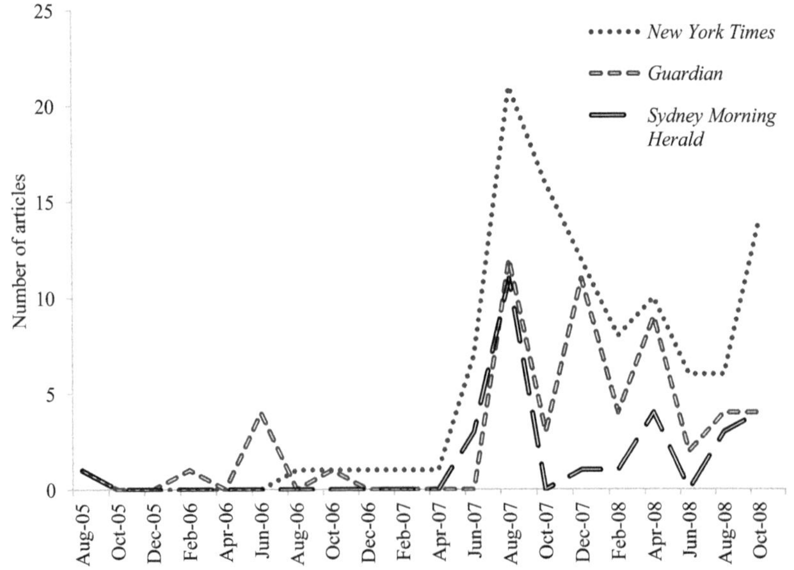

Figure 26. GFC: Distribution of articles that assign blame

were identified from the data set, including financial institutions, ratings agencies, and regulatory authorities. These are discussed below under three subject headings: lax monetary policy, financial deregulation, and aggressive lending.

Other Sources of Blame

Other sources of blame in descending order of frequency, are:

- Financial naivety (33);
- Ratings agencies (29);
- Human psychology that encourages groupthink (20);
- The financial products as if they existed as animate objects (18);
- Individual traders' activities (13);
- Wall Street greed (13);
- Compensation structures of companies that encourage reckless and speculative behaviour (12);
- A greedy public that played a significant role as they lived beyond their means (9);
- The financial wizards that designed products too complicated to understand and easily priced (8);
- Outright mortgage fraud (5); and
- The journalists that played a role in talking up the stock market (3).

Blame Game Topic

Each of the publications is critical of lax regulation and a corrupt financial industry. Free-market principles, since the 1980s, were suddenly called into question. Collectively, the publications were asking for someone and, in fact, something – the thing being the financial industry and government policy – to be accountable. They shared similar concerns, and while this could be seen as just another example of groupthink, it shows how the press together can lobby for social good. It also becomes clear that trying to place blame was part of trying to define the GFC and understand its true nature and dimensions.

This topic does provide some alternative views – on regulation, on the finance industry, and government economic policy. Each publication delivers its fair share of criticism. It would have prompted discussion. However, despite the preoccupation with blame, there are few ideas or suggestions for alternatives to replace or challenge the current political economic or financial system.

Also, there is little in the way of everyday advice. There is little advice to the average person on how to deal with the fallout from the crisis on a day-to-day basis, nor is there any focus on what needs to be done to prevent it happening again. Conversely, there are some explanations of how and why blame is placed on issues or individuals. There is also minimal use of jargon, and the articles would be easy for a lay audience to understand.

Therefore, collectively the blame game topic was very informative, challenging government philosophy and the moral heart of the financial industry. However, the explanations do not go far enough. They are also too late. As the discussion of lax monetary policy in particular indicates, the problem was gestating for a decade or two. Furthermore, as mentioned above, while there is a discussion of whom or what caused the GFC there are few suggestions of alternative policies or ideas to curb financial corruption in future. Thus, qualitative analysis reveals the financial press played a watchdog role in the sense that it certainly promoted accountability and democratic discussion. It failed, however, in its belated reporting and the limited everyday advice for the general public.

4. Bailouts

The topic of "bailouts" occurred in 130 articles, 15% of the total data set. The scale of some of the bailouts that came out of the US Federal Reserve, to the tune of US $900 billion, and the adding of an additional $3 trillion on its balance sheet to boost the economy, and the taxpayer-funded bailout of the Northern Rock in the UK, soon made headlines. For the US, the UK, and Australian governments, it was a sharp break from the laissez-faire free-market policies that had characterised business and economic policy for nearly three decades since the Thatcher and Reagan years in the 1980s.

Two peaks in coverage can be seen, in August 2007 and October 2008 respectively. (See Figure 27 below.) In August 2007, the month that central banks poured money in to failing banks, there are 30 articles. The following year, in October 2008, the month after the US Federal Reserve made the unprecedented decision to let Lehman Brothers fail, 37 articles appear.

Some of the more sceptical articles question the rationale and justification for the bailouts, with the *Guardian* the most scathing in its criticism of the huge bailouts and about the intervention by the US Federal Reserve and government. The topic of bailouts was not only a popular one, it was also a contradictory one because, although the press often reported on the topic in neutral terms, they saw the bailouts as a lifeline as much as they scorned them for using taxpayer money. Indeed, after the Lehman collapse in August 2007, all publications follow the same line and present the intervention as an act of taking control. To some extent, this view is justified, as the global financial system was balancing on a knife-edge by this stage. However, like the "blame game" topic, there was reporting that challenged the laissez-faire principles that had guided policy for so long. The GFC

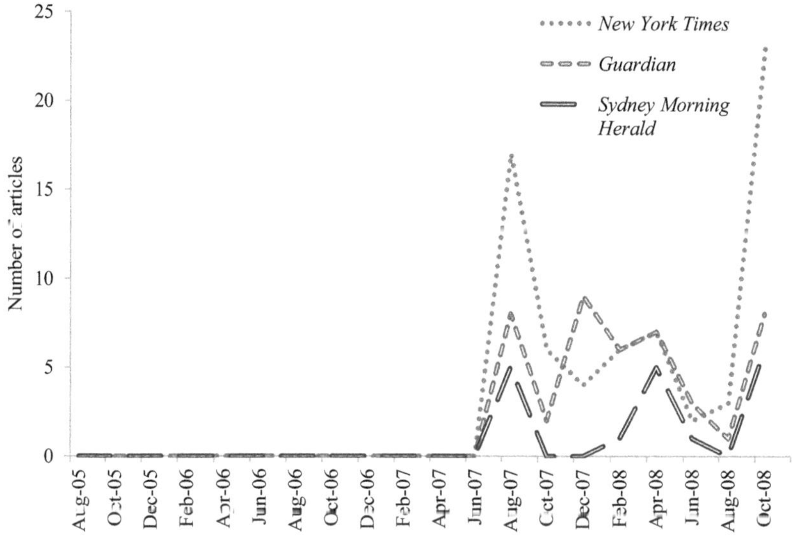

Figure 27. GFC: Distribution of articles that discuss a bailout

provided an opportunity to suggest alternatives and promote alternative views, but there are few examples of this by late 2008.

Each publication uses words, such as "injected" and "pumped," which are an extension of the narrative of a disease that began in the US and became contagious. However, each publication reports along different lines as they did with the framing of the "crisis." The *New York Times* provides a number of different views, and ultimately – particularly after the Lehman Brothers collapse – it rallies to support the rescue of central bankers through government bailouts. The *Guardian* reports with an element of schadenfreude on events in the US but also looks at the GFC in the context of the UK's own domestic economy, supporting remedial measures by the UK Treasury and Bank of England. The *Sydney Morning Herald* is mostly concerned with the domestic economy, rather than the global economy. It presents the bailouts in the US and Europe as solutions to problems it does not need to consider and uses language that is mostly alarmist and colloquial.

There is more information and advice regarding government spending on this topic than any other in the case study. In particular, given the anger generated around the use of taxpayer money, there is also discussion of average wages – for instance Morgenson's reporting in the *New York Times* about consequences for an individual forklift driver on August 6, 2007. However, this angle was not pursued, as justifications in favour of bailouts came to dominate the coverage. Also, there is minimal use of jargon, but there is also minimal explanation of the size, scale, and scope of the bailouts, as well as of the pros and cons of the arguments used to justify them. However, on August 14, 2007, economics reporter Gittins, from the *Sydney Morning Herald*, provides one of the most detailed explanations of how a "bailout" technically works.

Therefore, while the discussions that would prompt democratic debate and information that the public needed about large-scale funds being provided to banks were there, they tailed off too soon. Despite the size, scale, and scope of these phenomenal bailouts, and despite the creation of some "super" banks, there was relatively little discussion about whether the institutions should be allowed to fail. Instead, the majority of the reportage on a bailout focused on why the rescue was needed. Thus, this topic – on bailouts that directly impacted the general public through the use of taxpayer money – could have provided the financial press with ample opportunity to debate the bailouts, better inform the public and hold power to account. There is some evidence of articles that are geared to this aim, but any debate that involved suggesting policy alternatives, and arguing limits for the use of taxpayer money, was cut short by the end of 2008 after by the collapse of Lehman Brothers.

5. "Ordinary" Topics

The topic of "ordinary" public occurred in 128 articles, 14.5% of the total data set. All of the articles placed in this topic contained minimal jargon, addressed a non-elite, non-shareholder public, and referred to jobs, government spending, or personal finance. The number of articles that addressed at least one of these topics comprised 14.5% of the data set. There is increasing reference to these "ordinary" topics from the middle of 2007, with a peak from August 2007 onwards – the Minsky moment when the GFC crisis was revealed and became headline news.

According to Figure 28, the largest number of articles in one month is 21 and they appear in August 2007, the month that the subprime market was exposed. This deluge of articles suggests at first glance that nearly one-third of the coverage addressed a general non-shareholding public, and indeed there were many exemplary articles that did communicate directly with the "ordinary" public.

The reportage under "ordinary" topics tends to be quite objective and critical. The majority of the articles appear after August 2007 and inform the general public of the range of concerns as the economy begins to wobble. Some of the earliest and starkest warnings appear when journalists engage with this non-elite, non-shareholding audience. For instance, economics writer Porter, reporting in the *New York Times* in 2005, provides a warning of a housing boom and explains the boom's close association with risky products and vulnerable borrowers.

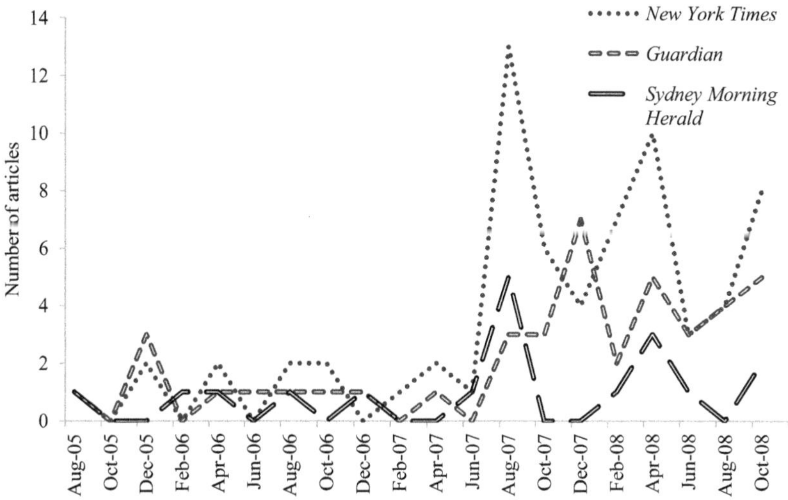

Figure 28. GFC: Distribution of articles for the "general public"

The stories collected under this topic show how individual-level narratives and engagement with an ordinary and non-shareholding audience often result in the most precise articulation of warnings of potential problems in the financial and economic systems. Also, rather ironically, some of the articles that were based on communication with the "ordinary" public also produced the starkest warnings, using individual-level narratives to connect dots between the subprime housing market and risky financial products. Furthermore, they usually come from economics writers and editors, like Porter at the *New York Times* and Gittins at the *Sydney Morning Herald*. However, the analysis also shows that this sort of coverage emerges too late in the genesis of the crisis to alert the public in advance to future problems and does not provide enough day-to-day guidance for the general public so that it can understand what is happening and cope with the consequences.

In summary, a watchdog role was not played in reporting on "ordinary" topics. The reportage was not fair and balanced with coverage appealing for and geared towards the general public. The ordinary public is either referred to as a barometer of financial and/or economic health or included as an illustration of the depth of the problems that had been caused by the GFC. Therefore, on this evidence, the financial press did not appear to have the "ordinary" public in mind as the main target audience. While the financial press had the capacity to communicate the situation and reflect what is truly happening to the public-at-large, the broadsheets were chosen for analysis elected instead to appeal to the interests of business and government.

Conclusion

Now we have assessed the ways three financial crises were reported in three countries it is possible to argue that publications increasingly gear their articles towards an investor audience and interpretations generally follow the same narratives regardless of the context of the country. There is a narrowing of interpretations of events that arguably limits democratic discussion.

Since the 1990 recession, there is a narrowing of sources used, with business sources comprising the majority of quotes in each publication. Analysts and PR sources also took up a large portion of direct quotes. The *Guardian* stood out, with the majority of its quotes coming from politicians and the Bank of England. Here as in the other case studies, each publication rarely features quotes from non-government organisations and members of the public.

Once again, as already noted in the previous case studies, the preference for business, analysts, and PR sources is exacerbated in the months immediately after August 2007 – the Minsky moment. And non-government organisations and members of the public are left outside the framing of the GFC in the crucial months when the crisis was defined.

The amount of coverage and warnings before the Minsky moment in August 2007 had drastically declined since the dot com boom. Of the total data set only 8 per cent of articles appear in the two years before August 2007. Therefore, there was minimal coverage on the topics that relate to the keywords before the month that the subprime bubble was exposed. The tone of the coverage from each publication turns toward scepticism at the tipping point of August 2007. This finding is understandable, as the economic data shows this is the point that the US, the UK, and Australian economies started to slow and inflation grew.

As with the other case studies, the most scepticism about the boom, and engagement with the general public, comes from economics writers. The analysis also shows that where warnings are given, economic journalists do direct themselves to a non-shareholding "ordinary" public. For instance, in the *New York Times*, the human-interest based articles in 2005, which quote members of the public directly, such as Porter on August 25, 2005, produced the starkest warnings of an impending economic downfall.

The explanations for the events of the GFC found mostly within the "connected dots" theme, appear almost exclusively in August 2007 and drop off quickly after that. Those that appear in August are thorough and detailed in most instances and would have served a general non-shareholding audience well. As in the other case studies, there is not much everyday advice for the general public to act on. Also, events are not reported to and for the general and non-shareholding public to the same extent as in the 1990 recession.

Overall there is a noticeable decline in quality standards since the 1990 recession: there is less "variety" in the sources used, and most are from inside the corporate sphere; there is minimal coverage overall before the Minsky moment, and there are not enough explanations geared towards the general public. Non-shareholders, whose savings and mortgages were under threat, were largely ignored by the coverage that could have been more effective in providing them with information and advice. All the results point to the fact that during the GFC the publications failed, to some degree, in their watchdog role.

Some General Conclusions from the Case Studies

This study has examined three decades of financial reporting from three countries focusing on their coverage before, during, and after three major financial and economic crises – the 1990 recession, the dot com boom of 2000, and the GFC of 2007–2008. We can begin to answer the questions posed in Chapter 1. Have there been any changes in the way financial news has been reported over the past three decades? What conclusions can be drawn from the coverage itself concerning the quality of the reportage? And how far does mainstream finance journalism go in fulfilling a watchdog role for the general public?

The analysis offered in this book shows that financial journalism has indeed changed in character and quality over the past three decades. The way sources, topics, and discourse frame events alters substantially between the 1990 recession and the GFC of 2007–2008. Topics and discourse include fewer alternative views and voices and are increasingly geared towards the interests of business and investors. The range of sources that are quoted and used for information narrows over the three decades, until the time of the GFC and business insiders start to dominate. Institutional investors and PR spokespeople also become a more pervasive source of influence from the 1990s onwards. Whereas financial journalism in mainstream newspapers once served a much broader section of society, it can be argued that now it serves the interests of business and investors.

This is confirmed by the pattern of coverage, of "ordinary" topics, that emerges from each study. The "ordinary" topics are important as they are an indication of the extent to which the financial press includes topics desired by the public – on jobs, unemployment, and government spending – and in such a way that cuts jargon and reports for a non-shareholding audience (Schifferes 2012).

The coverage of the 1990 recession included more articles geared towards the general public and a greater variety of voices that would have promoted democratic discussion. The pattern alters dramatically in the subsequent crises. However, all three graphs show a shift towards topics relevant to the general readership, such as jobs, government spending, and personal finance for non-shareholders when the economy starts to slow and unemployment starts to rise. Even so, there is very little in the way of everyday personal advice on how the average person should cope now and into the future.

Each case study also shows that on the comparatively rare occasions when journalists do go further afield and consult with sources, such as academics, non-government organisations, and members of the public, it is these sources that often provide some stark warnings of trouble ahead. It is individual-level narratives – mostly provided by the *New York Times* – where we are most likely to find everyday information about personal finance situations aimed at the general public. Another interesting feature that emerges is the different approaches of business journalists compared to economic journalists. It is the economics writers who usually express the most considerable scepticism and who engage most with the broader readership. Therefore, within the same publication, we see different approaches towards both topics and audiences.

Overall, the case studies build a convincing argument that the general public is increasingly irrelevant in financial reporting and that warnings and scepticism are always "a day late and several dollars short" (Kurtz 2008). The public cannot be confident, on this evidence, that the financial press are playing a watchdog role. Rather than serving the public interest, it is more likely to serve the business and political interests that power the economic engines.

It is all very well to draw conclusions from the written evidence, but this does not tell us what it is like to work as a financial journalist. It may be that the mainstream financial press has become increasingly reactive and less proactive. It may be that journalists have been ideologically captured by their sources and, hence, are less critical in their reporting. We may speculate on the impact of diminishing resources and increased time pressures on the work the journalists do.

Lessons can be drawn from the data that journalists should seek to speak to a broader range of sources, and even those non-elites on the ground, also that proprietors and editors should give scope and prominence to economic writers who purport to speak with a range of voices and target the wider populace. But what lessons have been learned since the GFC? And has quality improved? Are mainstream news outlets making a space for themselves in a digital media-scape, and do they stand out from specialist content yet? We move forward a decade in the next section to consider how financial journalism has developed over the past decade.

Note

1. Garnaut (2009) defines shadow banking in three ways. First, they are non-traditional banks and include investment banks, hedge funds, and monoline insurers—among others. Second, they

are traditional banks that use the same financial products and take part in the same activities—which often require the use of derivatives and a degree of speculation. Third, he describes the kinds of products that are used by the shadow banking system—'derivative products that enable institutions to shift risk, increase leverage and operate beyond regulatory scrutiny' (ibid., 41).

References

Barton, Laura. 2008. 'On the Money.' *The Guardian*, October 31. http://www.theguardian.com/business/2008/oct/31/creditcrunch-gillian-tett-financial-times.

Berry, Mike. 2018. *The Media, the Public and the Great Financial Crisis*. London: Springer.

Brummer, Alex. 2009. 'It Wasn't the Media's Fault.' *New Statesman*, February 12. http://www.newstatesman.com/society/2009/02/financial-crisis-rock-bank.

Caplen, Brian. 2009. 'Mea Culpa: How We Missed the Crisis.' In *Playing Footsie with the FTSE? The Great Crash of 2008 and the Crisis in Journalism*, edited by John Mair, and Richard Lance Keeble, 28–32. Suffolk: The Institute of Communication Ethics and Abramis Academic.

Chakravartty, Paula, and Dan Schiller. 2010a. 'Neoliberal Newspeak and Digital Capitalism in Crisis.' *International Journal of Communication* 4: 670–692.

Davies, Howard. 2010. *The Financial Crisis: Who Is to Blame?* Cambridge: Polity Press.

Dembiermont, Christian, Mathias Drehmann, and Siripon Muksakunratana. 2013. 'How Much Does the Private Sector Really Borrow? A New Database for Total Credit to the Private Non-Financial Sector.' *BIS Quarterly Review*, March 2013: 65–81. http://www.bis.org/publ/qtrpdf/r_qt1303h.pdf.

Elliott, Larry, and Dan Atkinson. 2009. *The Gods that Failed: How the Financial Elite Have Gambled Away Our Futures*. London: Vintage Books.

Fuller, Jane. 2009. 'Why Journalists Need to Relearn Old Habits of Scepticism, Fearless Reporting and Digging for Information.' In *Playing Footsie with the FTSE? The Great Crash of 2008 and the Crisis in Journalism*, edited by John Mair, and Richard L. Keeble, 87–91. Suffolk: The Institute of Communication Ethics and Abramis Academic.

Garnaut, Ross. 2009. *The Great Crash of 2008*. Melbourne: Melbourne University Press.

Hamilton, Martha. 2009. 'What We Learned in the Meltdown: Financial Journalists Saw the Trees but Not the Forest.' *Columbia Journalism Review* 47 (5): 36–39.

Kleinnijenhuis, Jan, Friederike Schultz, Dirk Oegema, and Wouter van Atteveldt. 2013. 'Financial News and Market Panics in the Age of High-Frequency Sentiment Trading Algorithms.' *Journalism* 14 (2): 271–291.

Kurtz, Howard. 2008. 'Press May Own a Share in Financial Mess.' *The Washington Post*, from Factiva.

Lewis, Justin. 2010. 'Normal Viewing Will be Resumed Shortly: News, Recession and the Politics of Growth.' *Popular Communication* 8 (3): 161–165.

Mair, John. 2009a. 'Top Journos Look behind the Headlines.' In *Playing Footsie with the FTSE? The Great Crash of 2008 and the Crisis in Journalism*, edited by John Mair, and Richard L. Keeble, 23–34. Suffolk: Institute of Communication Ethics and Abramis Academic.

Mair, John, and Richard L. Keeble, eds. 2009. *Playing Footsie with the FTSE? The Great Crash of 2008 and the Crisis in Journalism*. Suffolk: Institute of Communication Ethics and Abramis Academic.

Mickler, Steve. 2012. 'Blame Liberals: Conservative Columnists and the GFC in Australia and Canada.' *Communication, Politics and Culture* 45: 5–23.

Muller, Denis. 2017. 'Mixed Media: How Australia's Newspapers became Locked in a War of Left versus Right.' *The Conversation*, June 18.

Pew Research Center. 2008. 'The Changing Narrative: How the News Media Have Covered the Slowing Economy.' https://www.pewresearch.org/wp-content/uploads/sites/8/legacy/Economy-report.pdf (Accessed May 1 2020)

Phillips, Gavin. 2008. *Bad Money: Reckless Finance, Failed Politics, and the Global Crisis of American Capitalism*. New York: Penguin Group.

Roush, Chris. 2009. 'Unheeded Warnings.' *American Journalism Review* December/January. https://www.ajrarchive.org/Article.asp?id=4668 (Accessed May 1 2020)

Schifferes, Steve, and Stephen Coulter. 2012. 'Downloading Disaster: BBC News Online Coverage of the Global Financial Crisis.' *Journalism* 14 (2): 228–252.

Schiffrin, Anya, and Ryan Fagan. 2013. 'Are We All Keynesians Now? The US Press and the American Recovery Act of 2009.' *Journalism* 14 (2): 151–172.

Soros, George. 2009. *The Crash of 2008 and What It Means: The New Paradigm for Financial Markets*. New York: Public Affairs.

Starkman, Dean. 2009a. "Power Problem: The Business Press did Everything but Take on the Institutions that Brought Down the Financial System." *Columbia Journalism Review* 48 (1): 22–30.

Starkman, Dean. 2009b. 'How Could 9,000 Business Reporters Blow It?' *Mother Jones*, January/February. http://www.motherjones.com/politics/2009/01/how-could-9000-business-reporters-blow-it.

Starkman, Dean. 2015. *The Watchdog that Didn't Bark: The Financial Crisis and the Disappearance of Investigative Journalism*. New York: Columbia University Press.

Taibbi, Matt. 2010. *Griftopia: A Story of Bankers, Politicians, and the Most Audacious Power Grab in American History*. New York: Spiegel & Grau.

Tambini, Damian. 2008. *What is Financial Journalism For? Ethics and Responsibility in a Time of Crisis and Change*. London: London School of Economics and Political Science.

Tambini, Damian. 2010. 'What are Financial Journalists for?' *Journalism Studies* 11 (2): 158–174.

Tooze, Adam. 2018. *Crashed: How a Decade of Financial Crises Shaped the World*. London: Random House.

UK Treasury Select Committee. 2009. Panel of Robert Peston, BBC News; Jeff Randall, The Telegraph; Alex Brummer, The Daily Mail; Simon Jenkins, The Guardian; and Lionel Barber, The Financial Times. Inquiry into the Banking Crisis: Oral Evidence. Questions 1510–1540. February 4.

Wilson, Michael. 2008. 'Crisis? What crisis? But It's Great TV.' *British Journalism Review* 19 (3): 57–61.

CHAPTER SIX

Financial Journalism in the Digital Age – Does Alternative News Provide Alternatives?

The Digital and Online Reporting Environment – Providing Alternatives?

Since it emerged in the 1990s, there has been a large amount of hubris that the Internet will democratise the media and indeed, provide a more pluralist democracy. However, if we look at Hindman's (2018) work, it shows that 99 percent of page views are just to the top 10 websites for any given topic. Likewise, the latest research indicates that (currently) alternative digital news sources do not provide anything additional to that which is offered by mainstream financial news. It does not fill the gap in what is now touted as a "crisis" in journalism, nor does it improve the decline in quality and widen the breadth of discussion that has been discussed throughout the book. (see also Reuters' digital news report for lack of public trust in the news on social media; Newman et al. 2018.)

In addition to blogs and social media, there has been a proliferation of online content (Roush 2018), and some successful consumer sites such as moneysaving-expert.com. The overriding problem here is that many of these online offerings are highly specialised, and attract well-established and influential journalists from the mainstream: Alan Kohler (interviewed for this book), for instance, moved from the ABC and now focuses on his specialist business magazine. Likewise, Accesseos builds its brand around well-known writers and economists in the US.

There is currently little research on blogs – but there is suggestion that online niche and alternative sources of news like blogs provided something the mainstream did not before the GFC (Lowe, 2009), that they act more often as soothsayers, provide analysis of long-term trends and connect what is happening to historical developments. There has been a proliferation of well-read and influential blogs written by experts, such as Zerohedge.com. One part of Zerohedge's manifesto is to "sceptically examine and, where necessary, attack the flaccid institution that financial journalism has become." Certainly, these blogs are providing some alternative narratives and specialist analysis. The degree to which they are writing for and engaging a more general audience, however, is uncertain.

Take a sample of content from a typical Friday on the Zerohedge website in the year 2019. It shows the following subjects are the most widely read top three stories: on March 15 the top story is, unsurprisingly, about the tragic mass shooting at a mosque in New Zealand, which resulted in 50 deaths; the second and third most popular stories, with 120, 324 and 76, 688 views respectively, are about the technicalities that were involved in the crash of the Boeing 767 in Ethiopia, this time claiming 157 lives. Information from the three stories emanates from mainstream outlets – Bloomberg, the *New York Times* and the *Star* in Canada. So while the attraction of these stories is understandable, they are stories that were being well-covered by mainstream media. Stories about financial markets, business or the economy on Zerohedge are read much less, and their focus is narrow. A story on unemployment, for example, garnered only 6890 views and the least read story is about how traders are pricing QE4 with 1293 views. So the stories that lead and are popular with the audience are those with a politicised, tragic or spectacular nature. They do not necessarily provide additional analysis about the economy or finance that a wider public might engage with.

Continuing the focus on Zerohedge, the same trend can be seen in the year 2010, when the GFC had taken on an additional dimension in the Eurozone. On Friday, March 12, the site does not show the number of views, but we do have the number of comments to indicate levels of engagement. They show the top stories are the EU agreeing to bail out Greece, which emanates from the *Guardian*, and the sharing of a video from the bloggers Mike Shedlock and Marc Faber advising investment in gold and in Japan. Again the biggest stories are of a political or specialised nature, emanating from other (mainly) mainstream sources.

Another route for alternative and broadened discussion might, arguably, develop on social media. A strong argument emerges that we do not have enough research about economic news and social media. (See Damstra et al. 2018 for an excellent overview of the literature.) There is the general impression that the online social space might provide a different set of discourses, but it raises the question, who dominates the online space? Are alternatives lines of inquiry and discussion being provided? And it raises the much broader question of how the economy is mediated online, and what are the implications for the public sphere?

A study of journalistic coverage of the economy during the UK 2010 general election shows that the authority of an important UK institution, the Institute of Fiscal Studies, is retained online. Of the Tweets that mention the Institute for Fiscal Studies (IFS) in the UK general election 47.5 per cent assume the authority of IFS while only 6.1 per cent contested it (Anstead and Chadwick 2018). Similar results were found online as part of a study of economic journalists in Belgium. They found journalists covering the economy use Twitter for research purposes, but that they maintained their traditional sourcing channels. The authors lamented "It is still remarkable that citizens turn out to be totally irrelevant as sources." (Johnson, Paulussen and Van Aelst 2018, 883). There is further evidence elsewhere that sources used offline are similar online, which implies that traditional sources are still setting the news agenda, but the tenor of the content is more positive, as Twitter followers respond more to positive economic news (Soroka et al. 2018).

In light of the lack of research in this area, it seemed appropriate to conduct a short analysis of Tweets from a mix of official, left and right perspectives, mainstream and alternative economic voices from over the past three years (this author's analysis). They were Jeremy Warner, economics writer for the right-wing publication the *Telegraph*, the Bank of England, the bulwark of financial institutions, the BBC's Kamal Ahmed, alternative economic think-tank Rethinking Economics, the left-wing publication the *Independent*'s economics editor Ben Chu, and the Institute for Fiscal Studies. This author looked at the most and least favourited and re-tweeted Tweets to see who has the most traction, what the content of the Tweets say about the content provider, and what they focus on.

Jeremy Warner, who writes for the *Telegraph*, has the most retweets and the top retweet is of the earliest known original colour film of London. He is followed closely by the Institute of Fiscal Studies, which retweeted the *Economist*'s Tweet about the fiscal effects of Brexit. Like the retweets, those Tweets that are favourited are of a personal and political nature involving Brexit and Trump. The topic of austerity does not feature in anyone's top 10 retweeted or favourited Tweets. Jeremy Warner has the most traction again, and this time the public favourited a tweet about the free movement bankers would have as part of Brexit plans. The Bank of England is close behind, with a tweet about the scientist people would like to nominate as their favourite of all time. And BBC's Kamal Ahmed is not far behind, with a Tweet about the Panama papers and 66 criminal investigations. Clearly, the conversation the public follow and favour online is personal or political, and much less economic than one would expect from a cadre of economic commentators, editors and institutions.

Meanwhile, the digital news media environment is dominated by just a few companies. A Media Reform Coalition report from 2019 shows that only five companies are dominating 80 per cent of the online space. The overall implications, which duly deserve further investigation, are that the same voices and brands are shaping the news agenda; with public broadcasters and other media outlets doing much better online recently. (The *Guardian* and *Independent* turning a profit and expanding their online presence, for instance.) Moreover, the general population still turns to TV and mainstream news over social media (Newman et al. 2018), as discussed in Chapter 1.

Challenges and Lessons Learned: Views from Journalists

In surveys and interviews, journalists indicate a desire to reach a wider audience and write about complex subjects in a way a wide audience understands.

Still, too few surveys exist on this beat. Ragas and Tran (2018) conducted one of the largest and one of the first of financial journalists as recently as 2014. It focused on the US and tracked who the journalists thought were the most influential journalists on their beat. Another recent (small-scale) survey of financial journalists, again in the US (Strauß 2019), found that financial journalists perceived their roles as watchdogs. These results are corroborated to some degree by a survey of 65 financial, business and economic journalists conducted in 2018 in the UK, which demonstrates that journalists have a strong desire to play a watchdog role for the public (Knowles 2020).

Of the journalists surveyed, 33 per cent see the job of a financial journalist as being in a "public forum" role: to get ordinary people involved in debates. This is followed closely by 30 percent who see think their role is to be a watchdog investigating business malfeasance and asking questions on behalf of the public. Far less, only 13 per cent, believe they should work as passive mirrors, reflecting the markets.

But while there is a desire to report for the general public, there is also a sense that it is too difficult to write for this audience. The same survey shows journalists want to see the audience for financial journalism broadened, and they are concerned about the public's levels of financial and economic literacy.

This survey is also one of the first to use socio-demographic variables. It indicates that there are some big differences in modus operandi between the genders – an aspect that has rarely been considered before (Knowles2020). Also, the results indicate that the financial newsroom in the UK does not reflect society well, as there is little diversity in terms of journalists' demographics. The diversity of the cohort is limited, with 69% being Caucasian, 10% being black, 11% being mixed-race, and 5% being Asian. (Although this survey indicates a much more diverse newsroom in the UK than the one discovered by Thurman et al. 2016.)

Overall then, a layer of complexity is introduced when we include gender and other socio-demographic variables, which arguably warrant further investigation and indicate more research is needed to explore whether the financial and economic world is being represented fairly and accurately and engaging a wide audience globally.

Lessons Since the GFC

When the journalists interviewed for this book were asked what lessons have been learned since the GFC, they elicited a variety of responses. The main area of agreement, however, is that journalists have learned to be more sceptical about institutions and cognitive capture by politicians; and for this reason, they are better prepared to spot a crisis if one is developing.

For instance, Steve Long, ABC economics editor in Australia, thinks journalists have learned that you cannot trust authorities: "The lesson has to be that you have to have a critical eye on the claims being made by regulatory institutions and think critically about the structures that are in place." This is echoed by Rana Foroohar who says in the US journalists today are less trustworthy of financial analysts' reports: "When I was at Forbes in the 1990s, we read a lot of research that was being churned out by Goldman Sachs or Morgan Stanley, and we took it more seriously than it should have been taken. You can't trust anything that's coming out of banks."

Robert Peston thinks "one of the reasons the media were slightly wrong-footed and didn't see the risks developing was that there was a whole generation of journalists obsessed with stock markets, shares, the performance of companies, but 80% of the world's markets are capital markets." This has been resolved to some degree by "education about the importance of debt and capital markets, and these markets are now better covered. Personal finance journalists have learned to not be seduced by interest rates and more of an understanding of the importance of risk."

Of challenges moving forward, the role of the public relations industry stands out. Steve Long thinks the power of corporate PR and the spin industry is still substantial. Also, churnalism (the concept of news being literally churned out of a machine intent on profit-making over and above quality was established by Davies in his book *Flat Earth News* 2011) is something he thinks is a serious problem that is getting worse.

This concern with the effects of churnalism is echoed by Hamish McRae of the *Independent*, who thinks resources are tighter than they used to be, certainly in the print media. Also, the growing complexity of finance – for example, in pension legislation – increases the need for journalists to explain but also makes it harder to do so in a general way.

Starkman too points to resources, but also the broader conceptualization of financial journalism and what its aims should be. He thinks the biggest challenge ahead is "a continued cultural preference for access journalism and inability to broaden the definition of financial news."

So Will Journalists Be More Effective Soothsayers in the Future?

The journalists have mixed views on whether they will be able to spot whether a crisis is looming in the future.

For instance, Hamish McRae in the UK thinks, "the memory of our collective failure (though we were in good company) will make us more sensitive to danger signals when they start flashing. Look at how much discussion there is now about the next global downturn – its nature, timing and so on." Stephen Long in Australia thinks journalists "are now attuned to the sense that instability is part of the system. That crises are likely. So I think journalists are more sceptical and on the lookout."

Likewise, Robert Peston thinks: "We haven't seen an economic shock like this in decades, many journalists like bankers and companies had become complacent. Everybody is more alert to the risk of economic and financial risk than they were and are working harder to spot dangerous bubbles." Also, there is less sense that companies and private sectors always work for the economic and public good. He says, "we got to a period in the 90s and early this century where there was a reification and worship of companies, and I think there's an appreciation that wealth creation, and job creation, while important, … the media has become more sceptical and wary and properly analytical of the private sector."

This view is challenged to some degree by Dean Starkman, who thinks journalists are still [un]able to connect financial events to deeper underlying social problems, so no, they aren't better prepared. And Rana Foroohar makes the following cogent point about the lessons only experience can bring: "You have to have worked through the last crisis, but because this industry has been so disintermediated [with a proliferation of outlets online] and there's been so much churn, there are a lot of young people in the business that didn't go through the last crisis. I frankly don't know how they're going to respond."

Conclusion

Overall, this chapter picks up the themes discussed in Chapters 1 and 2 about the applicability of the normative relationship between journalism and democracy, and watchdog function of the media, to a digitally connected world. It shows that alternative blogs mainly provide specialist content, but also similar topics to those being covered in the mainstream. Financial and economic news is still dominated by mainstream voices in the digital world, with minimal take-up of alternative voices online.

Not only is the online sphere *not* providing a more lively and alternative space for discussion and fairer access to information, the public is also still very unsatisfied with mainstream business, finance and economic coverage, and they do not think financial journalists serve them or engage them. Their financial knowledge and economic understanding is low, and they are more dependent than ever on mainstream news to inform them. This lack of knowledge and disengagement is one journalists themselves are very aware of and are struggling to remedy.

The majority of the journalists interviewed for the book are confident that they, and others, are better equipped to spot another crisis if and when one is looming. To some degree things have come full circle; with media companies retrenching, expanding online and journalists adapting their practice to the new online environment. But without the engagement of a wide audience, we cannot guarantee that the public would be prepared to understand the broader political and policy implications of a crisis even if they were warned.

Wealthy individuals are able to capitalise on better quality information and a widening cleavage in understanding between them and the ordinary public who have less access to, and understanding of, detailed financial and economic information. This cleavage could have implications for social mobility and inequality as the global information gap and the differences in financial literacy levels between women and men, the young and old, the poor and the rich, continues to grow.

So it appears that the lessons of three crises we looked at for financial journalism are yet to fully materialise, and big challenges in the new world of digital journalism remain. The test will be how coverage has changed when the next financial crisis occurs.

References

Anstead, Nick, and Andrew Chadwick. 2018. 'A Primary Definer Online: The Construction and Propagation of a Think Tank's Authority on Social Media.' *Media, Culture & Society* 40 (2): 246–266.

Damstra, Alyt, Mark Boukes, and Rens Vliegenthart. 2018. 'The Economy. How Do the Media Cover It and What Are the Effects? A Literature Review.' *Sociology Compass* 12 (5): e12579.

Davies, Nick. 2011. *Flat Earth News: An Award-Winning Reporter Exposes Falsehood, Distortion and Propaganda in the Global Media*. London: Random House.

Johnson, Michiel, Steve Paulussen, and Peter Van Aelst. 2018. 'Much Ado about Nothing? The low Importance of Twitter as a Sourcing Tool for Economic Journalists.' *Digital Journalism* 6 (7): 869–888.

Knowles, Sophie. 2020. "Women, the Economy and the News: Undeserved and underrepresented?" *Journalism Studies*: 1–17: 10.1080/1461670X.2020.1762241.

Lowe, Kristine. 2009. 'How Blogs Challenged and Transformed Mainstream Media Coverage of the Credit Crisis.' In *Playing Footsie with the FTSE*, edited by John Mair and Richard Lance Keeble. London: Abramis Academic. pp. 92–98.

Nic, Newman, Richard Fletcher, Antonis Kalogeropoulos, David AL Levy, and Rasmus Kleis Nielsen. 2018. *Reuters Institute Digital News Report 2018*. Oxford: Reuters Institute for the Study of Journalism.

Roush, Chris. 2018. 'Current and Future Trends, Key Problems and Potential Solutions in Business Journalism.' Paper presented for the Symposium *Media, Crisis and Bubbles* at the University of Navarra, December 12.

Soroka, Stuart, Mark Daku, Dan Hiaeshutter-Rice, Lauren Guggenheim, and Josh Pasek. 2018. 'Negativity and Positivity Biases in Economic News Coverage: Traditional versus Social Media.' *Communication Research* 45 (7): 1078–1098.

Strauß, Nadine. 2019. 'Financial Journalism in Today's High-Frequency News and Information Era.' *Journalism* 20 (2): 274–291. DOI 1464884917753556.

Thurman, Neil, Alessio Cornia, and Jessica Kunert. 2016. 'Journalists in the UK.' Oxford: Reuters Institute for the Study of Journalism.

Tran, Hai L., and Matthew W. Ragas. 2018. 'Peer Perceptions of Media Elites and Hierarchical Differentiation among Financial Journalists.' *Journalism & Mass Communication Quarterly* 95 (1): 258–277.

CHAPTER SEVEN

Beyond the Crisis

> 'A sustained critique about the economy needn't be rooted in an ideological readjustment.'
>
> Nikki Usher 2017

The objective of this book, to explore the changing practice of financial journalism and its role as a watchdog, has revealed that the public had been provided with a narrowing worldview of the world of business, finance and the economy. This problem is not being resolved by the growth of digital media; although there are some additional and more specialist options now available if the public can pay a premium; and, indeed, if they can understand and interpret the information. If they cannot, we will continue to see a widening of the gap between the informed and the less informed who are not being served quite so well by their mainstream counterparts. To paraphrase a quote from a poster used by the *Financial Times*: those who are informed are richer.

The socio-political and media landscape has changed dramatically since the GFC. We have seen a stubborn commitment to austerity policies in the UK and across much of the world, but little in the way of analysis or contextualisation of the effects of the various policies associated with austerity in the media (Basu, Schifferes and Knowles 2018). Meanwhile, there has been very little widening of the discussion and discourse online in social media.

And the political transformation across the world has been profound: with populist politics gaining traction with some disturbing parallels to the rise of Fascism in Germany during an equally difficult economic downturn there. For an excellent discussion of the contemporary political, economic situation and its parallels see the recently revised *Darkness over Germany* (Buller 2017). Populist politics have spread across the US and EU and contributed to the debate that framed the UK referendum on leaving the EU and ultimately its divorce from their 50-year relationship.

The media industry has also seen its fair share of changes, with new formats and modes of delivery spurred on by smart technology and social media. Mainstream news, however, continues to prove its worth and its mettle. Some big titles have posted big profits recently as owners, editors and journalists adapt to changing mediums and conditions: their practice has changed, but not their modus operandi. A desire for more analysis and long-form, in-depth journalism can be seen in the trend that sees a rise in consumption of intelligent listening in podcasts.

In its Digital News Report (2017), Reuters discovered the majority of people they surveyed use mainstream news media, with social media having less influence on news consumption – and likewise, that distrust comes from mainstream media. The pay-wall introduced by the *New York Times* is proving to be successful as it makes inroads in to the Chinese market (Chyi 2013). The *Guardian* is extending its brand by opening newsrooms in Australia and the US, and recently it changed to a tabloid format. The *Sydney Morning Herald*, while also abandoning the broadsheet format, has retained the same editorial values. The merging of the finance reporting staff across all Fairfax publications, announced in October 2013, provoked concerns over a lessening of diversity. Carson's (2013) research in Australia has pointed to cross-media collaborations as a way forward for online mediums that still need the authority and clout that only mainstream newspapers can provide.

Others have expressed their support for good quality journalism and sage analysis by journalists. I draw here from Lionel Barber's 2018 James Cameron Memorial lecture at City University, London, and his belief that artificial intelligence will not usurp our need for journalistic analysis, insight and research. Also, where big media companies like Facebook have, on the one hand, failed the public by allowing companies like Cambridge Analytica to harvest and manipulate personal data, and ultimately to shape political campaigns, they have also been pouring money in to community journalism projects; and Google continues to provide free and valuable resources for newsrooms and schools.

Journalists are needed now more than ever, as politics continues to be driven by a zeitgeist that favours finance, capitalism and growth. Certainly, a deluge and splintering of information online does not solve the much broader structural and regulatory environment that shapes the world's most powerful institutions (Ewald et al. 2019). Before the GFC, this bias led to a siloing and silencing effect on regulators, bankers, rating agencies and politicians. And, as we saw in the case of HBOS, discussed in Chapter 2, journalists trying to report on events cannot do their job if there is a complicit pact between these entities to keep information which is in the public's interest out of the headlines, should it rock the markets.

We, therefore, return here to the last question posed in Chapter 1: if the financial media had such an important role to play in the story of the financial crisis, what lessons were learned and what has changed in the tumultuous decade that has passed since?

According to the journalists, the GFC has instilled in them a sense of mea culpa, and they are now better prepared to spot a crisis, and more likely to speak with a broader range of sources for information.

Perhaps of more concern are increasing barriers to engagement, namely in the low economic and financial literacy levels in young people and women, and low trust in media companies. (Discussed by Doyle in 2006, p. 436, and Newman et al. 2017 who show priming affects those who do not discuss the economy.) These more vulnerable and undeserving sections of society are the most susceptible to agenda-setting and framing (Damstra et al. 2018). Economy (2017), a charitable foundation in the UK, found that the public wants to be involved in discussions about the economy, but cannot decipher the language in the news which they describe as being too abstract, alien and expert-dominated.

Mainstream financial journalism has effectively evolved as a subgenre within mainstream newspapers that supports the financial community over and above the general public. At the same time, the watchdog role financial journalism plays for the general public is diminishing. Events and issues are now predominantly framed by business, analysts, and PR practitioners for whom time and resource-pressed journalists are easy prey. Viewing the world as these sources do—through a narrow lens of self-interest—the end result is a limited range of interpretations and versions of events, presented to the public in ways that diminish the ordinary person's access to the sort of information essential to facilitate democratic debate.

There is, therefore, a pressing need for both industrial and institutional support of mainstream financial journalism if it is to thrive and to do the job the public is entitled to expect from it. More resources need to be invested by media outlets so that journalists can hold their sources to account, provide independent analysis, and conduct investigations in to corporate misdeeds and changes in the financial industry. If deregulation is going to continue as a political mantra, then journalism resources need to be adequate to ensure the financial industry is accountable, that the public is appropriately informed, and that the public interest is safeguarded. Governments are starting to recognise the need to prepare their citizens for financial crises and place emphasis on financial education (OECD 2016). Like media companies, they too need to understand the crucial role being played by the media in shaping, mediating and direction discussions about economic topics.

In terms of industrial support, the publications analysed in Chapters 3, 4 and 5 subscribe to similar goals to provide independent, fair and impartial reporting in the public interest. The editorial codes at the *New York Times*, the *Guardian*, and the *Sydney Morning Herald* all enshrine specific values and practices. However, various content analyses and practitioner interviews clearly show the gap between ethical theory and ethical practice. If faith in the financial press is to be restored in a post-GFC, post-Leveson, and 'fake' news environment, then media proprietors and editors need to actively enforce ethical practices from the top down. Editorial codes need to encourage a move away from the over dependency on PR sources and material. The codes should clearly point out that using PR generated information is the last option, rather than the first option.

An excellent example of rich and diverse content is offered by the Brazilian newspaper, *Valor*, which has the specific editorial code to 'produce value' (Undurraga 2017). It strives to attain high levels of diversity through the encouragement of confrontational and diverging perspectives; it employs staff with varying economic perspectives and moves staff around their teams to encourage interaction and friction and avoid silo mentality (see Tett 2015 for a discussion of the effects of a silo approach to reporting).

This book has revealed an interesting difference in approach between financial and economics journalists that warrants further investigation – and maybe these differences of perspectives should be encouraged and embraced as they are at *Valor*. It is the economic journalists who tend to provide sage economic analysis, look at long-term trends, and report for the general public, as well as the market. They are needed to explain important economic shifts, as well as the political economy more broadly. They represent a sub-section of finance reporting that remains closer to the traditional ideals, values and audience for mainstream journalism.

This study also shows the public was once relevant and catered for, but that since the 1990s it has become increasingly invisible in the reportage and its interests have been overlooked. This is not a resourcing issue, but a question of ideology.

Beyond resources, it is the journalists who ultimately decide what the story will be, and the suggestion here is that they can exercise this power themselves to improve standards. There are examples of fine financial journalism—in each of the case studies—that provide warnings, explain complicated issues and developments with minimal jargon, and lobby on behalf of the non-shareholding public—for better tax conditions or more inclusion in government policy, for instance. Interviews and surveys also indicate that practitioners still see the general non-shareholding public as central to their news values—even if practical commercial and time pressures deflect them from achieving this goal.

The claims that economic academics are dull and hard to get usable quotes from deserves further research attention. These independent experts could play a major role in identifying and warning the public about future financial excesses and debacles, and it is important to investigate why they seem unwilling to engage in public discourse. Derida pointed out as early as 2002 that academics did not fit with the 24-hour news cycle, and it's discussed by economists today (Wren-Lewis 2018). There seems no way to stop the pace of the media cycle beyond a recent trend toward long-form journalism and analysis, but the old saying goes, if you can't beat them then join them. Academics and other experts need to learn to operate within the media system to ensure that their voices and perspectives are heard.

To some degree, and to end on a more positive note, the reporting of crises highlights a more basic and fundamental fact about journalism, and one which is discussed well by Nerone (2013): journalism, after all, is an "ism". It will continue to change and transform its practice, alongside tectonic technological and socio-political shifts, but its role and purpose will not be changed fundamentally from its purpose to serve the public interest, inform and educate. Academics, practitioners and the public alike all point to the vital role the media can, and should, continue to play in informing and educating the general public in an increasingly complex, global, digitalised, and financialised world. We need a less abstract and animated representation of the economic and financial world. It is real, it affects us daily, and, with some improved mediation, it can be understood by many.

References

Basu, Laura, Steve Schifferes and Sophie Knowles (eds). 2018. *The Media and Austerity Comparative Perspectives*. London: Routledge.

Buller, Amy. 2017. *Darkness over Germany: A Warning from History*. First published in 1943 by Longmans. London: Arcadia Books.

Carson, Andrea. 2013. 'Investigative Journalism, the Public Sphere and Democracy: The Watchdog Role of Australian Broadsheets in the Digital Age.' PhD dissertation. University of Melbourne.

Chyi, Hsiang I. 2013. 'World News Organizations' Web Strategies for the China Market: The Cases of the Wall Street Journal, Financial Times, and the New York Times.' Paper presented at the annual meeting for the *International Association of Media and Communications Researchers, Dublin, June 25–29, 2013.*

Damstra, Alyt, Mark Boukes, and Rens Vliegenthart. 2018. 'The Economy. How do the Media Cover It and What Are the Effects? A Literature Review.' *Sociology Compass* 12 (5): e12579.

Doyle, Gillian. 2006. 'Financial News Journalism: A Post-Enron Analysis of Approaches towards Economic and Financial News Production.' *Journalism* 7 (4): 433–452.

Economy. 2017. Exploring How People Feel about Economics. Research Report. https://www.ecnmy.org/research/report-2017/.

Ewald, Engelen, Ismail Ertürk, Julie Froud, Sukhdev Johal, Adam Leaver, Michael Moran, Karel Williams. 2019. 'Misrule of Experts? The Financial Crisis as Elite Debacle.' *Economy and Society* 41 (3): 360–382.

Nerone, John. 2013. 'The Historical Roots of the Normative Model of Journalism.' *Journalism* 14 (4): 446–458.

Newman, Nic, Richard Fletcher, Antonis Kalogeropoulos, David Levy, and Rasmus Kleis Nielsen. 2017. 'Reuters Institute Digital News Report 2017.' Oxford: Reuters Institute for the Study of Journalism.

OECD. 2016. 'OECD/INFE International Survey of Adult Financial Literacy Competencies', OECD, Paris. http://www.oecd.org/finance/oecd-infe-survey-adult-financial-literacy-competencies.htm (Accessed May 1 2020)

Tett, Gillian. 2015. 'Silos and Silences. Why So Few People Spotted the Problems in Complex Credit and What that Implies for the Future.' *Financial Stability Review* 14 (2010): 121–129.

Undurraga, Tomas. 2017. 'Making News of Value: Exploiting Dissonances in Economic Journalism.' *Journal of Cultural Economy* 10 (6): 510–523.

Usher, Nikki. 2017. 'Making Business News: A Production Analysis of the New York Times.' *International Journal of Communication* 11: 20.

Wren-Lewis, Simon. 2018. '"Mediamacro": Why the News Media Ignores Economic Experts.' In *The Media and Austerity: Comparative Perspectives*, edited by Laura Basu, Steve Schifferes and Sophie Knowles. London: Routledge. pp. 170–182.

Appendix: Methodology for Assessing the Financial Press

> The irony about this argument is of course that there's a record out there to be checked; the record is of course what was published and aired over the seven years that preceded the crisis, the crash. The trouble is, the record is huge. (Starkman, cited in Correy 2009)

What follows here is a catalogue and summary of the various ways financial media and financial practitioners' modus operandi have been analysed previously. This appendix outlines the key ways the articles are analysed: by establishing a Minsky moment, by looking at sources used for information, tone, and what themes are covered in each article. The level of transparency that is provided is intended to establish intracoder reliability.

Introduction and Rationale

There has been no longitudinal study of financial journalism since Steve Barkin's (1982) analysis of content from 1930–1970. Since that time, not only have there been three significant economic crises, but also the media industry itself has undergone unparalleled change both structurally and technologically. Studies that measure the GFC range from studies on the main frames and narratives used to represent the crisis, to investigations into the modus operandi of the financial journalists themselves (Mair and Keeble 2009; Pew Research Center 2008; Roush 2009; Schifferes and Coulter 2012; Starkman 2009a; Tambini 2010). There is still a need for more thorough, comprehensive, and empirical research into financial journalism: "Despite the wide anecdotal criticism there is not much academic research on business/economic journalism" (Schiffrin and Fagan 2013, 153). Merrill (2019) notes there is a serious lack of ethnographic research on this beat. This has been covered in the US, to some degree, by Nicki Usher's (2013) research at the *New York Times*. We also need more surveys of journalists and more perspectives from the public themselves – something Berry has started to do in his focus group research in the UK that highlights some devastating priming effects of news media (2018).

Importantly, the main question being investigated here is whether mainstream financial fulfils the traditional watchdog function expected of journalism in a democracy.[1] The publications analysed here are established quality mainstream dailies that arguably have a pronounced influence on setting media agenda. The relevance of mainstream news outlets continues, be it in various, splintered versions and accessed via news aggregators, smart phones or social media. Legacy media, therefore, still proliferates and dominates the public's consciousness. Also, the digital versions of the same newspapers are currently doing very well (with the *Guardian* expanding into Australia, for instance, and receiving a Pulitzer Prize for its coverage of US National Security Agency leaks by whistle-blower Edward Snowden).

Three-Year Periods: The Lead-up to the "Minsky Moment"

As watchdogs, journalists would provide a degree of scepticism and warning before a moment of 'crisis' becomes evident. Roubini and Mihm (2010, 91) describe this financial crisis moment as the point when there is sudden aversion to risk and "sudden desire to dismantle the pyramids of leverage." This, they explain, was once known as "discredit" or "revulsion", but it is now better known as the "Minsky moment", which is named after Hyman Minsky, the post-Keynesian economist who believed in a balance of government regulation and the impact of financial markets on the real economy, and is known for his Financial Instability Theory (Minsky 1992). A two year period prior to the Minsky moment was chosen as sufficient to assess the attitude of the media to the growing economic threat. And data was collected for a year after the Minsky moment, to analyse the patterns and standards of reportage in its wake.

The 1990 Recession

November 1990 was chosen as the Minsky moment because it was the month that the recession was officially called in the US, and shortly after in Australia and the UK. There was no one single cause of the 1990 recession, so this was the most apparent indication and signalling of economic problems.

The Dot Com Boom

In the case of the dot com boom, March 2000 was the month that the NASDAQ, the market comprising all of the new Internet companies, peaked before starting its rapid decline from its phenomenal high. While the recession was not formally announced until the following year, from March 2000 the financial markets began a year-long nosedive, as new media companies that were listed on them fell one-by-one.

The GFC

The economist and historian Roubini and Mihm (2010) identify the spring of 2007 as the Minsky moment for the GFC. In August 2007 the French bank BNP Paribas halted trading and signalled its problems deriving from its links with the US subprime market. Two Bear Stearns hedge funds had also failed by August 2007 (Soros 2009, xx). It was, therefore, tangible that something was occurring happened in the financial markets. While the recession had not been called officially, from this date the risk to the financial and economic systems was certainly evident.

The Data Set

Using Factiva, 1,205 articles in total were collected that were written by financial, business, and economics journalists, based on key words that pertained to the particular case study: 384 were collected for the 1990 recession; 275 for the dot com boom and bust; and 546 for the 2007–2008 GFC. The idea of tracking the development of a large company, such as Enron or Nokia, in the financial media was tempting. However, this study is longitudinal and concerned with tracking patterns of reportage rather than individual companies. The 1990 recession, the dot com boom and bust, and the GFC had different characteristics and causes, and therefore, required different key words. Each article was scrutinised to ascertain whether the key word was directly relevant to the story content. If the word was completely out of context the article was disregarded. A final list of six key words per case study was compiled based on the ones that produced the largest number of relevant results.

Previous Studies of Financial Media

Quantitative

Early quantitative studies on financial media emanated mostly from the US. Barkin (1982) produced one of the first longitudinal content analyses on financial journalism, covering a lengthy period from 1931–1979. He argues that before his study there was little research which analysed business news alongside some economic realities. Before his own analysis, studies such as Hynd's (1980) were based on studies of questionnaires of readers or editors. So Barkin embarked on a content analysis with the intention of finding out how the substance of financial news had changed and whether stock market coverage dominated. A longitudinal glance from the 1930s to 1980 shows a decline in coverage about the national economy in each publication, while coverage of international business increased and consumer news was persistently underreported. Growing interest in the international economy is attributed to an increase in international trade and the rise of the Organization of the Petroleum Exporting Countries (OPEC)[2] (ibid., 439). Overall, Barkin thinks coverage is more international and varied, and on this basis quality has improved.

Another study looked at the amount and type of coverage in a decade already covered by Barkin, from 1968–1978 (Feldman and Aronoff 1980). They analysed five US metropolitan dailies and found that the *New York Times* was the newspaper that increased its coverage most markedly across the decade. The length of the article was coded as an indication of the depth of the article. They found that a lot of articles focused on energy topics, while business stories migrated outside of the business section into general news, and those retained for the business section contained a more in-depth analysis of economic topics. Taken together, the results suggest that economic and business content was increasing and diversifying in the US up until 1980, with more coverage devoted to international topics. While these studies were pioneering in their scope, they define quality according to the size and breadth of articles.

In what is one of the earliest content analyses on financial journalism, Griggs' (1963) study of the 1957 US recession examines where articles were placed in the months leading to the recession – finding few articles about the recession on the front pages. Covering only the three months leading up to the recession, he recorded the space and content dedicated to financial news as the recession came closer, the amount included in the front pages of the newspaper, and the extent to which coverage was optimistic or pessimistic. More than half of the content remained in the business section, and coverage did not increase over time. Coverage did, however, become more neutral as time went on, with equal amounts of optimistic and pessimistic coverage when the recession began.

More recently in his analysis of the GFC, Starkman (2009b), like Griggs, defines quality financial journalism in terms of a watchdog role for the public, providing sceptical coverage and forewarning of troubles ahead. His study covers a long period from 2000–2007, which provided ample time for the financial press to provide warnings. Arguing that the capture of financial journalists by their sources, or "Stockholm Syndrome," infects the financial press, he aimed to discover through content analysis whether or not the financial press had in fact missed the story (ibid., 24). Of the 730 articles collated the most warnings appeared from 2000–2003. It was not until 2006, and then markedly in 2007, that the press "scrambled" as they tried to keep up with the quickly developing story of the GFC (ibid., 5).

Unlike earlier studies, this study casts a wider net, including a transnational comparison. In doing so it provides new data on international trends in finance reporting during an era when not just the finance industry but the media industry underwent a complete transformation in terms of scope and reach.

Canaries in the Coalmine, or Overly Negative/ Positive? Coding Tone

Concern over whether the financial press is overly optimistic or overly pessimistic has been a constant preoccupation for researchers, many of whom have therefore analysed content based on "tone." This relates to the extent to which coverage is optimistic, neutral, or sceptical. Mainly, this method has been used to establish whether the financial media were too optimistic in their coverage before a recession and too pessimistic during the unfolding of events.

An analysis of coverage of the months leading to the 1929 stock market crash from the Financial Markets section of the *New York Times*, shows coverage was fairly balanced (Bow 1980). More than half of the articles analysed were neutral, and the ratio of optimistic to pessimistic articles was balanced. The reverse was true for a study of the BBC's coverage of the months that immediately followed the GFC (Schifferes and Coulter 2012). The content analysis covered three months from September to December 2008. The study also explores audience traffic and usage, as well as some of the main actors quoted by the BBC. It finds a lack of neutrality and instead "dramatic swings in sentiment over the course of the study period." (Schifferes and Coulter 2012, 12)

Other studies have tracked the amount and type of economic coverage and then tested it against variables, such as consumer sentiment and official economic statistics (Blood and Phillips 1995; Wu, Stevenson, Chen and Guner 2002). Overall, these studies prove to some degree the influence that the news media can have on markets and consumer sentiment. They lend weight to the argument in favour of the powerful effects of economic news.

For instance, Blood and Phillips (1995, 2) assessed whether media coverage of the economy was, as had been alleged, "unfairly negative" during the 1992 US Presidential elections. They found that the growing number of recession headlines had more of a "depressing effect upon consumer sentiment than official statistics (ibid., 17). Like Blood and Phillips (1995), Goidel and Langley (1995, 321) identify a causal link between negative news items and a more depressed consumer sentiment. Their results show that the tone of news coverage does indeed correlate with real economic conditions, while positive articles are not always as reflective of actual economic conditions as neutral and negative articles.

Similarly The Pew Research Center (2008) researched the leading narratives that framed the coverage of the GFC in the US. Like the studies of Blood and Phillips (1995), and Goidel and Langley (1995), it shows there is a correlation between more negative economic coverage and a drop in public confidence. The data suggests that the narratives on the economy lagged behind the key economic indicators. For instance, when the GDP slowed at the end of 2007, there was little media coverage before the release of official data. Therefore, the study concludes that the media have an overreliance on government data, which is sometimes delayed (ibid., 17). Furthermore, coverage did not increase until 2008 when economists predicted a slowdown, indicating reliance on official sources of information too.

This method of recording the tone of articles has not been tested on Australian financial media. However, it has been argued that the Australian financial press was overly optimistic in the 1980s in their coverage of business personalities, such as Alan Bond. (Kitchener 1999; O'Ryan and Shoesmith 1987; Toohey 1993)

In the case studies, coverage of three financial crises is analysed on a three-point scale. Every three months of news coverage is averaged and plotted on a timeline to show the tone of articles before and after the Minsky moment. There is also a review of economic data to compare the tone of reportage against the real economic situation that society was facing.

The Reporting of Economic (Un)Realities

The extent to which the financial press present a true version of the economy has been a source of criticism. Three sets of economic data were selected to give a simple but overall understanding of the economic situation in each country during each case study. The key economic indicators analysed were the GDP, and unemployment and inflation rate for each country. The principle source used to gather economic data is Trading Economics, which is a database that collates information from credible sources, like the Australian Bureau of Statistics and the UK office for National Statistics, and then plots it in graphs.[3]

First, the GDP of a country indicates the level of the country's wealth by totalling the value of goods and services during a given

Second, inflation factors in the extent to which the prices of good are rising or falling. Trading Economics (ibid.) tracks inflations through the CPI index, which "measures changes in the price level of consumer goods and services purchased by households. The CPI is calculated by taking price changes for each item in the predetermined basket of goods and services and averaging them."

Third, unemployment rates are analysed to indicate the level at which people were employed. The unemployment rate is defined as follows: "The unemployment rate can be defined as the number of people actively looking for a job divided by the labour force" (ibid.).

Indexing/Coding the Quoted Sources

The sources that are used by journalists for information and quotes have the opportunity to shape the way reportage is framed. For instance, the work of Schiffrin and Fagan (2013) in the US, Manning (2013) in the UK, and Thompson (2013) in New Zealand, recently linked the sources that are quoted by the financial press with biased and pro-business discourse. The methods used in previous studies range from the coding of cited sources to speaking with the sources of information. Collectively, the studies suggest that coding the amount and types of sources that are used by the financial press are essential to measuring the standards, quality, and fairness of the reportage.

To address the criticism that financial journalism is dependent on sources from business and PR, discussed in Chapter Two, this study recorded the first two sources quoted as a gauge of whether or not there is a preoccupation with business interests and their version of events. This methodology is based on earlier studies conducted by Lidberg and McHoul (2003, 106), and the rationale is that the more important a source is, the earlier it will tend to be mentioned in the article. This provides both an insight into the journalists' newsgathering norms and an indication of the diversity of voices. The recording of sources is also intended to establish the extent to which PR spokespeople are quoted, and conversely the extent to which non-elite sources and workers' voices are left out. (Kollmeyer 2004)

The sources that are quoted in the six months after the Minsky moment are recorded and analysed separately to test Lewis' (2010) argument that the crisis presented a moment of clarity that saw the journalists break free from their traditional newsgathering practices and conventional sources used for information. This study tracks whom the press consulted for explanations and interpretations in these formative months that arguably shaped the public's understanding of the crises.

Few studies have compared sourcing patterns across countries and across more than one event (Dimitrova and Stromback 2009, 75).

Qualitative Analysis

Framing Analysis

There is still no one way to approach framing analysis, as there are no straightforward guidelines. Scheufele (1999), and Chong and Druckman (2007) provide detailed literature reviews that highlight the debate that still exists around this area of research. Entman (2007, 166) considers the potential effects that framing has on democracy, seeing it as contributing to content bias. This has far-reaching implications for democracy, because "those officials favoured by the slant become more powerful" and "those who lose the framing contest become weaker" (ibid., 170).

The case studies explore whether the financial press are ideologically neo-liberal and pro-business in their reporting practices, and thus, whether business interests are served over and above the 'ordinary' public. To do this the articles had to be read on several occasions to identify the most salient topic – or topics, as they sometimes overlapped in the same article. The main ways in which the topics were discussed – the narratives used – and the language used to describe events, were identified and then coded within the main topic (the category) using NVivo.

Coding Main Topics

According to Entman (1993), the first step in framing theory is to identify an event or issue. Second, the researcher must isolate an attitude to an event or issue that he/she wants to explore. Third, the researcher must compile an initial list of frames that become the coding schemes. The fourth step is to collect sources for analysis. It is argued elsewhere that coding manually can pick up nuances that a computer might miss out (Chong and Druckman 2007, 108). Chong and Druckman (ibid., 111) also determine a frame's importance for individuals mainly by strength and repetition.

Using this rationale the main topics were identified manually and the articles were coded twice to ensure intracoder reliability and some measure of validity. Some of the topics overlapped and were coded a few times in different categories. This way, all of the main topics discussed by the publications were included, and the main areas of concern and overlapping debate became obvious. The most salient topics were the most referred to by each publication; this was also determined quantitatively by NVivo.

Content specifically for the more 'general' public was defined according to the preferences that emerged from a poll of the London public conducted by City University—discussed in Chapter One—which revealed that the public wants financial journalism for non-shareholders with minimal jargon on topics such as government spending, jobs, and personal finance (Schifferes 2012).

Coding Narratives

A number of studies have analysed the main topics and narratives that feature in mainstream financial coverage in the US, the UK, and Australia (Preston and Silke 2012; Rae and Drury 1993). The Pew Research Centre's (2008) study of the US media coverage of the GFC, from January 2007 to June 2008 tracked some of the main narratives that were employed by online, broadcast, and print media as a percentage of the news they collected—5,000 stories from 48 outlets. By coding narratives the Pew Research Centre (2008) reveals similarities in storylines and a certain level of groupthink.

Analysing Discourse

Discourse analysis is another qualitative way to analyse the content and identify the way narratives are shaped and language is used by the financial press. Discourse analysis seems to be more prevalent as a research method in the UK and Australia, than in the US, which is more concerned with quantitative data.

Two content analyses from Australia, Greenfield and Williams (2002), and Mickler (2012). deal with financial journalism in the context of its rhetorical framework. Greenfield and Williams embrace the larger spheres of influence that can affect news discourse, including media ownership. They argue that this approach goes beyond previous studies of the historical development of the Australian financial press, and the pressures and challenges that affect financial coverage (Schultz and Matolcsy 1993), its sourcing patterns (Tiffen 1989), or the narratives that have informed it (O'Ryan and Shoesmith 1987). Instead, they build on studies, such as Gittins (1995), Craig (2001), and Schiller (2000) that also consider the impact financial journalism has on stock market fluctuations.

Mickler (2012) builds on this approach more thoroughly and deconstructs the writings of conservative opinion-makers in Australian and Canadian mainstream newspapers. Referring to Foster from Canada's *The National Post*, he provides evidence that the author hails capitalism for creating global wealth, yet also manages to vindicate its role in the GFC. (ibid., 16)

Conclusion

Overall, this study adopted the viewpoint of Griggs (1963) and Starkman (2009a), that the business sections of mainstream newspapers should provide forewarning to the public. Like Griggs (1963) and Starkman (2009a), it tracks the type and amount of "warnings," and the "tone" of reportage. Tracking the tone of coverage, as employed by Griggs (1963), Bow (1980), and Schifferes and Coulter (2012), it addresses key concerns that the financial media are too optimistic, and then too negative in downturns. The primary sources of information are coded, to measure the diversity of views and opinions that shape coverage. It also explores, through analysis of the narratives and discourse, whether the financial press provides a diverse range of views and interpretations of events. In doing so it tracks whether mainstream financial reportage has been framed for business at the expense of the wider public (Greenfield and Williams 2002; Mickler 2012; Preston and Silke 2012).

Overall, the study is designed to provide information relating to the key areas of concern: the nature and style of financial reporting over three decades, and if and how mainstream financial journalism has changed; the extent to which the information provided by mainstream financial journalism keeps the general public appropriately informed and warns before periods of economic crisis; and the level of independence of the financial press from business.

Notes

1. The *Sydney Morning Herald*, traditionally a broadsheet, turned tabloid in March 2013. However, it retained its reporting standards and values (see the article, *Crikey*, by Knott, which assesses the successes and failures of the first 'compact' edition: http://www.crikey.com.au/2013/03/04/the-verdict-is-in-as-fairfax-goes-compact-smh/?wpmp_switcher=mobile). To cut costs and ease readability *Guardian* followed suit, but not until January 2018.
2. OPEC is an intergovernmental organisation of petroleum exporting countries founded in 1960. It aims to promote fair pricing and regulation of crude oil. For a complete outline and history of the organisation's development, see: http://www.opec.org/opec_web/en/about_us/24.htm.
3. See: www.tradingeconomics.com.

References

Barkin, Steve. 1982. 'Changes in Business Sections, 1931–1979.' *Journalism Quarterly* 59 (3): 435–439.

Berry, Mike. 2018. *The Media, the Public and the Great Financial Crisis*. London: Springer.

Blood, Deborah, and Peter Phillips. 1995. 'Recession Headline News, Consumer Sentiment, the State of the Economy and Presidential Popularity: A Time Series Analysis.' *International Journal of Public Opinion* 7 (1): 2–22.

Bow, James. 1980. 'The Times' Financial Markets Column in the Period around the 1929 Crash.' *Journalism Quarterly* 57 (3): 447–450.

Chong, Dennis, and James N. Druckman. 2007. 'Framing Theory.' *Annual Review of Political Science* 10: 103–126.

Correy, Stan. 2009. 'The Media in Boom and Doom', The Background Briefing Show, ABC, Australia, Feb 22. https://www.abc.net.au/radionational/programs/backgroundbriefing/the-media-in-boom-and-doom/3162636 (Accessed Feb 20 2019).

Craig, Geoffrey. 2001. 'The Global Financial News, Information & Technology Corporations.' *Southern Review: Communications, Politics & Culture* 34: 4–13.

Dimitrova, Daniela, and Jasper Stromback. 2009. Look Who's Talking. *Journalism Practice* 3 (1): 75–91.

Entman, Robert M. 1993. 'Framing: toward Clarification of a Fractured Paradigm.' *Journal of Communication* 43 (4): 51–58.

Feldman, Howard D., and Craig Aronoff. 1980. 'Trends in Newspaper Coverage of Business and Economics, 1968–1978.' *Newspaper Research Journal* 1 (4): 54–65.

Gittins, Ross. 1995. 'The Role of the Media in the Formulation of Economic Policy.' *The Australian Economic Review* 28 (4): 5–14.

Goidel, Robert, and Ronald Langley. 1995. 'Media Coverage of the Economy and Aggregate Economic Evaluations: Uncovering Evidence of Indirect Media Effects.' *Political Research Quarterly* 48 (2): 313–328.

Greenfield, Cathy, and Peter Williams. 2002. 'The Politics of Finance Journalism: Approaches to the Field and a Rhetorical Instance.' Paper presented at the annual meeting for the *Australian & New Zealand Communication Association, Queensland, July 10–12, 2002.* http://www.anzca.net/conferences/past-conferences/41-anzca02.html (Accessed May 1 2020)

Griggs, Harry. 1963. 'Newspaper Performance in Recession Coverage.' *Journalism and Mass Communication Quarterly* 40 (4): 559–564.

Hynds, Ernest. 1980. 'Business Coverage is Getting Better.' *Journalism Quarterly* 57: 297–304.

Kitchener, Jennifer. 1999. 'Business Journalism in the 1980s.' In *Journalism: Print, Politics and Popular Culture*, edited by Ann Curthoys, and Julianne Schultz, 229–244. St Lucia: University of Queensland Press.

Knowles, Sophie. 2020. "Women, the Economy and the News: Undeserved and underrepresented?" *Journalism Studies* (2020): 1–17.Knowles, Sophie, and Steve Schifferes. 2020. "Financial Capability, the Financial Crisis and Trust in News Media." *Journal of Applied Journalism & Media Studies* 9(1): 61–83.

Kollmeyer, Christopher. 2004. 'Corporate Interests: How the News Media Portray the Economy.' *Social Problems* 51 (3): 432–452.

Lewis, Justin. 2010. 'Normal Viewing Will be Resumed Shortly: News, Recession and the Politics of Growth.' *Popular Communication* 8 (3): 161–165.

Lidberg, Johan, and Alec McHoul. 2003. 'Freedom of Information as a Journalistic Tool – A Comparative Study between Western Australia and Sweden.' *UTS Law Review* 15: 101–118.

Mair, John, and Richard L. Keeble, eds. 2009. *Playing Footsie with the FTSE? The Great Crash of 2008 and the Crisis in Journalism.* Suffolk: Institute of Communication Ethics and Abramis Academic.

Manning, Paul. 2013. 'Financial Journalism, News Sources and the Banking Crisis.' *Journalism* 14 (2): 173–189.

Merrill, Gary. 2019. *The Political Content of British Economic, Business and Financial Journalism: A Deficit of Perspectives.* London: Springer.

Mickler, Steve. 2012. 'Blame Liberals: Conservative Columnists and the GFC in Australia and Canada.' *Communication, Politics and Culture* 45: 5–23.

Minsky, Hyman. 1992. 'The Financial Instability Hypothesis.' *The Jerome Levy Economics Institute* Working Paper No. 74.

O'Ryan, Gabrielle, and Brian Shoesmith. 1987. 'Speculation, Promise and Performance: Businessmen as Stars.' *Australian Journal of Cultural Studies* 4 (2): 163–173.

PEW. Pew Research Center. 2008. 'The Changing Narrative: How the News Media have Covered the Slowing Economy.' http://www.journalism.org/files/legacy/Economy%20report.pdf.

Preston, Paschal, and Henry Silke. 2012. 'Market 'Realities': Decoding Economic Ideology in the Press.' *Critical Media Review.* http://criticalmediareview.wordpress.com/2012/08/05/market-realities-decoding-economic-ideology-in-the-press-paschal-preston-henry-silke-dcu/.

Rae, John, and John Drury. 1993. 'Reification and Evidence in Rhetoric on Economic Recession: Some Methods Used in the UK Press, Final Quarter 1990.' *Discourse Society* 4 (3): 329–356.

Roubini, Nouriel, and Stephen Mihm. 2010. *Crisis Economics: A Crash Course in the Future of Finance*. London: Penguin Books.

Roush, Chris. 2009. 'Unheeded Warnings.' *American Journalism Review* December/January. https://www.ajrarchive.org/Article.asp?id=4668 (Accessed May 1 2020)

Scheufele, Dietram. 1999. 'Framing as a Theory of Media Effects.' *Journal of Communication* 49 (1): 103–122.

Schifferes, Steve. 2012. 'Trust-Meltdown for Business Journalism.' *British Journalism Review* 23 (2): 55–59.

Schifferes, Steve, and Stephen Coulter. 2012. 'Downloading Disaster: BBC News Online Coverage of the Global Financial Crisis.' *Journalism* 14 (2): 228–252.

Schiffrin, Anya, and Ryan Fagan. 2013. 'Are We All Keynesians Now? The US Press and the American Recovery Act of 2009.' *Journalism* 14 (2): 151–172.

Schiller, Dan. 2000. *Digital Capitalism: Networking the Global Market System*. Massachusetts: MIT Press.

Schultz, Julianne. 1993. 'Reporting Business – A Changing Feast.' In *Reporting Business*, edited by Julianne Schultz, 1–8. Working Paper. Sydney: Australian Centre for Independent Journalism.

Soros, George. 2009. *The Crash of 2008 and What It Means: The New Paradigm for Financial Markets*. New York: Public Affairs.

Starkman, Dean. 2009a. 'Power Problem: The Business Press did Everything but Take on the Institutions that Brought Down the Financial System.' *Columbia Journalism Review* 48 (1): 22–30.

Starkman, Dean. 2009b. 'How Could 9,000 Business Reporters Blow It?' *Mother Jones*, January/February. http://www.motherjones.com/politics/2009/01/how-could-9000-business-reporters-blow-it (accessed January 10, 2012).

Tambini, Damian. 2010. 'What are Financial Journalists for?' *Journalism Studies* 11 (2): 158–174.

Thompson, Peter A. 2013. 'Invested Interests? Reflexivity, Representation and Reporting in Financial Markets.' *Journalism* 14 (2): 208–227.

Tiffen, Rodney. 1989. *News and Power*. Sydney: Allen and Unwin.

Toohey, Brian. 1993. 'The Entrepreneur as Folk Hero.' In *Reporting Business*, edited by Julianne Schultz, 33–38. Working Paper. Sydney: Australian Centre for Independent Journalism.

Usher, Nikki. 2013. 'Ignored, Uninterested, and the Blame Game: How the New York Times, Marketplace, and the Street Distanced Themselves from Preventing the 2007–2009 Financial Crisis.' *Journalism* 14 (2): 190–207.

Wu, Denis, Robert Stevenson, Hsiao-Chi Chen, and Nuray Z. Guner. 2002. 'The Conditioned Impact of Recession Headline News: A Time-Series Analysis of Economic Communication in the United States, 1987–1996.' *International Journal of Public Opinion Research* 14: 19–33.

Index

A

B

E

F

G

H

I

J

K

L

M

N

O

P

Q

R

S

T

GLOBAL CRISES AND THE MEDIA

Simon Cottle, *General Editor*

From climate change to the war on terror, financial meltdowns to forced migrations, pandemics to world poverty, and humanitarian disasters to the denial of human rights, these and other crises represent the dark side of our globalized planet. They are endemic to the contemporary global world and so too are they highly dependent on the world's media.

Each of the specially commissioned books in the *Global Crises and the Media* series examines the media's role, representation, and responsibility in covering major global crises. They show how the media can enter into their constitution, enacting them on the public stage and thereby helping to shape their future trajectory around the world. Each book provides a sophisticated and empirically engaged understanding of the topic in order to invigorate the wider academic study and public debate about the most pressing and historically unprecedented global crises of our time.

For further information about the series and submitting manuscripts, please contact:

Dr. Simon Cottle
Cardiff School of Journalism
Cardiff University, Room 1.28
The Bute Building, King Edward VII Ave.
Cardiff CF10 3NB
United Kingdom
CottleS@cardiff.ac.uk

To order other books in this series, please contact our Customer Service Department at:

peterlang@presswarehouse.com (within the U.S.)
order@peterlang.com (outside the U.S.)

Or browse online by series:

www.peterlang.com

www.ingramcontent.com/pod-product-compliance
Ingram Content Group UK Ltd.
Pitfield, Milton Keynes, MK11 3LW, UK
UKHW021839100926
8556IPUK00004B/431